I0102940

Four Cardinal Errors:
Reasons for the Decline of the American Republic

STEVEN YATES, PHD

BRUSH FIRE PRESS
INTERNATIONAL

Brush Fire Press International
P.O. Box 923
Drayton, SC 29333

Copyright © 2011 Steven Yates, PhD

All rights reserved.

ISBN: 0615516416

ISBN 13: 9780615516417

Library of Congress Control Number: 2011934964

Brush Fire Press International

To the memory of William Clyde Yates Jr.
(November 21, 1923–December 23, 2009):
World War II submarine veteran, patriot,
husband of fifty seven years to Alice M. Yates, father to
my sister and myself, provider, mentor.

ACKNOWLEDGMENTS

The author would like to thank publisher Paul Walter and staff of the online news and commentary site *NewsWithViews.com* for publishing the articles that evolved into the various chapters of this book. Since late 2004 I have had a running dialogue with Mr. Terry Hayfield over the various themes and areas of reference in this work, sometimes agreeing and sometimes disagreeing; it was Mr. Hayfield that prompted me to study Joseph Schumpeter's work. My conclusions, obviously, are my own and not Mr. Hayfield's. Jack Utz, Nelson Waller, Rev. E. Ray Moore, Patrick Tyndall, and Christina Jeffrey looked at a more recent draft and made a number helpful comments. I am also grateful to Kris and John Langville, Ilona and Paul Blakeley, Dr. John Cobin, and the folks at Roper Mountain Baptist Church for their support, encouragement, and (sometimes inadvertent) suggestions. (I apologize if I have missed anyone.) Finally I am very grateful to Joan Kremer at CreateSpace.com for a truly superb editing job. All remaining errors are, of course, my own responsibility.

Lastly, I and the rest of the Brush Fire Press International team (Kathy Patriot, Kris Anne Patriot, and let's not forget Susan S.) all wish to thank Lisa-Renée Rodriguez for her design of our logo.

INTRODUCTION

The United States of America is a unique place. Governments are usually founded on grabs for power and then conquest. Some see this as a universal phenomenon, with only the details and rationalizations differing. But the Founding Fathers of the United States, despite their differences of emphasis and disagreements over details, tried to found a government on a new model. Based on insights into human nature that are rarely seen, they recognized that too little centralization meant anarchy and too much meant tyranny. They strove for a balance that recognized both the need for authority and distrust of too much authority—their own included. Our country's founders established a set of *founding principles*: individual freedoms, private-property rights, free enterprise, personal morality and responsibility, and constitutionally limited government—all embodied in the phrase "life, liberty, and the pursuit of happiness."

The idea that political power could and should be limited by political principles took centuries to develop. It began at least with the Magna Carta of 1215, which King John's feudal barons forced him to sign at sword point, and which declared that the king's power is not absolute, but is limited by the rule of law. This idea continued in later documents, such as the 1628 Petition of Right and the 1689 Declaration of Rights. British kings sometimes learned the hard way that they could not rule as they saw fit. Yet when all was said and done, the British were unable to check the power of the Crown.

The United States showed some promise of doing things differently, beginning with our Declaration of Independence of July 4, 1776:

> We hold these truths to be self-evident, that all men are created equal, that they are endowed by their Creator with certain unalienable rights, that among these are life, liberty, and the pursuit of happiness—that to secure these rights, governments are instituted among men, deriving their just powers from the consent of the governed.

When the Articles of Confederation proved to have created too weak a governing union, political men of the day assembled in Philadelphia and emerged with a new document, the U.S. Constitution—not a perfect document, perhaps, but articulating arguably the best balance that could have been achieved by imperfect human hands seeking to guide an imperfect world. James Madison penned the basic insight in the oft-quoted "Federalist No. 51":

> But what is government itself, but the greatest of all reflections on human nature? If men were angels, no government would be necessary. If angels were to govern men, neither external nor internal controls on government would be necessary. In framing a government which is to be administered by men over men, the great difficulty lies in this: you must first enable the government to control the governed; and in the next place oblige it to control itself.

Was such a project even possible? Theoretical anarchists say not. They say that any state, even one with powers ostensibly limited by specific principles, will gradually define its powers more and more broadly until once again it controls everything and we are back where we started. If they are right, it explains much. Yet surely we shouldn't just assume they are; surely a people can, in principle, hold governing power in check. But what if other factors interfere with their doing so? Does that explain why a civil society with such unique founding principles as ours embarks on a course that can only be described as suicidal in the long run?

Some philosophers of history believe that civilizations have life spans just as individuals do, and that they go through equivalent cycles of birth and rapid growth, to maturity, reckless expansion, eventual decadence, and finally decline and fall. Oswald Spengler's *Decline of the West* is an example. In some broad sense, this may be true—even if the civilization is left to itself and not attacked from the outside. Rome overwhelmed numerous weaker cultures and then gradually disintegrated from within. Arguably, the United States did the same thing, overwhelming and destroying Native American cultures—much to our shame, since our founding principles should have taught us better. Our ancestors erred in not applying the principles consistently. Historically, though, stronger powers have always overwhelmed and usually destroyed weaker ones. That this happens is unfortunate, but not especially controversial. Failure to apply a set of principles consistently does not invalidate the principles themselves.

The foes of a civilization can be foreign or domestic—or foreign posing as domestic. One of the key assumptions of this book is that a civilization *can* be attacked through a Trojan-horse strategy, without armies or other evidence of invasion. Civilizations founded on defining principles are vulnerable in that they *must* transmit these principles to the next generation, and then the generation after that, and so on. Failure to do so *will* compromise the principles. A civilization's guiding institutions can then be made to turn on the civilization itself so that it appears to act as its own destroyer, even if the primary destructive force comes from outside. Moreover, the process set in motion can operate with sufficient slowness that the internal rot can be very well-advanced before anyone notices—akin to termites destroying a large house. Much of the damage is done before it is discovered.

I will argue in the chapters that follow that this is what has happened to the American republic. We are not necessarily at the end of a Spenglerian life cycle. The decline of the United States has been engineered from outside its borders. Our country had elements—such as a sound currency and a spirit of independence among many of its people—that those with enormous wealth and power in Europe (especially within the British Crown) saw as threats to their hegemony. The latter sought to destroy those elements from the start. Their efforts met with only the most limited success for quite a while. The United States of America rose as a world power. The liberty created by a limited government became a tremendous calling card, attracting people from all over the world. The system had tremendous resilience and forward momentum. It was very strongly believed in by those who settled here, working the land and the seas, working in factories and on railroads, or working in any number of other endeavors that formed the warp and woof of the first hundred and fifty years of U.S. history. This country was not going to be taken down overnight, and not without a struggle of epic proportions! But what was most remarkable and foundational in American culture eventually did succumb.

We are not talking about military forces, of course, but intellectual and financial ones. Among our founders were those who sought to consolidate power in a central banking system that would protect a mercantile class right from the start. Alexander Hamilton was one of them. Sometimes our own political class embraced wrong ideas, thinking they could improve on our founding principles. Wrong ideas had taken root in education by the mid-1800s. Our system may have been resilient, but those who worked against it were very persistent. Their efforts, over the long haul, gradually sapped both our strength and our national integrity.

We made our share of mistakes, as every civilization does. The destruction of Native American cultures and our acceptance of slavery were the two worst errors in our early years. America's enemies have gotten as much mileage as they could out of these flaws, using the latter in particular to undermine our national self-confidence in our founding principles. However, I will argue that other mistakes—what I call the *Four Cardinal Errors*—have almost destroyed our Republic. All other errors can be reduced to one or more of these four. Furthermore, the original motive for each error came from outside, but set in motion processes that would destroy the Republic from within.

Cardinal Error One: the Republic failed to gain full freedom and economic sovereignty from British bankers, headquartered in that wealthy district known as the City of London (a different entity from the surrounding city of the same name), and this state of affairs went unrecognized. Our founding documents—and warnings from alert and thoughtful men such as Thomas Jefferson—proved insufficient to prevent incursions by power-hungry European bankers. Alexander Hamilton, Jefferson's arch-foe, opened the door by creating the Bank of the United States, and John Jay opened it further with the Jay Treaty. No one ever closed it completely again—not even Andrew Jackson, who, despite shutting down the Second Bank of the United States, did not call for criminalizing that special brand of financial trickery known as *fractional-reserve banking* and run its practitioners out of this country. Eventually, this fraudulent system was imposed on the country again. It gradually replaced currency backed by precious metals (gold and silver) with currency backed by nothing except legal-tender laws and people's willingness to use it. Its value began to drop, as the value of fiat currencies invariably does. This story is reviewed in chapter 1.

Cardinal Error Two: the Republic embraced, over time, an educational system whose premises were alien to those of free citizens in a free republic. This system ceased to transmit our founding traditions. Eventually it proved incapable of transmitting any sort of learning, freedom-based or otherwise, to future generations. It devolved into what amounts to effective obedience training and to a "refutation" of our Founding Fathers' principles with the claim that they owned slaves. This issue is explored in chapter 2.

Cardinal Error Three: Americans slowly but steadily lost the tacit religiosity of our founding traditions—a religiosity that was more a way of life, or of being in the world, than an explicit doctrine. It was replaced, again over a long time, with a materialism also imported from Europe. This materialism, too, became a way of being and not an explicit doctrine, but with far different consequences. What remained of Christianity was neutered by falsehoods and sometimes outright absurdities. It lost ground steadily among the educated. The kinds of personal, social, and professional ethics that make for strong families, strong communities, and honest business practices were undermined until we reached our present state, where the bottom line is: nothing matters except the bottom line, and no one can really trust anyone. These matters will occupy chapter 3.

Cardinal Error Four: Americans did not recognize the British Fabian Society for what it was. Thus, they were blind to agents of Fabian permeation who gradually assumed control over dominant institutions and occupations in this country, in both education and labor. Early modern British thought considered the individual to be the locus of rights and responsibilities. Collectivist thinking had dominated on the Continent at least since Rousseau; the idea of a society fully planned and ruled by a power elite thinking of itself as "philosopher-kings" goes back to Plato, of course. Gradually, with few holdouts, collectivism and power-elitism subverted the English-speaking world as well. How this occurred is the topic of chapter 1.

Finally, as Fabian organizers joined forces with international bankers, both would lay in place, piece by piece, institution by institution, the groundwork for the complete replacement of nation-states by an emerging "global governance," sometimes called—not always by its detractors—a "new world order." I call this coalition of Fabian intellectuals, bankers, and those who came to surround them (intellectuals, diplomats, politicians, etc.) the Western *superelite*—to distinguish its status from any national elite in the form of a political class.

The superelite has no loyalties to anything except money, power, and itself. The key is its advancement of an aggressively global, but British-led, materialistic capitalism—a brand of capitalism not to be confused with free enterprise. Rather, the superelite's materialistic capitalism depends on central banking and money creation via fractional-reserve banking, and grows through constant turmoil—what the Austrian-born economist

Joseph Schumpeter called *creative destruction*. In the absence of these elements, this brand of capitalism falls into crisis. In the final analysis, it is unsustainable. With the right political maneuvering, it will make people dependent and will socialize itself with the support of a significant fraction of the population, though not for the reasons Karl Marx gave. Unlike genuine free enterprise, which seeks to operate independently of government and favors small, local endeavors, this brand of capitalism is very much oriented toward government, while the major players build huge corporate empires and exploit government's regulatory structure to thwart competition. It promotes wild spending by governments, corporations, and individuals; it encourages all to live beyond their means. The elite players are helped both by new technological developments and a technocratic mind-set holding that the masses in a society of increasing complexity must be controlled. Devices for control are many, but include encouraging fear in the masses—be it fear of terrorism or just of environmental degradation. In other words, either we embrace a Platonist plan directed by the "philosopher-kings," or chaos and destruction will result. These are the topics covered in chapter 5.

We are now on a high-velocity train steaming toward full-fledged globalist society—a brand of what I call *techno-feudalism*, directed as much by global corporations as by governments. Chapter 6 discusses whether this high-velocity train *can* be braked and genuine free enterprise restored. What should responsible individuals do, especially given the abundant evidence of the unsustainability of the debt-based, banker-dominated system that made its failings most evident with the financial crisis that hit the entire Western world hard in the fall of 2008? Clearly, changes will be necessary. One change may very well be the end of the culture of accumulation that has been part of mass-consumption capitalism as it has understood itself since before the mid-twentieth century. Such changes will not mitigate the fact that we are probably in for a very rough ride—one that started for many families long before this book saw the light of day. The avalanche of unemployment and foreclosures may be just the beginning. Some writers predict calamity as the government and the Federal Reserve attempt to monetize the skyrocketing national debt, bringing on catastrophic hyperinflation; others predict a slow diminishing in the American standard of living, resulting in an elite-controlled techno-feudalism: an oligarchy with a minimal middle class of those who administer policies of the elites, and a veritable army of struggling proletarians—the "global workforce"—without a power base of its own.

Has the destruction of the American republic been deliberate? I should state up front: I am not an insider; I have no special insight or source of knowledge. What I offer here is a set of inferences that lead to the best explanation, nothing more and nothing less. The contention that a superelite exists explains more than any other perspective. The alternative view, that there is no such group of insiders, or superelite, is that the visible political classes, the movers and shakers of European nations and the United States, are not very bright, for they have been operating under assumptions that are clearly false and taking the entire Western world on a suicidal course, based as it is on fiat money and the idea that banks can print their way and governments can spend their way into prosperity.

One of my fundamental premises is that *it is no more possible to create wealth and prosperity out of thin air than it is to violate the law of conservation of mass and energy in physics*. Ignore physical law—for example, by stepping out a third-floor window thinking you can fly—and there will be immediate consequences, to say the least. I wouldn't recommend clicking your heels three times trying to make it true! Unfortunately, violations of the equivalent law of economic reality only exact their consequences after a much lengthier period—at least a generation, if not longer. The systems involved are just too complex for matters to be otherwise.

The consequences of bad decisions by one generation can frequently be staved off by quick fixes for decades. Thus, for much of the past century, most economists believed that government spending would stimulate economic activity indefinitely, because it can do so in the short run by running deficits. Central bankers appear to have believed they could print money to stimulate economic activity without eventually destroying the value of the currency. Now the bills are coming due. The tech bubble was replaced by a housing bubble, and all visible efforts appear to be directed toward inflating the next bubble, which may be nothing more than a massive and very dangerous expansion of accrued debt—a debt bubble, if you will. This is our present reality, and it is very dangerous, because when this bubble bursts, it could bring about the worst depression in history—from which the superelite will attain refuge behind the walls of gated communities.

The superelite believe they can control events, of course. They will find out otherwise. No one can control the laws of reality. One can only learn about them, acknowledge them, live in accordance with them, and (for the political class) design and develop policies in accordance with them. Anything else is suicidal in the long run. There are, therefore, good reasons for exposing and opposing the superelite behind this untrammeled globalism, or "new world order," which some proclaim to be just over the horizon.

Is it possible to expose the superelite and thwart for a time the scenario of techno-feudalism controlled by global oligarchy? One would think that exposing and thwarting the superelite agenda would be easy. As we'll see in due course, some of those I consider members of the superelite have *written down in black and white just what it is they are doing, or plan to do*. I am not especially optimistic, however, for several reasons.

First, quantities of resources vaster than most of us can imagine are now being poured into building up the new order. If the superelite face a known threat, they may respond by pulling their resources out of this country and precipitating a depression for which their critics will get the blame; their control over the mass media could ensure this.

Second, despite the magnitude of the present crisis, the number of people willing to peer behind the curtains isn't terribly large. "Public education" has done its job extremely well, especially by teaching nothing of personal or national financial and monetary literacy. Most Americans appear to believe the economy will simply improve and that "things will all work out"—or that the economy must be getting better because the Dow-Jones average is going up!

Third, and finally, some people consider this line of thinking nothing but "conspiracy theory." I've seldom used the term *conspiracy*; detractors from works such as this use it a lot! There are some, after all—many securely entrenched in federal or corporate jobs—who trust authority (because they identify with power), believe their masters have everything in hand, and resist the dissemination of information demonstrating otherwise. These critics assume that works such as this are irrational and perhaps even dangerous in that they embody, or encourage, a "conspiracy theory" of modern and recent history—presumably meaning by this phrase the idea that very wealthy and powerful men have gathered behind closed doors and developed and carried out nefarious plans of various sorts without the knowledge of those their plans would affect. If that is what is meant by *conspiracy*, then one would have to be *extremely ignorant* not to realize that there have been not one but many conspiracies of various sorts, some of which became highly visible once exposed. We do not even need to explore famous but controversial claims regarding such events as the 1963 John F. Kennedy assassination, about which many unanswered questions remain. It is clear, for example, that the 1953 coup that overthrew the democratically elected government of Mohammed Musadegh in Iran and instilled the Shah was the work of the CIA, an event for which the Western world has paid dearly, since it was under the Shah's brutal regime that the Islamic terror underground incubated (cf. Stephen Kinzer, *All the Shah's Men: An American Coup and the Roots of Middle Eastern Terror*, 2003). Was that not a conspiracy? The Gulf of Tonkin "incident," on August 4, 1964, appears to have been fabricated, and the result was one of the most destructive wars in recent U.S. history. Was it not a conspiracy? Watergate was a conspiracy that destroyed the Nixon presidency. Iran-Contra was a conspiracy that for a time threatened Reagan's presidency. It appears very likely that a conspiracy within the CIA ensured that the so-called war on drugs would fail (cf. Michael Levine's *The Big White Lie*, 1994). It is now known that in each case, the major players were operating behind the scenes.

   An honest study of recent history discloses many conspiracies, and of course we have no idea how many events have resulted from conspiracies that were never uncovered and revealed to be such. So what is it that the skeptics are so fervently skeptical about? What is it about powerful people operating in secret, hiding information behind disinformation, fabricating alternative accounts of events, etc., that drives critics into hysterical attacks on "conspiracy nuts" and "tin-foil hat" wearers?

For some reason, when the topic turns to banking and finance, especially at an international level, we are not supposed to talk *conspiracy*. Yet we can look at both long-term tendencies and find that certain family dynasties have been able to amass stratospheric levels of wealth by questionable means. These families all appear to share a single vision: that of a globalist world order dominated by them. We can document how they hold very private and exclusive meetings every year where they and elite national leaders work out the details of "global governance." G. Edward Griffin has assembled overwhelming evidence that the Federal Reserve resulted from just such a meeting (see *The Creature from Jekyll Island*, 1994). Indeed, as this manuscript was nearing completion, the leading bureaucrats of today's Federal Reserve held a reunion at Jekyll Island commemorating the hundredth anniversary of the 1910 meeting that we are not supposed to believe was significant, and which, for decades, was not officially admitted to have taken place. The creation of the Federal Reserve was a turning point in U.S. history, as we shall see: the first of four turning points in just the last hundred years. (The other three were the embrace of Keynes's economics in the mid-1930s; Nixon's closing the gold window in 1971; and the international signing, sealing, and delivering of NAFTA in 1992—prior to its actual passage by the U.S. Congress in 1993.)

Consider the idea that many trends and specific events of recent decades are not accidents, but the work of powerful men operating behind the scenes, often within private financial corporations or think tanks, who essentially own heads of state and much of the mass media, and that the long-term goal of these trends is the destruction of this nation and its independent middle class—while perhaps leaving as much as is possible of its military and corporate infrastructure intact as part of a "new international economic order." Perhaps *this* is the idea the skeptics fear, since it is gaining traction with an increasingly large segment of the American public in this Internet age with its freer flow of information. Is this the idea they fear and call dangerous, demonize as "extremist," or ridicule with comparisons to silly notions such as Elvis being alive or the moon landings being faked? Ridicule is illogical, but as Saul Alinsky observed (*Rules for Radicals*, 1971), it is very difficult to counter effectively. Public ridicule tends to leave its targets flustered, incoherent, and apt to damage their own credibility still more by retaliating with unfocused emotional attacks of their own. Ridicule convinces audiences whose educational levels are sufficiently poor that they do not recognize disinformation when they see it—especially if they find it entertaining!

Worse yet, we have reached the point where preoccupations like these will get you branded an *extremist*, as opposed to merely a "conspiracy nut," and by government officials, not the scoffing coworker. A number of years ago, the FBI issued a brochure listing what its agents were to consider the marks of an extremist. One of these was what it called an excessive preoccupation with the U.S. Constitution, supposedly our federal government's founding document. Many of those whom government officials and self-anointed watchdog groups (e.g., the well-heeled Southern Poverty Law Center) have branded as extremists—not just those on the "right" but sometimes the "left" as well—worry, rightly or wrongly, about a day when the U.S. federal government will "crack down" in some fashion, as with a declaration of martial law. They believe the Federal Emergency Management

Agency (FEMA) has already constructed the equivalent of con-centration camps surrounded by barbed wire and accessible by rail lines, as were the death camps in Nazi Germany. I concede I am unsure how seriously to take such fears—FEMA's perfor-mance following Hurricane Katrina makes one wonder if those folks could herd cattle into a barn. What we should worry about *immediately* are: the continued restrictions of our freedoms in the name of "security," the declining value of our currency and the danger of a dollar collapse and hyperinflation, the continued belief in federal spending as the road to "economic recovery," and the continued support for fiat-money creation (now, in the Bernanke era, euphemistically called "quantitative easing").

If fiat-money creation was the key to prosperity, Zimbabwe would be the wealthiest nation in human history!

All this is beside the point, however, because what is de-scribed here no longer fits any "classic" model of a conspiracy as something the conspirators by definition hide from you and so you can't know about. It has not fit that model for decades. The better arguments against "conspiracy theories" presume that such theories lack evidence, or "smoking guns," that they place critics in the logically impossible situation of having to prove a negative ("Show me the conspiracy *doesn't* exist!"), and that, therefore, those who believe in such things are paranoid or in some other way deluded—or, at best, that they employ bad methodology or a defective, "crippled" epistemology. But in fact there are many well-documented and easily referenced "smok-ing guns." Here is one prominent recent example:

> For more than a century ideological extremists at either end of the political spectrum have seized upon well-publicized incidents...to attack the Rockefeller family for the inordinate influence they claim we wield over

> American political and economic institutions. Some
> even believe we are part of a secret cabal working against
> the best interests of the United States, characterizing my
> family and me as "internationalists" and of conspiring
> with others around the world to build a more integrated
> global political and economic structure—one world, if
> you will. *If that's the charge, I stand guilty, and I am proud
> of it.* (David Rockefeller Sr., *Memoirs*, 2002, p. 405;
> italics mine)

How much clearer could he be? It is true that such "smoking guns" are relatively rare, and tend to turn up in books very few people read; David Rockefeller's autobiography was hardly on the bestseller list along with Harry Potter, a Jackie Collins sex opera, the latest fad diet, or Sarah Palin's autobiography. However, these and other words of the "conspirators" are available to anyone seeking them out. Dogmatic declarations that no credible statements by "insiders" exist or that there is no evidence of the process described in this book are simply uninformed.

One must suspect intellectual dishonesty on the part of those who allege mental derangement in writers who draw attention to these "smoking guns" with references that any reasonably intelligent person can check. A recent article in an academic journal (Cass Sunstein and Adrian Vermeule, "Conspiracy Theories," *Journal of Political Science*, 2008) recommends that the federal government begin infiltrating and working to neutralize groups that promote "conspiracy theories." This blows the lid off the issue! One must suspect that those with real power know that the "conspiracists" are turning out to be right. They appear to be threatened by the fact that in an Internet-based culture—with e-mail, websites, uncensored blogs, social networking (Facebook, Twitter), and so on—*no longer can superelite "insiders" effectively hide themselves and their operations.*

It is with good reason that they feel threatened. All too many Americans now know who they are and that their activities have almost ruined a civilization that took centuries to build! Moreover, it is becoming clear that what the superelite wants and what middle America values could not be more different (see Angelo Codevilla's *The Ruling Class*, 2010).

To begin summing up, the present predicament of U.S. civilization is dire. If readers listen to the pundits on television or read daily mainstream newspapers, it is easy to become confused about what the economy is doing, or at least to think our fearless leaders have a handle on what they are doing. What counts are long-term tendencies, not what the Dow did yesterday, or whether the official unemployment rate ticked down a fraction of a percentage point last month, or that such-and-such corporation created four hundred jobs, or because Congress passed a certain bill. The plain truth is, America today is in a state of advancing decline on multiple fronts.

During the past twenty years, this country has hemorrhaged millions of good-paying manufacturing jobs and replaced them with low-paying service jobs, most of which do not require a college education. Since 2008, the situation has rapidly worsened. The "official" unemployment rate has not been under 9 percent since April 2009; the real unemployment rate, which includes "discouraged workers" who have given up, is over 20 percent! At the time of this writing, there were more than five applicants for every job opening, and that includes so-called services jobs. Our poverty rate is higher than it was in the 1960s when the Johnson Administration declared the so-called "war on poverty." Governments at all levels—federal, state, and local—are technically broke! Tens of thousands of houses, many foreclosed upon, stand empty; in some cases, entire neighborhoods are standing empty except, of course, for low-level drug dealers and street gangs. Some areas of large cities have become no-man's-lands looking like scenes out of *Blade Runner*! The predicament is worsened by our open borders, which have admitted millions of illegal aliens to compete with Americans for jobs—this while our government is supposedly fighting a "war on terror"! I have sometimes asked people: how does a government claim to be fighting a "war on terror" with its southern border wide open, and expect to be believed? (After all, not all immigrants entering this country illegally originated in Mexico!)

Which of the two dominant political parties controls the White House or Congress has not mattered in the least during the past fifty years of fiscal irresponsibility, deindustrialization, and globalism. Consider what is probably *the single most important political observation of the past century,* another of those "smoking guns," which accounts for the lack of real competition within our political system, even as it again illustrates the superelite mind-set:

> The chief problem of American political life for a long time has been how to make the two Congressional parties more national and international. The argument that the two parties should represent opposed ideals and policies, one, perhaps, of the Right and the other of the Left, is a foolish idea acceptable only to doctrinaire and academic thinkers. Instead, the two parties should be almost identical, so that the American people can "throw the rascals out" at any election without leading to any profound or extensive shifts in policy....Either party in office becomes in time corrupt, tired, unenterprising, and vigorless. Then it should be possible to replace it, every four years if necessary, by the other party, which will be none of those things but will still pursue, with new

vigor, approximately the same basic policies. (Carroll
Quigley, *Tragedy and Hope: A History of the World in Our
Time*, pp. 1247–48)

Have we not seen, since before Quigley published *Tragedy
and Hope*, essentially the same basic policy direction furthered in
Washington, D.C.—more globalism and more control over the
lives and business activities of individuals—regardless of which
party controlled Congress or the White House?

Unfortunately, modern government schools—"public education"—stifle independent thought and intellectual curiosity
through regimentation and "group activities," often before their
victims are out of grade school. Lack of a sound education that
includes some history, some philosophy, some theology, some
civics, and above all, something about the role of money in human life (i.e., one's own life) and how to manage one's money—
as opposed to the production of trained technicians, salespeople,
and bureaucrats—has given us a population that knows how to
use a Blackberry but cannot ask crucial questions about what
government officials or elite bankers are up to in any cogent or
coherent manner. Many people today cannot name their repre-
sentative in Congress or their two senators, much less the current chairman of the Federal Reserve. They are even less likely
to be able to tell you what credit-default swaps and derivatives
are, or how banks worked mortgage-backed securities (even if
they have been foreclosed on!). A flourishing multibillion-dollar
entertainment industry keeps America's masses in a cloud of
permanent distraction by parading celebrity after celebrity on
the "boob tube."

In light of these facts, there may be no need for martial-
law-type moves. Thus I will not discuss FEMA camps and the
like. I find it quite plausible that the "new world order" of the

superelite will eventually overwhelm the United States, just as it replaced European nation-states with the European Union without firing a shot—because most Americans will be too busy watching *American Idol*-type fare or sports events while it happens. Most Americans will not support presidential candidates who are labeled outside the "approved" range of opinions, much less outside the two dominant political parties: witness Dr. Ron Paul's run for the Republican nomination in 2008. Dr. Paul (R-Tx.) was the one candidate who could have given us a "profound and extensive shift in policy." What we ended up with were two candidates neither of whom was qualified to lead this country but had pedigrees acceptable to globalists.

One final note: libertarian readers will be disappointed that this is not just another anti-government tract. Libertarians, unfortunately, are captives of a pair of specific illusions: *private* equals *voluntary*, or absence of coercion; and *large corporations really want free markets*. Libertarians believe that if you do not like a corporation's products or services, then what you should do is refuse to buy those products or services. This approach goes only so far. We will be discussing private entities capable of controlling huge portions of the economy through control over the monetary system and hence over relevant parts of the political system, establishing monopolistic control over markets, services, or employment—and over control of ideas via the endowment process in universities and ownership of major newspapers and other mass-media outlets. Hence we need to watch private entities as closely as governments.

Whatever criticisms can be made of our government—and they are extensive!—I am *not* an anarchist who is anti-government (even though some critics may well brand me as such because I discuss criticisms of our government favorably).

The anarchocapitalist's illusion is that we could go, in principle, from too *many* rules and an ambience of entitlement, to no rules *at all* other than whatever is established in a "free" marketplace (which would not be free, but controlled by those with the most land and money), and an every-man-for-himself economy (which would most likely result in a Hobbesian state of nature). A minimal state that answers to a written constitution and has the machinery to create and maintain an uneasy balance between competing interests is probably the best arrangement human nature is going to allow, and even that will depend on a vigilant segment of the public capable of keeping that state on its constitutional leash.

The fundamental locus of control we are concerned with here is not government as such, but the superelite class that stands above governments—because it has the resources to buy governments, keep them in its very deep pockets, and use them to further its goals and policies. This means corporate power and also private foundation power. There is a difference between the *power of the sword*, which is the power of governments to achieve their goals by passing laws and enforcing them at gunpoint, and the *power of the purse*, which is the power of those with incredible levels of wealth to achieve their goals by distributing their wealth to those who will then work to achieve them, while withholding it from those who will not. The result is that opponents twist in the wind—without ever figuring out why, if they are locked in the conceptual box that labels America as a democracy with a truly free-market economy. If you abolished government altogether, you would not abolish the superelite class or restore free enterprise—and the superelite would simply re-create government, having allowed enough chaos in the meantime that its efforts would be resoundingly supported by the public.

The United States of America began with a unique set of principles, rose higher than any nation in history, but has fallen terribly over the past century. Its fall has accelerated during the past four decades, and it is in danger of falling much farther. I submit that we have fallen because of the Four Cardinal Errors. Our system has never needed "profound or extensive shifts in policy" more than we need them today! Whether we can achieve these shifts by means of our present political system, or with our present American public, remains to be seen. But as the economic situation in America worsens, and with more and more people waking up to our present reality, we will see what happens. In the meantime, let us look at how we got here.

1

Cardinal Error One. Our original Republic, founded in 1776, failed to keep British-European bankers out of its affairs even though these bankers served the interests of the Crown, not the United States of America. Our Republic embraced their fraudulent money system based on fractional-reserve lending. The result was a form of capitalism bound to be hijacked.

. . .

For roughly a thousand years, the British Crown has been the wealthiest and most powerful secular entity in the Western world. Its modern enclave is the City of London, which has been called the wealthiest square mile in the world and should not be confused with the surrounding city also called London (see E.C. Knuth, *The Empire of the City: The Secret History of British Financial Power*, orig. 1944; cf. Joan Veon, "Who Runs the World and Controls the Value of Assets," 2007). The City of London is a private enclave with its own governance: a private corporation called the City of London Corporation. The Bank of England was chartered there in 1694 by William Paterson under the direction of King William III of the House of Orange. Fifteen years later, the British government borrowed from the bank to finance its wars. The Bank of England received a legal monopoly on the banking industry. This quickly led to the empowerment of an entrenched ruling class capable of exercising control over the British government.

Although we fought a war for independence, we never obtained full freedom and economic sovereignty from this British system. This will likely come as a surprise to most readers. Please allow me to elaborate.

I.

Concentrations of power have always been dangerous. This is as true of private wealth as it is of state power. Sadly, advocates of *laissez-faire* economics have yet to realize that the ultra-wealthy have never wanted *laissez-faire*. When used to buy and retain the loyalty of heads of state and their minions, private wealth *is* power. The Rothschild dynasty, though doubtless not the first, built up an enormous system of private wealth in the final third of the 1700s and on into the 1800s. The founder of that dynasty, Mayer Amschel Bauer, was born in 1743, a child prodigy who grew up on *Jüdenstrasse* in Frankfurt-on-the-Main in what is now Germany. As a boy he learned from his father, Amschel Moses Bauer, how to handle currencies and currency exchanges. The elder Bauer ran a counting house that also dealt in rare coins. His son appears to have been avidly interested from his earliest days. Amschel Moses Bauer had hung a red shield over the entrance to the business. The Bauers, who had migrated to the area from the East, were Ashkenazi Jews. The red shield, which sported a six-pointed star, was a symbol of revolutionary-minded Jews and thought by some to be occult or even satanic in nature. The color *red* has remained deeply significant for leftist revolutionary movements.

Young Mayer Amschel's parents died from the plague when he was eleven. The boy was sent to nearby Hannover, where he went to work at Oppenheimer, a major bank. His talents obvious, he was promoted to junior partner status while still in his teens. At Oppenheimer, he made contacts that would prove invaluable later, such as with General von Estorff, who shared his interest in rare coins and for whom he ran errands. Despite the opportunity with Oppenheimer, Mayer Amschel returned to Frankfurt and bought the family business back. The red shield was still there. He'd begun to understand its role in his Ashkenazi heritage. Mayer Amschel changed his legal last name to *Rothschild* (*Rot[h]*, red, and *Schild*, shield). He established a *Wechselstube* where the various currencies circulating in the duchies and fiefdoms that made up what was then Germany could be exchanged, charging a commission for each exchange. He began to profit handsomely from these exchanges. He also began making use of his Hannover contacts. General von Estorff, who was now attached to the court of Prince William of Hanau, invited Mayer Amschel to meet the prince. Mayer Amschel sold the prince some of his rarest medals and coins. It was the first transaction between a Rothschild and a head of state. Mayer Amschel then offered the prince a discount for any new business he could direct Mayer's way. Soon Mayer had become the personal banker of Prince William and other members of his court.

News of Mayer Amschel Rothschild began to spread, especially after September 21, 1769, when he was granted permission to hang a sign on the front of his business declaring himself, in gold lettering, to be "M.A. Rothschild, by appointment court factor to his serene highness, Prince William of Hanau." Mayer sought the patronage of other heads of state through a prolific letter-writing campaign. Here is a typical example of his letters:

> It has been my particular high and good fortune to serve your lofty princely Serenity at various times and to your most gracious satisfaction. I stand ready to exert all my energies and my entire fortune to serve your lofty princely serenity whenever in future it shall please you to command me. An especially powerful incentive to

this end would be given me if your lofty princely seren-
ity were to distinguish me with an appointment as one
of your Highness' Court Factors. I am making bold to
beg for this with the more confidence in the assurance
that by so doing I am not giving any trouble; while for
my part such a distinction would lift up my commercial
standing and be of help to me in many other ways that
I feel certain thereby to make my own way and fortune
here in the city of Frankfurt. (Frederic Morton, *The
Rothschilds*, p. 26)

Such letters were very successful. Soon he was doing business with other heads of state in the region. While his brothers
Moses and Kalmann looked on, the smiling and ambitious Mayer
began to profit handsomely from these exchanges. He was on
his way to becoming fabulously wealthy: the rise of the House
of Rothschild had begun. In 1770, he married Gutle Schnaper,
the daughter of a respected Frankfurt merchant. She was just
sixteen. She immediately began to bear him children. In 1785,
Mayer Amschel Rothschild moved with his family into a large
five-story house they would share with the Schiffs, another
wealthy banking family whose most famous progeny was Jacob
Schiff.

Mayer Amschel Rothschild had five sons and five daughters.
His five sons were known as "the five arrows": Amschel Mayer
(born in 1773), Salomon Mayer (born in 1774), Nathan Mayer
(born in 1777), Kalmann "Karl" Mayer (born in 1788), and Jacob
"James" Mayer (born in 1792). Mayer Amschel trained each son
in the practice of moneylending, and eventually placed each
in a central bank in a major city in Europe: Amschel stayed in
Frankfurt, Salomon went to Vienna, Nathan to London, Karl to
Naples, and James to Paris. Remaining in close communication,
the five Rothschild sons became the first internationalists whose

only loyalties were to money, power, and family concerns. They married the daughters of prominent families and sired children of their own.

The growing Rothschild network not only came to dominate the world's financial and monetary systems but also gave fractional-reserve banking a central role in the rising capitalist civilization. Bankers considered it a golden goose. In fact, it is the most gigantic swindle in all of history. Fractional-reserve banking involves lending out more money than the bank has in reserve—creating money literally out of thin air. A paper-money system makes this possible, which is why Jefferson was so opposed to a paper-money system. Fractional lending makes possible what I call *pseudoprosperity*: lives of leisure built up on an edifice of debt—personal, corporate, and governmental. In the right intellectual and political environment, the apparent ready availability of money obtained with minimal effort creates in people a sense of entitlement. This is dangerous, as we are learning the hard way. The Rothschilds did not invent the practice, of course, but they honed it to a fine science, and it would prove to be a pathway to levels of wealth previously undreamt of—for themselves!

Some knowledge of how fractional-reserve banking works is necessary to any understanding of how the Western superelite have built up such enormous levels of wealth over the past three centuries. Let's use a parable first: We are playing poker at Paul's house, with Paul acting as banker. There are seven of us, and we've each given Paul $20 for twenty poker chips. So Paul's cash box—the "bank"—contains exactly $140. Each of us has twenty $1 poker chips. We can leave the game whenever we want, exchanging our winnings for dollars. We're enjoying the game, so no one leaves. The $140 remains in the box. The poker chips are functioning as *backed* currency. They are backed by the cash each of us contributed when we joined the game, kept secure in the box. Now suppose Paul's brother Peter shows up. Peter wants to borrow some money. Suppose Paul lends him $120 from the box. Strictly speaking, of course, Paul has no right to lend Peter the money; it isn't his to lend! He ought to obtain an additional $120 to lend his brother, or use $120 of his own money. But more importantly, the poker chips in the "bank" cannot retain their value as backed currency if Paul loans Peter the $120. He does so anyway, leaving just $20 in the box. Paul has *debauched* the value of the poker chips and also placed him-self in an awkward position should one of us wish to leave the game with winnings totaling more than $20. Paul would have to default on his contract, which was to keep our money safe for the duration of the game. A bank that defaults on its contract *fails*. The banker is out of business.

Suppose one of the early bankers stored $140 in gold from seven customers (all having deposited $20 worth of gold) and issued seven $20 paper currency certificates each stating this face value, totaling $140 in *face value*, as we shall call it. The certifi-cates might even say, "Will pay to bearer on demand, $20." This suggests a hard distinction between money (the gold on deposit in the bank vault) and the paper currency (backed by the gold on deposit). Now a would-be borrower appears and wants to borrow $120, as Peter did from Paul in the poker-game illustra-tion. The banker decides to "put the money to work." The money may not be his, but he has observed that his customers would rather carry around paper certificates than heavy bags of gold coins. Most customers leave their gold in his vault, akin to the poker players leaving their money in the cash box. The banker thus considers it a safe gamble to issue additional $20 certificates for up to $120 of what he has stored, under the assumption that the original customers will not want all their gold back at once. Do the arithmetic, and we see that the banker has issued certificates totaling $260 (the original $140, plus $120 in loans)—this despite his having just $140 in his vault. He has created the other $120 out of thin air, *ex nihilo,* as God is supposed to have created the world. Only our banker is not God, and his certificates are no longer fully backed by one of God's precious metals. They are loaned out, accepted, and used as if they were, by a borrower who suspects nothing.

Through this process of *fractional lending,* the certificates have become *fractional money*, meaning the worth of the gold behind them is a fraction of their face value. The actual worth of any particular certificate after the banker's loan is therefore a fraction of its original worth before the loan. The supply of certificates in circulation has been *inflated*, which gives us the true meaning of *inflation*: more paper currency chasing the same quantity of goods and services, with each unit of paper currency worth less—and capable of buying less. The goods purchased thus cost *more* in terms of currency units.

One additional matter must be factored into the equation: *interest (usury)*. The early bankers decided they were entitled to payment for the work involved in moneylending. Let's say I am a banker in a hypothetical economy with just $200 in currency available to be loaned out. I loan both Peter and Paul $100. Now let's say that in addition to my payment, I charge 5 percent interest per year on each $100 loaned out. At this point, we should recall that a finite amount was loaned out: $200. But I have contracted to receive back more than I lent out: $210. At the end of the year, Peter has more money than he borrowed (say, $105), so he can repay the loan plus the year's interest. Paul, however, has only $95, so he cannot pay back either the loan or the interest. To pay, he has to borrow again. Thus *debt* is created—a debt that cannot be repaid because *the currency necessary to repay it does not exist!* After all, $210 is owed, but only $200 is in circulation!

I can, of course, create and loan Paul additional money as *credit* so he can repay that debt—but at the price of incurring a fresh debt. The new loan is not interest free. Its interest rate may even be higher. Paul has bought some time; he may consider this a good deal. Thus Paul's debt accumulates over time, as will that of other borrowers on whom I can place a *lien*. A lien placed by a bank on someone's property means that ultimately, the bank owns the property and can, in principle, seize it if the debt is not repaid. This is called *foreclosure*. I can take Paul's house and resell it to obtain payment for the debt. Of course, it may not be desirable to do this. If I prefer Paul to be complacent, I can continue loaning him money. His debt grows still higher. He believes himself to be free, but the truth is, I own him. Bankers know the truth: *the borrower is a slave of the lender*.

Now imagine this situation writ large, in an actual economy that has adopted fractional lending in the context of modern central banking, where, regardless of what products and how much are produced, there is a large, but still finite, amount of paper currency in circulation. Only the bankers are able to see that individuals, corporations, or entire nations can fall into debts from which they can never extract themselves—since *that extra 5 percent was never loaned out and cannot be repaid*. In this hypothetical economy, if some can repay specific debts, others cannot. And with each extension on a loan, interest accumulates. Debts grow higher. A *national debt* begins to rise. If not checked, the rise becomes uncontrollable.

Borrowers believe, of course, that they can redeem their paper certificates for their full face value if they want; yet they are being charged interest on their full face value! Typically they do nothing, because the paper certificates continue to be easier to use than heavy metal coins. They trust the system. This works to their detriment. The banker collects the profits and can extend the loans indefinitely, collecting still more profits. This is fractional-reserve banking plus usury. If we understand how this works to create a money system based on debt, we are in a position to understand the hugest swindle in modern history.

Early bankers loaned fractional money and charged interest on its full face value. The more fractional money they loaned, the less it was actually worth—and the more interest they could charge. Their clients included governments. Countless duchies, fiefdoms, and princedoms were spread across what is now Germany, so the bankers had plenty of customers. They would extend the loans, attaching conditions to the extensions. In this way, the bankers gained not just wealth but power. Their borrowers accrued debts that could never be repaid since, again, the currency for repaying the interest didn't exist. So they fell under the bankers' private power—the power of the purse. It was a system guaranteed not just to expand governments—the power of the sword—but simultaneously to control them, so that specific agendas the bankers wanted could be enacted. The bankers, of course, kept their mouths shut. They quietly honored their own core commandment: *tell no one.* Following money trails is hence one of the first skills needed by an investigator into the shadowy movements that have grown up around international banking. The Rothschild dynasty offers a case in point.

Most people would never figure out the fractional money system. It is not taught in schools. Its workings are concealed within an esoteric vocabulary and when described at all, are described in long, ponderous statements guaranteed to make one's eyes glaze over. Money creation, therefore, became a road to both wealth and power for a banker class that came to exist in a world all its own, above even kings and princes. This class became the core of the superelite we see today. Mayer Amschel Rothschild has been quoted (supposedly he said this around 1790): "Let me issue and control a nation's money and I care not who writes the laws" (see G. Edward Griffin, *The Creature from Jekyll Island*, p. 218).

Incidentally, there were also five Rothschild daughters, each of whom married into another wealthy family, extending Rothschild influence but without using the name. That influence grew and spread. Within a couple of generations, there were people advancing Rothschild interests who very likely had no idea who they were really working for. In Fabian terminology, they were permeated. (For who the Fabians were/are, see chapters 4 and 5.)

The British Crown housed in the City of London was, as noted above, already one of the largest repositories of wealth and power in the West. The Crown's East India Company and its offshoots spanned the globe after the demise of its predecessor, the Dutch East India Company, arguably the first modern multinational megacorporation to achieve quasi-governmental levels of power. It was inevitable that the most talented of Mayer Amschel's sons—Nathan Mayer—would establish his bank (N. M. Rothschild and Sons) in 1811 in the heart of Crown territory, which soon became the center of Rothschild influence as well.

Nathan Mayer appears to have had a cold-as-ice demeanor. Consider:

Eyes are usually called the windows of the soul. But in Rothschild's case you would conclude that the windows are false ones, or that there was no soul to look out of them. There comes not one pencil of light from the interior, neither is there one gleam which comes from without reflected in any direction. The whole puts you in mind of an empty skin, and you wonder why it stands upright without at least something in it. By and by another figure comes up to it. It then steps two paces aside, and the most inquisitive glance that you ever saw, and a glance more inquisitive than you would ever have thought of, is drawn out of the fixed and leaden eye, as if one were drawing a sword from a scabbard. The visiting figure, which has the appearance of coming by accident and not by design, stops just a second or two, in the course of which looks are exchanged which, though you cannot translate, you feel must be of most important meaning. After these the eyes are sheathed up again, and the figure resumes its stony posture. (Frederick Morton, *The Rothschilds*, p. 65)

As such descriptions hint, the Rothschilds were ruthless in their business dealings. They had no friends as such, just allies of convenience—who often found themselves discarded when their usefulness had ended. Nathan Mayer's talent for working the system soon made him the richest man operating in the City of London. The most legendary of his supposed exploits involves an insider-trading stunt involving the Battle of Waterloo: he orchestrated a selloff on the London Stock Exchange leading observers to believe that Great Britain was losing, then bought back in when stocks were at their low point. Upon news that Great Britain had won the Battle of Waterloo, their value skyrocketed. Nathan Mayer became a billionaire overnight!

Nathan Mayer was training his own son, Lionel Nathan, born in 1808. Other Rothschild brothers were doing the same with their progeny. The third generation and then the fourth carried the family name into activities other than banking: railroads, mining (diamonds and precious metals), oil, vineyards, horse breeding and racing, and so on, eventually including major media outlets like Reuters, purchased by a Rothschild late in the 1800s after an attack on the family. Many of these purchases were entirely innocuous: pastimes for the idle rich. For to be a Rothschild was to be fabulously wealthy.

The first five Rothschild brothers had learned early on how to engineer financial panics. In other words, they could create crises to which they would offer a solution that inevitably enlarged their wealth and power. They became masters of the most important manifestation of Hegelian dialectic: *thesis, antithesis, synthesis*. In practice, the Hegelian triad emerges as: *crisis, reaction, response*. Create a crisis (or through inaction allow one to emerge); the crisis brings about a panicked reaction on the part of people ("Do something!"), to which the bankers offer the response they wanted all along. This practice included fomenting wars in which Rothschild money bankrolled both sides, often to topple rulers who had forgotten their place, as it were. The incipient superelite had no qualms about stirring up wars. They understood the most important fact about modern warfare: it costs money. Wars require governments to borrow to rebuild their economies, resulting in still more debt and dependence. (Hegelian dialectic in the above sense is very much in evidence today; witness former White House Chief of Staff and current Chicago Mayor Rahm Emanuel's remark about never letting a crisis go to waste. He is hardly alone with this kind of sentiment.)

Prior to his death in 1812, Mayer Amschel had left a detailed will. What it specified is worth considering here:

(a) all key positions in the House of Rothschild were to be held exclusively by male members of the family;

(b) first and second cousins were to intermarry, keeping the vast Rothschild fortune within the family;

(c) under no circumstances were there to be audits or public inventories of the Rothschild estate, thus ensuring complete secrecy;

(d) a perpetual family partnership was to exist, with male members managing their portion of the estate and female members receiving their share of the interest, subject to management by the male members;

(e) the eldest son of the eldest son would become head of the family, unless the majority of the sons agreed otherwise.

This last provision worked in Nathan's favor, as Nathan was clearly the most talented (and most ruthless). With the mutual consent of the other Rothschild sons, after Mayer's death he assumed control over the Rothschild dynasty, moving its seat of operations into the City of London. He would pass the reins of the dynasty to his eldest son, Lionel, who financed Great Britain's purchase of Egypt's interest in the Suez Canal in 1875 and also become the first Jew to serve in the House of Commons. Lionel then passed control to his eldest son, Nathan ("Lord Natty"), the first Baron Rothschild, who became the first Jewish member of the House of Lords. "Natty" helped bankroll Cecil Rhodes's endeavors in southern Africa, enterprises that built the Rhodes fortune. One of Lionel's other sons, Leopold, helped administer the Rhodes estate after Cecil Rhodes's death in 1902. He also helped arrange the Rhodes Scholarship program through

Oxford University. Rhodes scholars are furthering long-term Rothschild goals, whether they know it or not; most, of course, probably do not.

The family did experience setbacks. In 1814, Nathan spearheaded an effort that would have transformed the Rothschild network into a *de facto* world government. Czar Alexander I of Russia exposed the plan and warned others. This led to its being opposed in Europe, and the effort failed. A livid Nathan vowed vengeance on the Czar and his descendents. One hundred and three years later, the banker-financed Bolshevik Revolution led by Vladimir Lenin would destroy traditional Russian civilization.

These incidents were few and far between, however. In 1823, the Rothschilds assumed control over the finances of the Vatican, and thus of the Catholic Church worldwide. The aging Amschel Meyer, still in Frankfurt, schooled Otto Bismarck in the science of power. Bismarck, of course, became dictator of Prussia. His personal banker was Gerson von Bleichroder, who served Rothschild interests. Von Bleichroder bankrolled Prussia's wars with Austria and France, leaving both in ruins. An American named Junius Spencer Morgan was brought in to finance France's rebuilding. Morgan became wealthy through the power of debt. Alphonse de Rothschild (James's son) and his younger brother Edmond began the herculean work of planning a Jewish homeland. While its exact location was initially uncertain, the Rothschilds finally settled on the Middle East. In 1917, the Balfour Declaration sent by Foreign Secretary James Arthur Balfour to Walter, Lord Natty's eldest son and the second Baron Rothschild, conveyed His Majesty's support for creating the Jewish homeland in Palestine. The State of Israel was established by the United Nations in 1948. The Middle East has arguably been in a state of crisis ever since.

By the 1900s, it is fair to say, Rothschild influence spanned the globe! The Rothschild financial behemoth had become a vast "shadow government" behind the scenes. It ensured that money power would dominate future economic development around the world. Sympathetic biographer and Harvard University mainstream historian Niall Ferguson wrote how the Rothschilds "represented a new materialist religion." (Chapter 3 explores materialism in more depth.) Ferguson quotes journalist, essayist, and poet Heinrich Heine, who remarked as far back as 1841: "Money is the god of our time, and Rothschild is his prophet" (*The Rothschilds*, Vol. 1, 1998, p. 17). By 1900, no one outside the Rothschild behemoth could be sure how much wealth it controlled. The figure clearly ran into the hundreds of billions even then. There are estimates placing the total amount of money it controls, measured in current American dollars, at more than $100 trillion!

The Rothschild behemoth still exists, of course, although it keeps a much lower profile and feigns an appearance of disinterest in politics or global finance. Napoleon—whose fall was engineered by the Rothschilds—said in 1815, "When a government is dependent for money upon the bankers, they and not the leaders of the government control the situation, since the hand that gives is above the hand that takes…financiers are without patriotism and without decency; their sole object is gain" (quoted in Robert McNair Wilson, *Monarchy or Money Power*, 1933, ch. 9). As we said: the borrower is the slave of the lender.

II.

Whatever zest for exploration and desire for religious free-dom motivated many people to move to the New World, it is clear that the American colonies began their existence subservient to the Crown. For a time, however, they printed their own currency independently of British banks, and they had grown prosperous. The banks, led by the Bank of England, petitioned King George III to outlaw the practice, and the result was the Currency Act—actually, two separate acts (one in 1751, the second in 1764) designed to bring colonial finances back under British control. The colonial economy took an immediate nose-dive. Benjamin Franklin took the lead in urging the repeal of the Currency Act of 1764, the most immediate cause of economic difficulties in the colonies. Many colonists began to chafe at the differential treatment they received at the hands of the Crown. A number of taxes were imposed through the Stamp Act (1765) and the Townsend Acts (1767). These taxes were repealed in 1770 (except for a tax on tea) when they prompted a boycott of British goods. The British military began to increase its presence in the colonies. This annoyed the colonists further. In Massachusetts Bay Colony on March 5, 1770, a mob began throwing sticks of firewood and snowballs at a group of British soldiers. When one soldier was struck and fell, the others pan-icked and fired into the crowd, killing three people instantly and wounding several others. Two more colonists later died from their wounds. The event became known as the Boston Massacre.

It is important to understand the colonial mind-set. The col-onists considered themselves British citizens. Outcries against "taxation without representation" were obviously not calls for revolt or independence, but demands to be treated the same as their countrymen across the Atlantic. Yet hostilities between the two were about to escalate. Some colonists had begun smuggling in tea from Holland to circumvent the tax on tea. The Tea Act, which Parliament passed in 1773 in retaliation, made British tea cheaper than Dutch tea by repealing duties. The colonists refused even to unload British tea, which rotted on ships in harbors in Charleston, Philadelphia, New York, and Boston. On December 16, a group of colonists disguised themselves as Mohawk Indians, boarded the ships of the British tea merchants, and dumped some ten thousand British pounds worth of tea into the harbor: the Boston Tea Party. A furious King George III passed what became known as the Intolerable Acts of 1774, one of which closed the Boston port until Great Britain's East India Company had been repaid for the destroyed tea and until the king was satisfied that the colonies would fall back in line.

Colonial leaders instead assembled the First Continental Congress, which petitioned the king for an end to the Intolerable Acts, organized another boycott of British goods, and supported further resistance in the Massachusetts Bay Colony. On April 19, 1775, violence broke out at both Lexington and Concord. On August 23, the king proclaimed the colonies to be in "open and avowed rebellion." (Note that word *proclaimed*. We will see it again.) The Second Continental Congress convened and issued its reply on December 6. It still referred to "this unhappy and unnatural controversy, in which Britons fight against Britons." The colonists *still* considered themselves British citizens. They preferred reconciliation to revolution. Independence stirrings were inevitable, however. In January 1776, former British civil servant and pamphleteer Thomas Paine published a bold and incisive tract titled *Common Sense*. Paine's tract, initially published anonymously—"written by an Englishman"—brazenly attacked the authority of the monarchy and made an eloquent case for independence over reconciliation: "The authority of Great Britain over this continent, is a form of government, which sooner or later must have an end." And later: "A government of our own is our natural right." Since it spoke the plain language of the common man, *Common Sense* was widely read and circulated throughout the colonies, prompting wide discussion of its main proposal, which was full independence from the Crown.

The Declaration of Independence was adopted by the Second Continental Congress on July 4, 1776. The war for independence had already begun. The thirteen colonies formed a Perpetual Union of Sovereign States under the Articles of Confederation, completed in 1777 and ratified by all the states in 1781. The Articles created a highly decentralized government. They allowed a central government to establish foreign policy, declare war, and raise an army to continue the war for independence, but without taxing authority. Instead, the federal government had to request money from the states. Nor could it impose uniform tariffs or assume unpaid state war debts. The Treaty of Paris in 1783 formally ended the war but languished in Congress for months because the Confederation had no means to compel attendance by state representatives. By the mid-1780s, some began calling themselves Federalists and argued that the government established under the Articles of Confederation was too weak. To be sure, a number of additional volatile issues had erupted (e.g., Shays' Rebellion in Massachusetts). Moreover, the British had not honored their promise in the Treaty of Paris to leave the former colonies. It was unclear how these issues were to be resolved peacefully under the authority of the Articles. Was the Perpetual Union established under the Articles too weak and hence inherently unstable?

In 1786, Charles Pinckney of South Carolina proposed revising the Articles of Confederation. In 1787, all of the states except for Rhode Island sent representatives to what became the first Constitutional Convention in Philadelphia. They met behind closed doors. Their stated intent was to revise the Articles. They emerged after three months of intense debate and discussion with a new document, the Constitution of the United States of America. One could make a case that the Constitutional Convention of 1787 peacefully overthrew the government established by the Articles of Confederation and gave the world something it had never seen before: *federalism* with *dual sovereignty*. Historian Forrest McDonald observes:

> The constitutional reallocation of powers created a new form of government, unprecedented under the sun. Every previous national authority either had been centralized or else had been a confederation of sovereign states. The new American system was neither one nor the other; it was a mixture of both. (*Novus Ordo Seclorum: The Intellectual Origins of the Constitution*, 1986, p. 276)

Certain powers, enumerated and very specific, were accorded to the federal government; others, unenumerated and indefinite, were retained by the states. When asked by a woman what kind of government this Constitution created, monarchy or republic, Benjamin Franklin famously replied, "A republic, if you can keep it." One thing was for sure: the Constitution had created a stronger central government than its predecessor. Not everyone was comfortable with this fact. It is unfortunate that both Thomas Paine and Thomas Jefferson were in Europe. Had they participated in the Constitutional Convention, it is quite possible that the resulting Constitution and all subsequent history might look very different. A divide emerged within the former colonies between those who distrusted concentrations of power, British or otherwise, as inherently dangerous—Paine, Jefferson, and those history would label the Anti-Federalists—and those who sought a centralized, hierarchical regime perhaps free of British rule but structured along British mercantilist lines— James Madison, George Washington, and especially Alexander Hamilton, who represented the elite interests of bankers and wealthy landowners. Allegations exist that Hamilton was serving Rothschild interests.

To be adopted, the new Constitution needed ratification by nine of the thirteen states. Madison, John Jay, and Hamilton penned the *Federalist Papers,* making a public case for ratification. Hamilton's desire to protect commercial interests (i.e., banking interests) was clearest in "Federalist No. 12." The Anti-Federalists smelled a rat and argued against ratification. Anti-Federalist authors such as Richard Henry Lee and Robert Yates circulated numerous broadsides contending, for example, that the Constitution contained too many loopholes through which those who wanted a still larger central government would eventually climb.

Among Anti-Federalist worries was the lack of an explicit statement of rights that any legitimate government was obligated to respect. They reached a compromise: a Bill of Rights was appended to the document—its first ten amendments. In light of history, this wasn't enough. History validated the fears of the Anti-Federalists. But alas, we get ahead of ourselves.

The Constitution created a new system of government, one stronger and more centralized than that of the Articles, but still limited *if* its provisions were followed. The federal government was to have three branches, each with specific delegated powers—or, better, responsibilities, since the overriding aim of having a Constitution was to contain power by creating a balance of powers within the federal government itself—and *dual sovereignty,* in which the powers of the federal government were few and carefully defined, while the rest were left to the states and the people.

This did not resolve a growing divide between those who wanted more power consolidated at the center and those who did not. Among the responsibilities assigned to Congress was to "coin money and regulate the value thereof." Article I Section 8 did *not* authorize Congress to delegate this responsibility to any private entity. Yet this clause in the Constitution was abrogated almost at once. Here is where Alexander Hamilton enters our story. His contributions to the *Federalist Papers* (e.g., "Federalist No. 11") argued for an essentially mercantilist economic system. He would become secretary of the Treasury under President George Washington. In 1790, he used his position to spearhead the passage of the Assumption Act, which allowed the federal government to assume state debts. He then drew up plans for a central bank that would administer and fund debts under the Assumption Act and submitted his plan to the president. The bank would be called the Bank of the United States.

Over Thomas Jefferson's explicit objections, Washington allowed the Bank of the United States to be created in 1971 and chartered for twenty years. Jefferson's warnings about central bankers, doubtless based on firsthand observations from his time in Europe, are well known. A quote attributed to Jefferson has been circulating for some time on the Internet:

> If the American people ever allow private banks to control the issue of their currency, first by inflation, then

by deflation, the banks and corporations that will grow up around them will deprive the people of all property until their children wake up homeless on the continent their Fathers conquered....I believe that banking institutions are more dangerous to our liberties than standing armies....The issuing power should be taken from the banks and restored to the people, to whom it properly belongs.

This quote is apocryphal. The existence of several minor variations suggests that Jefferson never wrote or uttered these exact words. His letters, however, contain many well-authenticated remarks about banks that make his stance clear. Doubtless he understood the fractional reserve system. Doubtless, too, he had observed Rothschild influence while in Europe. Jefferson had no trust in banking institutions or in what we today call fiat money. "Paper is poverty," Jefferson told Edward Carrington in a 1788 letter, "it is only the ghost of money, and not money itself" (*The Writings of Thomas Jefferson*, vol. 7, p. 36). On several other occasions, Jefferson warned of the dangers of paper money and of banks. He wrote to John W. Eppes in 1813, "Private fortunes, in the present state of our circulation, are at the mercy of those self-created money lenders, and are prostrated by the floods of nominal money with which their avarice deluges us" (*Writings*, vol. 13, p. 278).

Portions of the apocryphal quote are authentic and appear in various letters, such as the one he wrote to John Taylor in 1816: "I sincerely believe...that banking establishments are more dangerous than standing armies, and that the principle of spending money to be paid by posterity under the name of funding is but swindling futurity on a large scale" (*Writings*, vol. 15, p. 23). Regarding the Bank of the United States, he wrote in 1791, "The incorporation of a bank and the powers assumed [by legislation doing so] have not, in my opinion, been delegated to the United States by the Constitution. They are not among the powers specifically enumerated" (*Writings*, vol. 3, p. 146). In 1803, he wrote to Albert Gallatin:

> The Bank of the United States…is one of the most deadly hostility existing, against the principles and form of our Constitution….An institution like this, penetrating by its branches every part of the Union, acting by command and in phalanx, may, in a critical moment, upset the government. I deem no government safe which is under the vassalage of any self-constituted authorities, or any other authority than that of the nation, or its regular functionaries. What an obstruction could not this Bank of the United States, with all its branch banks, be in time of war! It might dictate to us the peace we should accept, or withdraw its aids. Ought we then to give further growth to an institution so powerful, so hostile? (*Writings*, vol. 10, p. 437)

In 1819, he wrote to William C. Rives:

> Certainly no nation ever before abandoned to the avarice and jugglings of private individuals to regulate according to their own interests, the quantum of circulating medium for the nation—to inflate, by deluges of paper, the nominal prices of property, and then to buy up that property at 1s. in the pound, having first withdrawn the floating medium which might endanger a competition in purchase. Yet this is what has been done, and will be done, unless stayed by the protecting hand of the legislature. The evil has been produced by the error of their sanction of this ruinous machinery of banks; and justice, wisdom, duty, all require that they should interpose and

arrest it before the schemes of plunder and spoliation desolate the country. (*Writings*, vol. 15, p. 232)

Finally, Jefferson wrote:

> The art and mystery of banks…is established on the principle that "private debts are a public blessing." That the evidences of those private debts, called bank notes, become active capital, and aliment the whole commerce, manufactures, and agriculture of the United States. Here are a set of people, for instance, who have bestowed on us the great blessing of running in our debt about two hundred millions of dollars, without our knowing who they are, where they are, or what property they have to pay this debt when called on; nay, who have made us so sensible of the blessings of letting them run in our debt, that we have exempted them by law from the repayment of these debts beyond a given proportion (generally estimated at one-third). And to fill up the measure of blessing, instead of paying, they receive an interest on what they owe from those to whom they owe; for all the notes, or evidences of what they owe, which we see in circulation, have been lent to somebody on an interest which is levied again on us through the medium of commerce. And they are so ready still to deal out their liberalities to us, that they are now willing to let themselves run in our debt ninety millions more, on our paying them the same premium of six or eight per cent interest, and on the same legal exemption from the repayment of more than thirty millions of the debt, when it shall be called for. (*Writings*, vol. 13, p. 420)

That central banking, the chief instrument of the power of the purse, was *very dangerous* to liberty, property, free enterprise, and a people's capacity to grow their prosperity—to a free society generally—couldn't have been said more clearly in these and other remarks by Thomas Jefferson. It may already have been too late, however. The Hamiltonians, as they became known, pursued mercantilism modeled on that of Great Britain. They favored strengthening the federal government for this purpose. The Jeffersonians feared that if this happened, the people would be right back where they had started, under a regime no less repressive than the one they had just fought! But the Hamiltonians had powerful backers!

It is likely that the banking elite of the time—the Rothschild dynasty, of course, but also its allies, such as Schiff and Warburg—wanted to destroy the fledgling republic across the ocean. They would bring it back under Crown control (i.e., *their* control), or else! The Treaty of Paris of 1783 had officially ended the war, but the Crown's overbearing presence remained, including on U.S. soil. Washington, seeking to avoid renewed hostilities with the still-powerful British war machine, sent John Jay to London with a new treaty intended to diffuse the danger of renewed conflict. This treaty—more Hamilton's doing than Washington's or Jay's, and unfortunately almost forgotten by historians today—became known as the Jay Treaty and was very controversial in its time. It was signed in London on November 19, 1794. Back in the states, it was submitted to the U.S. Senate on June 8 the following year and provoked an angry debate. It was finally passed on June 24 (the vote was 20–10). The House passed it on August 14, 1795. Then it was sent back to Great Britain. British Parliament ratified it on October 28, 1795. King George III proclaimed the Jay Treaty on February 29, 1796.

Time out! Remember that word *proclaimed*? What, precisely, do we mean by *proclaimed?* There was no basis in the American Constitution for a recognition of *proclaimed*! *Proclaiming* was something British royalty did, not people's representatives in a constitutional republic!

This is bound to be startling, even to Patriots who believe they've seen everything! In the final analysis, given that it was *proclaimed*, the Jay Treaty *is more a British document than an American one*. The Crown ended the American War for Independence on February 29, 1796—with a treaty that *nowhere explicitly acknowledges U.S. sovereignty and independence!* Rather, it establishes on its own terms "a firm inviolable and universal Peace, and a true and sincere Friendship between His Brittanick Majesty, His Heirs and Successors, and the United States of America." Had Americans just fought a war for independence only to have established a vaguely defined "Friendship" with the Crown, one that is "inviolable"?

A disturbing question that should pull us all out of our comfort zones: did the new nation end up subservient to the Crown, just as the colonies had been? Was Crown dominance over the former colonies restored by the Jay Treaty, with the real end of the War for Independence in 1796, not 1783? *Were Americans merely allowed to believe they had attained full sovereignty?*

One final note about the Jay Treaty. Articles V, VI, and VII of the treaty establish the first international mixed commissions, to resolve disputes not yet resolved through negotiation. This set an important precedent for later "commissions of inquiry" with autonomous decision-making power. Do make a note of this. We will encounter it again as well.

III.

Alexander Hamilton's Bank of the United States began operating in 1791. Hamilton defended British-style mercantilism in "Federalist No. 11" and "Federalist No. 12." Unlike Jefferson and the Anti-Federalists he wanted a centralized and activist government. Hamilton's goals certainly aligned with those of the Rothschilds. The future of the United States was opened to the very meddling by European bankers about which Jefferson had warned. A few historians believe Nathan Mayer Rothschild ordered the War of 1812 as retaliation for our refusal to recharter Hamilton's bank the previous year. ("Teach those impudent Americans a lesson," he is alleged to have said. "Bring them back to colonial status." So much for the inviolability of the "Friendship Treaty" from the British point of view.) What we do know: the Second Bank of the United States was created in 1816, again with a twenty-year charter. Rothschild agents John Jacob Astor, Stephen Girard, and David Parish were placed in charge and immediately began to meddle in American enterprise to further Rothschild goals.

President Andrew Jackson—popular hero of the War of 1812 following his victory in the Battle of New Orleans—would shut down the Second Bank of the United States in 1834, before its charter expired. Jackson's antibank stance being known, the Second Bank's supporters in Congress made an effort to renew the bank's charter in advance of its expiration. Jackson got wind of it. Furious, he confronted a delegation of bankers and roared:

> Gentlemen! I too have been a closer observer of the
> doings of the Bank of the United States. I have had men

watching you for a long time, and am convinced that
you have used the funds of the bank to speculate in the
breadstuffs of the country. When you won, you divided
the profits amongst you, and when you lost, you charged
it to the bank. You tell me that if I take the deposits from
the bank and annul its charter, I shall ruin ten thousand
families. That may be true, gentlemen, but that is your
sin! Should I let you go on, you will ruin fifty thousand
families, and that would be my sin! You are a den of
vipers and thieves. I have determined to rout you out,
and by the Eternal (bringing his fist down on the table),
I will rout you out! (quoted in Stan V. Henkels, *Andrew
Jackson and the Bank of the United States*, 1928, pp. 3–4)

This was the culmination of Jackson's protracted battle with
Rothschild agent Nicholas Biddle, another prodigy who had
assumed the bank's presidency in the 1820s. Biddle led the
bankers' retaliation against Jackson in 1837 by contracting the
money supply and causing a depression that severely damaged
the remainder of his presidency. The effort backfired; Biddle
had been overheard describing details of a campaign to destroy
Jackson's presidency through money manipulation. An investigation for alleged fraud ensued. Biddle was acquitted, but legal
problems dogged him for the rest of his life. Jackson survived
an assassination attempt on January 30, 1835. Two guns, aimed
at his chest at point-blank range, both misfired. His would-be
assassin admitted to working for "foreign interests."

Despite having lost their power center on this continent, the bankers were not about to give up. Rothschild agent
August Schoenberg came to American shores and changed his
last name to *Belmont*. He began purchasing government bonds,
rose in wealth and stature through his firm August Belmont and
Company, and eventually became an adviser to the White House.

John Slidell, another Rothschild agent, was a merchant in New York before relocating to New Orleans to build up a law practice and later serve in the Louisiana House of Representatives. Finally, Judah Benjamin was a Rothschild agent who would rise to become Jefferson Davis's chief adviser.

It is very difficult to determine to what extent Rothschild money built the American industrial revolution. What we do know: Northern states were transformed starting in the mid-1800s. Railroads began to crisscross the countryside. Industrialization gradually took people off land they had farmed and sent them into burgeoning cities. This created a fundamentally different culture. Invariably, people began to lose touch with the land and would gradually lose the ability their ancestors possessed to live off the land. They would also begin to lose touch with one another. People in farming communities grew up together and knew one another their entire lives. They cared about and trusted one another. Those who ended up in cities became increasingly anonymous, as did their transactions.

The North's commitment to industry versus the South's retaining an agrarian economy also helped set the stage for dividing America into two separate nations that could be more easily brought under Rothschild/Crown control. Some authors have alleged that the Rothschilds were prime movers in attempting to divide the nation (see A. Ralph Epperson, *The Unseen Hand*, ch. 15, "The Civil War"; see also Des Griffin, *Descent Into Slavery*, ch. 5, "The Rothschild Dynasty"). In this view, slavery—meaning *chattel* slavery, of course—was the most convenient wedge issue: the agrarian Southern economy depended on it; the industrializing North had eliminated it and become the seat of a strong abolition movement.

Abraham Lincoln *may* have figured out what was really going on and found himself between the proverbial rock and hard place. He's been elevated to the status of a hero by many historians for saving the union, but condemned as a villain by others for ending federalism, permitting the ascension of the federal government as a centralized power over the states (Fourteenth and Fifteenth amendments), and setting the conditions for the emergence of the United States as the next empire (see Thomas DiLorenzo's *The Real Lincoln*). He almost assuredly knew he'd made enemies by printing greenbacks to finance the Northern war effort, instead of turning to the bankers. Lincoln himself appears to have believed his life would end violently. "'I am sure,' he said to his partner once, 'I shall meet with some terrible end'" (quoted in Epperson, *The Unseen Hand*, p. 154). Had he made enemies who had no scruples about murdering those who interfered with their plans? Not long before his assassination he wrote:

> We may congratulate ourselves that this cruel war is near its end. It has cost a vast amount of treasure and blood....It has indeed been a trying hour for the Republic; but I see in the near future a crisis approaching that unnerves me and causes me to tremble for the safety of my country. As a result of the war, corporations have been enthroned and an era of corruption in high places will follow, and the money power of the country will endeavor to prolong its reign by working upon the prejudices of the people until all wealth is aggregated in a few hands, and the Republic is destroyed. I feel at this moment more anxiety for the safety of my country than ever before, even in the midst of war. (letter to William F. Elkins, Nov. 21, 1864; in A.H. Shaw, ed., *The Lincoln Encyclopedia*, 1950, p.40)

This quote—like many—has been disputed. Lincoln's personal secretary, John Nicolay, repudiated it, calling it a "bald, unblushing forgery" (*New York Times*, Oct. 3, 1898, p. 1). Allegedly, what prompted Lincoln's remark was Congress's passage of the National Banking Act of 1863. Its spirit is consistent with other remarks attributed to Lincoln by his law partner William H. Herndon, who left an extensive collection of his thoughts and remarks (*The Hidden Lincoln*, 1938).

While a century and a half have doubtless erased all possibility of definitive proof, allegations exist that Lincoln was killed by a conspiracy originating overseas, and that John Wilkes Booth was just the triggerman. There are actually several "conspiracy theories" surrounding Lincoln's death. It is known that a plot to kidnap Lincoln predated the end of the war. Booth left some of the details in a diary in which he called Lincoln a "tyrant." Did Lincoln's assassination result from a "simple" conspiracy directed by Booth and a handful of trusted associates based in the Confederacy—or was it the product of a larger campaign, perhaps instigated outside this country? At least one such theory has been furthered in the essay "The Rothschilds' International Plot to Kill Lincoln" (*New Solidarity*, 1976). This theory holds that Lincoln was killed because of his monetary policies. Lincoln had rejected offers from Rothschild-controlled central banks and instead printed $450 million worth of debt-free greenbacks to finance the war effort. According to this view, the European superelite now firmly entrenched in the central banks saw Lincoln as a major threat and, accordingly, took him out of the picture.

Whether or not this theory is true, the money power Lincoln referred to certainly existed. It would play Americans—including leaders in both government and emerging industries—like musical instruments. Here are some specifics: In the banking community of the late 1800s, a rising star appeared. His name was Jacob Schiff. We mentioned him briefly earlier; he was a Rothschild agent and key descendent of the Schiffs with whom the first Rothschilds had shared their residence. Jacob Schiff arrived in New York not long after the War Between the States ended. His instructions were to buy into a banking house that could be used to rebuild banking cartel influence. Schiff had three other assignments. First, he was to enlist the service of men as unscrupulous as he was who were willing to service banking interests in America; he used his financial resources to place them in positions of influence in the federal government and in corporations. Second, he was to create conditions for ethnic strife in America, especially between blacks and whites. And third, he was to work to erode the hold Christianity had over ordinary Americans. Schiff bought a partnership in the Kuhn and Loeb firm and became a full partner in 1875. He bought out the interests of senior partner Kuhn, moved the firm to New York, and changed the name to Kuhn, Loeb, and Company. For all practical purposes, he became the sole owner.

Of course, Schiff was far from being a major player. Well before the War Between the States—in 1837, the year August Belmont arrived—a wealthy American bond salesman named George Peabody went to London and approached Nathan Rothschild. Aging, unmarried, and with no heirs, Peabody sought a partner to continue his business. The man for the job turned out to be Junius Spencer Morgan. Morgan had served the Rothschilds in rebuilding France and so was a known quantity. In 1854, Morgan became a full partner in the firm eventually named Peabody, Morgan, and Company. Peabody became the Union's main financial agent in Great Britain, but in 1864 retired and turned the business over to Morgan, who renamed it J. S. Morgan and Company.

Junius Spencer Morgan had a son, John Pierpont Morgan, who became better known by his initials: J. P. Morgan. It was a given that the elder Morgan would school his son in international finance just as Mayer Amschel Rothschild had done with his sons, and those men with their sons. In 1864, the younger Morgan became a partner in one of his father's New York acquisitions, Dabney, Morgan, and Company—the American branch of the British firm. During a meeting in London in 1869, the younger Morgan learned about the immense financial benefits of allying with the Rothschilds. With the addition of Philadelphia financier Anthony Drexel in 1871, the firm became known as Drexel, Morgan, and Company. The elder Morgan died in 1890. Drexel passed on in 1895, leaving J. P. in charge. The company his father had acquired became J. P. Morgan and Company.

J. P. Morgan had by this time schooled his own son, J. P. "Jack" Morgan Jr., and the latter was ready to become a partner. Jack went to England in 1898 to learn how the English system worked, to convert the elder Morgan's J. S. Morgan and Company into a distinctively British concern, and to begin preparations for the resurrection of central banking in the United States. This meant cultivating an alliance with the Rothschild behemoth—despite the "anti-Semitic" appearance the growing Morgan empire would cultivate as a front.

Capitalism, courtesy of the so-called robber barons (led by John D. Rockefeller Sr., whose Standard Oil, emerging originally in Ohio, had become the wealthiest oil corporation in the United States) was getting the bad name the Fabians would exploit. Rockefeller was alleged to have said, "Competition is a sin," as he bought out competitors or drove them out of business through secret deals with railroads, which would then refuse to carry his competitors' product. With "finance capitalism," things would get worse. In 1901, Morgan bought out Carnegie's steel corporation operation for $500 million, making Carnegie temporarily the richest man in America. John D. Rockefeller Sr. became a major stockholder in the new company, the United States Steel Corporation. His progeny would also soon discover that there was more money to be made in banking than in oil. Carnegie turned philanthropist and created the network of foundations that still bear his name. A globalist by instinct, he coined the expression *league of nations*. Given the international web of controls that was again enveloping America's finances, a globalist mind-set with enormous resources to back it up was inevitable.

With the fluctuations in the economy (for which the bankers were responsible), the time was ripe for another try at a full-fledged central bank. Jacob Schiff had been working on the problem. He knew he would have to finance the elections of men in both houses of Congress who would support the creation of such an entity and be influential enough to get it passed. Then—even more important—he would need someone in the White House who would sign such a bill into law once Congress passed it. It would not be easy, but he found an ally in the Senate, Nelson Aldrich of Rhode Island. He also nurtured a relationship with "Colonel" Edward Mandell House, ambitious son of wealthy Texas landowner and Rothschild agent Thomas House, and this brought him into the orbit of Dr. Woodrow Wilson, who had been president of Princeton University. Wilson, it was clear, was the man he wanted. Already a progressive surrounded by Fabians, the bankers began "educating" him through an "educational" fund for professors and administrators at major universities who would endorse the idea of a central bank.

In 1907, the bankers used their combined resources to pre-cipitate a financial panic—the Panic of 1907—and blame it on the decentralized banking that had been prevalent since the time of Lincoln. Within days, countless small banks failed. Morgan stepped in, offering to cover their debts with money produced through the same fractional-lending system that had gotten them into trouble. Congress, under pressure to "do something," authorized the creation of $200 million in private, no-reserves money *ex nihilo*—out of nothing. Morgan, whose wealth and power took a quantum leap, was hailed as a hero.

The stage was set for the Coup of 1913, as we might call it; for this is what it was, a bloodless coup brought about by the banking wing of the superelite. *Coup of 1913* refers to the crea-tion of the Federal Reserve System. G. Edward Griffin, in his classic treatise *The Creature from Jekyll Island* (1994), recounts the circumstances of this momentous event, after which America would never be the same. Before Griffin came Eustace Mullins, who spent years researching *Secrets of the Federal Reserve* (1952), the first such expose, for which he was blacklisted and labeled "anti-Semitic." (It is interesting to note that the powerful Anti-Defamation League, used to discredit *ad hominem* those who would seek to expose the superelite bankers, most of whom were indeed Ashkenazi Jews, was also established in 1913, as was the Internal Revenue Service which would become the most feared federal agency.)

Creating a new central bank would not be easy, however. There was a lot of distrust. In 1908, the Aldrich-Vreeland Act created a National Monetary Commission with very broad powers to spend money and further the study of banking and currency. As a result, in 1910, the Aldrich Bill came out. This bill formally proposed an entire reorganization of the banking system, but did not make it out of committee (for the specifics, see H. P. Willis, *Business and Banking*, 1925).

Also in 1910, however, and unbeknownst to Congress or the public, a small, select group convened at Jekyll Island off the coast of Georgia—purposefully outside the limelight. Secrecy was so tight that invitees left their homes under cover of night and traveled alone using just their first names. Not until 1935 would a decisive statement appear, made by one of the participants, Frank A. Vanderlip, that any meeting had ever taken place. The list of attendees was a who's who of the banking wing of the superelite: J. P. Morgan; John D. Rockefeller Sr.; "Colonel" House; Jacob Schiff; Nelson Aldrich; Frank Vanderlip (vice president of the Rockefeller-owned National City Bank); Henry P. Davison of J. P. Morgan (who became the Federal Reserve's first chairman); Paul Warburg, by this time owner of Kuhn and Loeb; Bernard Baruch; and a few others. This group laid out specific plans for the new central bank. Like its predecessors, the bank would be a private corporation, controlled by the international cartel of corporations owned and operated by the superelite—then known as the "money power." After a week of intensive work, they emerged with the new system. The last thing they wanted to call it was a *central bank*. The term had a bad name. So they settled on *Federal Reserve*.

The planners returned home and penned the Federal Reserve Act, which once passed by Congress and signed by the president would make the new central bank legal. They would have to wait until after the 1912 election; then President Howard Taft would almost certainly veto the thing. Woodrow Wilson had been urged (by House) to support the central bank as necessary for economic stability. Wilson, initially, did not seem a strong candidate for president. He was an academic by temperament.

His instincts doubtless told him something was up, for in *The New Freedom* (1913) he wrote:

> Since I entered politics, I have chiefly had men's views confided to me privately. Some of the biggest men in the United States, in the field of commerce and manufacture, are afraid of somebody, are afraid of something. They know that there is a power somewhere so organized, so subtle, so watchful, so interlocked, so complete, so pervasive, that they had better not speak above their breath when they speak in condemnation of it. They know that America is not a place of which it can be said, as it used to be, that a man may choose his own calling and pursue it just as far as his abilities enable him to pursue it; because to-day, if he enters certain fields, there are organizations which will use means against him that will prevent his building up a business which they do not want to have built up; organizations that will see to it that the ground is cut from under him and the markets shut against him. For if he begins to sell to certain retail dealers, to any retail dealers, the monopoly will refuse to sell to those dealers, and those dealers, afraid, will not buy the new man's wares. (p. 13–14)

Wilson apparently kept whatever reservations he might have had to himself, because the superelite, using their financial resources, lent support to Theodore Roosevelt's third-party Bull Moose candidacy and divided the opposition. Wilson won handily. Carter Glass, chairman of the Banking and Currency Committee, introduced what became known as the Federal Reserve Act in September 1913. Prospects for the Glass Bill, as it was initially called, were not especially good at first. But the "money power" kept the pressure on. On December 23, 1913—with much of Congress having departed to be with their families for Christmas—the select few who remained passed the Glass Bill. Wilson immediately signed it into law. The superelite had their central bank in America—a state-sponsored private corporation controlled by other private corporations, many of which were based outside this country—in the City of London. Its actual list of shareholders remains a closely guarded secret to this day. Arguably, the Coup of 1913 was a turning point for the United States —the culmination of the First Cardinal Error. The Federal Reserve ("independent within the government," according to its own literature), as has often been observed, is neither federal nor does it have any reserves.

Congressman Charles August Lindbergh Sr. (R-Minnesota), father of the famed aviator and longtime foe of the "money power," warned his colleagues at length:

> [The Federal Reserve Act] establishes the most gigantic trust on earth.... When the President signs this bill the invisible government by the money power, proven to exist by the Money Trust investigation, will be legalized....
>
> The bill is of such far-reaching injustice that I feel it my duty...to make some observations on the system that has made it possible to prevent Members of Congress from preparing a good bill and forcing a vote upon it. The Money Trust caused the 1907 panic, and thereby forced Congress to create a National Monetary Commission, which drew a bill in the interests of the Money Trust, but Congress did not dare to pass the bill as coming from that Commission. The main features of that bill, however, were copied into this bill.... This is the Aldrich bill in disguise, the difference being that by this bill the Government issues the money, whereas

by the Aldrich bill the issue was to be controlled by the banks. No one should be deceived by that change, however, for by this bill the Government can let no one but the banks have the money....

The greatest crime of Congress is its currency system. The schemiest legislative crime of all the ages is perpetrated by this new banking and currency bill. The caucus and the party bosses again operated and prevented the people getting the benefit of their own Government....

The banks have been granted the special privilege of distributing the money, and they charge as much as they wish. The President's new bill gives the bankers even greater powers than they had under the old laws....

What is the fundamental basis of the new bill? It is...that property shall be preserved as having greater potential force than the human family....No human being can compete with [the potential power of compounding interest on a dollar]. Nothing can compete with the dollar except $2...and so on up, the greater the sum the greater the cinch. The bankers control it....

The President's bill directs all the money into the control of the banks—the money loaners. It will be used by them to exploit the borrowers and users of money. If not enough can be collected into these centers, then the Government will print more to place there. The banks and special centers will get the exclusive control of all the stocks of money. They will form the greatest trust in the world. The bill does not limit the charge that the banks can make borrowers.

> I hope that the public may soon take as much inter-
> est in banking and currency legislation as the bank-
> ers do, for the public is just as much interested and
> the importance to the public is as much greater as the
> number of people constituting the public exceeds that
> of the bankers. Congress can only be forced by public
> opinion. Until it is, it will legislate in favor of the banks
> and against the people. (*Congressional Record*, December
> 22, 1913, pp. 1446–51)

More prophetic words have never been spoken! That year, right
before Christmas, the institutional machinery was established
that would gradually devalue our currency over the course of
the next several decades until the dollar had lost approximately
97 percent of its value.

As the decades progressed, the Federal Reserve became an
accepted part of the country's economic landscape, taken for
granted. There were, however, a handful of notable holdouts.
Some developed scathing criticisms of the Fed. The most visible
of these was Congressman Louis T. McFadden of Pennsylvania.
On June 10, 1932, with the country gripped by the emergency
that would become the Great Depression, McFadden stood and
addressed Congress:

> Mr. Chairman, at the present session of Congress we
> have been dealing with emergency situations. We have
> been dealing with the effect of things rather than with the
> cause of things. In this particular discussion I shall deal
> with some of the causes that lead up to these proposals.
> There are underlying principles which are responsible
> for conditions such as we have at the present time and
> I shall deal with one of these in particular which is tre-
> mendously important in the consideration that you are
> now giving to this bill.

Mr. Chairman, we have in this country one of the most corrupt institutions the world has ever known. I refer to the Federal Reserve Board and the Federal Reserve Banks. The Federal Reserve Board, a Government board, has cheated the Government of the United States and the people of the United States out of enough money to pay the national debt. The depredations and iniquities of the Federal Reserve Board has cost this country enough money to pay the national debt several times over. This evil institution has impoverished and ruined the people of the United States, has bankrupted itself, and has practically bankrupted our Government. It has done this through the defects of the law under which it operates, through the maladministration of that law by the Federal Reserve Board, and through the corrupt practices of the moneyed vultures who control it.

Some people think the Federal Reserve banks are United States Government institutions. They are not Government institutions. They are private credit monopolies which prey upon the people of the United States for the benefit of themselves and their foreign customers; foreign and domestic speculators and swindlers; and rich and predatory money lenders. In that dark crew of financial pirates there are those who would cut a man's throat to get a dollar out of his pocket; there are those who send money into States to buy votes to control our legislation; and there are those who maintain international propaganda for the purpose of deceiving us and of wheedling us into the granting of new concessions which will permit them to cover up their past misdeeds and set again in motion their gigantic train of crime. (*Congressional Record*, June 10, 1932, pp. 12595–96)

This, of course, was a staggering indictment! But subsequent history—leading, I would argue, up to the Meltdown of 2008 as I will call it—lends it support. The superelite have been interested only in money and power—the power of the purse wielding control over the power of the sword. Congressman McFadden died under somewhat mysterious circumstances just a couple of years after these remarks. His death was officially diagnosed as caused by "intestinal flue." This followed three previous attempts on his life: twice he was shot at by unknown assailants who missed, and an attempted poisoning following a political banquet failed. It looks very much as though *someone* felt strongly motivated to take him out!

Arguably, too, the superelite sought control over the power of the *pen*: the growing mass media. Just as the Rothschilds had purchased controlling interest in Reuters (which later bought the Associated Press in the United States), there is evidence that the superelite began to acquire control over mass media in the United States just a few years after the Federal Reserve began to operate. In 1917 the following appeared in the *Congressional Record*:

> In March, 1915, the J. P. Morgan interests, the steel, shipbuilding, and powder interests, and their subsidiary organizations, got together 12 men high up in the newspaper world and employed them to select the most influential newspapers in the United States and sufficient number of them to control generally the policy of the daily press of the United States.
>
> These 12 men worked the problem out by selecting 179 newspapers, and then began, by an elimination process, to retain only those necessary for the purpose of controlling the general policy of the daily press

throughout the country. They found it was only necessary to purchase the control of 25 of the greatest papers.
The 25 papers were agreed upon; emissaries were sent
to purchase the policy, national and international, of
these papers; an agreement was reached; the policy of
the papers was bought, to be paid for by the month; an
editor was furnished for each paper to properly super-
vise and edit information regarding the questions of
preparedness, militarism, financial policies, and other
things of national and international nature considered
vital to the interests of the purchasers.

This contract is in existence at the present time, and
it accounts for the news columns of the daily press of the
country being filled with all sorts of preparedness arguments and misrepresentations as to the present condition of the United States Army and Navy, and the possibility and probability of the United States being attacked
by foreign foes.

This policy also included the suppression of everything in opposition to the wishes of the interests served.
The effectiveness of this scheme has been conclusively
demonstrated by the character of the stuff carried in the
daily press throughout the country since March, 1915.

They have resorted to anything necessary to com-
mercialize public sentiment and sandbag the national
Congress into making extravagant and wasteful appro-
priations for the army and navy, under the false pretense
that it was necessary. Their stock argument is "patriotism." They are playing on every prejudice and passion of
the American people. (Proceedings and Debates of the
2nd Session of the 64th Congress, Vol. LIV, *Congressional*

Record of the House of Representatives, Feb. 9, 1917, pp. 2947–48)

The speaker was Oscar Callaway of Texas. Did his remarks reflect paranoia or actual history? They did prompt a call for a Congressional investigation by one J. Hampton Moore of Pennsylvania. What became of this investigation is unknown, but the superelite were not in the habit of allowing themselves to be investigated by members of Congress, any more than they were in the habit of leaving paper trails lying around. One can, however, look at media as it developed in the West to see compelling evidence of increasing controls—how today's mainstream media has been owned by progressively fewer and fewer corporations until, today, the number has dwindled to five. These corporations do not report the truth about the extent of inflation or unemployment. They use entertainment to distract listeners and viewers from what we are not supposed to see or hear. *Manufacturing Consent* by Edward S. Herman and Noam Chomsky (1988), insightful though it is, peels back only the top layers; it is limited in its absence of references to either Callaway or the Rothschilds.

To sum up this perhaps unwieldy discussion, the history books tell us we fought a war for independence from the British Empire and established our sovereignty. But we were unable to prevent British bankers from meddling in our economy, all of which was technically legal. Not long after the passage of the National Banking Act during Lincoln's tenure, the following appeared in a letter attributed to Lord Rothschild to his associates in New York:

> The few who understand the system (interest-bearing money) will either be so interested in its profits, or so dependent on its favors that there will be no opposition

> from that class, while on the other hand, the great body
> of people, mentally incapable of comprehending the
> tremendous advantages that capital derives from the
> system, will bear its burdens without complaint, and
> perhaps without even suspecting the system is inimical
> to their interests. (quoted in *The Unseen Hand*, p. 157)

The question is: were we *ever* as sovereign and independent as our national mythology has led us to believe? One might argue for an alternative view of U.S. history. In this alternative view, the so-called Revolutionary War did not end in 1783 with the Treaty of Paris but in 1794 with the Jay Treaty, a treaty that did not go into effect until it was *proclaimed* (not when it was *passed by Congress*). Alexander Hamilton had already opened the door to British bankers in 1791. They continued their efforts, decade after decade, to control what became British-American capitalism by controlling its finances. Their efforts were hardly unknown. A very detailed account of the struggle to contain banker activity can be found in the recently republished *The Coming Battle* by M. W. Walbert (1997; orig. 1899). It is clear that most such activity was directed by that powerful family ensconced in the heart of British Crown territory, the City of London: the Rothschilds. They were aided by others: the Schiffs and the Warburgs, eventually the Morgans and the Rockefellers. Their project was herculean and long term, their members did not always agree on every point, and success was hardly guaranteed, no matter how many stealth operators and financial resources they threw into it. To bring it about, they needed both educational arrangements and a guiding philosophy other than Christianity, which taught that the "love of money is the root of all evil"! Then they needed cadres of organizers who could infiltrate every endeavor and bend it to their service. That is, they needed agents as catalysts for the United States to commit the Second, Third, and Fourth Cardinal Errors. In the twentieth century, they would find an abundance of such agents.

2

Cardinal Error Two. In the 1840s, an educational system whose working premises were alien to those of a free republic was brought into this country and eventually embraced not just by the powerful, but by the majority of the American people. "Public schools" became part of the warp and woof of American life. Today the majority of Americans take them for granted. They shouldn't.

• • •

I.

Nearly all education in early America was private in any reasonable sense of the term. The Constitution did not contain a word about the subject. The kinds of private education that important Founders such as James Madison received are well documented (see Mary-Elaine Swanson, *The Education of James Madison*, 1992). Also well-known to education historians are the dame schools that appeared in many communities: a group of families would hire a single teacher, or "dame," and entrust the education of their children to her. The first several generations in early America after the Revolutionary War were quite well educated. Literacy rates were high, and in some communities, close to 100 percent. Quite unlike today, the best-selling books of the time were dense, complex stories of exploration and conflict packed with historical detail and philosophical discussion by characters of depth. James Fenimore Cooper's works are examples. After the 1840s, so slowly as to be almost unnoticeable, this would begin to change.

As far back as Benjamin Rush, one of the signers of the Declaration of Independence, an undercurrent of sentiment held that government ought to play a key role in educating the young for participation in the unique form it was to assume on U.S. soil. There was no agreement on what that role was, however, and given the high literacy rate, no one considered the matter a priority. Horace Mann, who in 1837 had become the first secretary of education of the Commonwealth of Massachusetts, traveled to Prussia in 1843 and returned to his home state with word of what he considered an amazing school system he had observed there. Prussian schools, steeped in the philosophy of

Georg W. F. Hegel, not John Locke or Thomas Jefferson, operated on the assumption that *the individual belongs to the state
instead of to himself and to his God*. They "educated" Prussian children accordingly.

Bad methodology for teaching reading had already appeared.
Thomas Gallaudet, who had worked at educating deaf-mutes at
Hartford, Connecticut, devised the first "look-say" method, which
treated words as akin to pictures. One of Gallaudet's beliefs is very
prescient of what was to come: "Mind, like matter, can be made
subject to experiment." He sought to introduce children to words
before introducing them to the alphabet. Noted educator-turned-
critic and author John Taylor Gatto isolates three important
threads running through the school of thought that Gallaudet and
his followers promulgated: (1) learning should be scientific, and
learning places akin to laboratories; (2) words can and should be
learned ideographically (as if they were pictures); and (3) reliev-
ing boredom and tedium should be an important part of pedagogy. Gatto notes that as these themes became institutionalized,
they would all require vast bureaucracies to develop and enforce;
evidence would also emerge that ideographic methods did permanent damage to students' abilities to learn new words and hence
to both read and understand—but we get ahead of ourselves.

Mann received a matching grant from the Commonwealth
of Massachusetts to set up the Prussian-derived school system inside its borders. He incorporated Gallaudet's methods,
which he had endorsed as early as 1838. The system seemed
likely to encourage loyalty and obedience. New York became
the second state to adopt the new system. Other states gradually followed. Thus began what became known as "public
education"—state-sponsored, or government, schools—in
America. They were then called "common schools."

Although Americans would run this system, it was not American. Its assumptions were Prussian. Our word *kindergarten* is, in fact, a Prussian word. The word best translates as *child garden*—a reference to the growing of children as if they were vegetables in a garden, to be tended, nurtured, and directed down the paths the owners of the garden want them to follow. The system seemed to work. In 1852, Massachusetts became the first state to pass a compulsory school attendance law. Other states would soon follow. A few pastors/authors (e.g., R. L. Dabney and Archibald Cox) warned of danger. They were ignored. And at first, government schools seemed harmless enough. They seemed benign and even beneficial. The enormous task of educating children was removed from extended families and delegated to the state-sponsored system.

State sponsorship spread to higher education with the Morrill Act of 1863, rejected during the 1850s by President James Buchanan as unconstitutional, but signed into law by Lincoln as a wartime measure. The Morrill Act created the land-grant system of what were then called agricultural and mechanical (A&M) colleges. These institutions began to train people in their late teens and early 20s in the rote technical and business skills wanted by those furthering the industrial revolution—the incipient but rapidly growing corporate world. This meant setting aside, in public institutions anyway, the classical model of formal learning that makes for an independent-minded, thinking citizen. Neither the government nor the emerging corporations wanted that.

Thus began our gradual shift from a nation of independent craftsmen and entrepreneurs (farmers, doctors, lawyers, carpenters, bricklayers, inventors, writers, teachers, traders, etc.) to a nation of employees and guilded professionals. The latter could be more easily controlled. Professionalization included instituting specific educational or other credentials, licenses, and so on, to restrict entry into occupations and then to police those admitted. Ostensibly this was to ensure quality control. The practice became known as occupational licensure, and began to transform professions, one after another, into organized guilds, setting up an "establishment," including gatekeepers, for each profession. The key effect was a gradual centralization of every profession. Education was no exception. The end of the era of the autonomous schoolhouse was approaching. For example, teacher certification had already begun; according to Diane Ravitch, by 1867 most states required teachers to pass a locally administered test to obtain a certificate. Such practices would expand and serve as instruments of control after the turn of the century. Teachers would relinquish control over textbooks to school officials. Traditional texts such as the *New England Primer*, in use since the days of colonial America and religiously focused, would be replaced by more "up-to-date" texts incorporating secularism.

As the Gilded Age moved American capitalism forward, we entered the era of the "captains of industry" (others called them "robber barons") who came to dominate specific industries. Some we have met: John D. Rockefeller Sr. in oil, Andrew Carnegie in steel; there was also Cornelius Vanderbilt in shipping and railroads, Edward Harriman in railroads, and so on. It is on John D. Rockefeller Sr. that we need to focus just now. In 1881, Rockefeller joined with his older brother William and nine associates to create a trust. By this time, he had control over better than 90 percent of the oil industry, had extended enormous influence into railroads, and was becoming visible in banking. He had also made his share of enemies. To counter his reputation as a ruthless monopolist, he turned to philanthropy. Many of his concerns focused on education. His best-known philanthropic endeavor was founding and endowing the University of Chicago in 1892, although he would donate money to many other emerging colleges and universities. Arguably, his founding of the General Education Board in 1902 and the Rockefeller Foundation in the pivotal year 1913 would prove even more significant for the future of education in America. Rockefeller money would soon spread far and wide in the United States, as we will see below, in service of the goal of long-term social control.

Let me reiterate a theme stated at the outset. We will encounter evidence for this again and again. A widespread misunderstanding about corporations is found among free marketers of various stripes, be they Friedmanites, Misesians, or Randians (disciples of Ayn Rand): the idea that those at their helm really believe in free-market ideology, *desire* free markets, and therefore support the *laissez-faire* school of capitalist economics. While this may well be true of many entrepreneurs, the "captains of industry" of the late 1800s and early 1900s were as interested in their own brand of economic power as any politician was in political power; again, wealth *was* power—the power of the purse, which could control the power of the sword by buying the loyalties of politicians in both political parties. Rockefeller did not want *free* markets, he wanted markets he could control. There can be no doubt that he cooperated with the Rothschilds. Some have speculated that he and other "captains of industry" were aided directly by the Rothschilds; this is possible, but Rockefeller had accumulated more than enough resources of his own to further goals of social control. Social engineering in the schools was an important key. What evidence supports this claim? Let us find out!

II.

Shortly before the turn of the century, Rockefeller and his associates discovered young John Dewey, a then-obscure psychology professor who had been hired by the University of Chicago and had penned a well-received text on education. Dewey had studied under G. Stanley Hall at Johns Hopkins University. Hall, in turn, had been the first American student of pioneer "experimental psychologist" Wilhelm Wundt of the Leipzig School. The Wundt school of thought is worth a brief digression. It held that human beings were no different in kind from other biological organisms. Members of the Wundt school were radical empiricists. What counted was what they could observe. What they could *not* observe was any mind or soul. They believed they observed specific kinds of stimuli yielding specific responses that could be studied, replicated, and ultimately controlled. Change the stimuli, they reasoned, and you change the response, or behavior. By repeatedly supplying the right stimuli, desired behaviors could be artificially induced and then "frozen" in place as permanent habits. Conditioning was therefore possible. Human beings were malleable, like potter's clay.

This idea began to take psychology by storm in the English-speaking world. Wundt's pupils and their pupils applied this idea to children, for children were exceptionally malleable. We speak of children being impressionable. It seemed to the Wundtians that if they could control a child's environment from the outset, they could produce a certain kind of child. Establish schools on this basis, and professional educators could raise cohorts of readily conditioned children. Conditioned children would grow up to be controllable adults. Perhaps they could even be conditioned to believe themselves free! Dewey, having been trained by Hall and also having absorbed ideas from Hegel, Marx, and Darwin, was the perfect choice for developing what the emerging superelite in America wanted.

It all began with a meeting on January 15, 1902, involving John D. Rockefeller Sr., his eldest son, John Jr., and one Frederick Taylor Gates, who shared Rockefeller's views and had been handling more and more of Rockefeller's philanthropic endeavors since 1887. Gates would lead John Jr. to an interest in education that would surpass his father's. The 1902 meeting resulted in the founding of the General Education Board—private money guiding the public agenda. The Board's *Occasional Letter No. 1* stated:

> In our dreams, we have limitless resources and the people yield themselves with perfect docility to our molding hands. The present education conventions fade from their minds, and unhampered by tradition, we work our own good will upon a grateful and responsive rural folk. We shall not try to make these people or any of their children into philosophers or men of learning, or men of science. We have not to raise up from among them authors, editors, poets, or men of letters. We shall not search for embryo great artists, painters, musicians, nor lawyers, doctors, preachers, politicians, statesmen, of whom we have an ample supply.
>
> The task we set before ourselves is very simple as well as a very beautiful one, to train these people as we find them to a perfectly ideal life just where they are. So we will organize our children and teach them to do in a perfect way the things their fathers and mothers are

> doing in an imperfect way, in the homes, in the shops, on
> the farm. (quoted in Paolo Lionni, *The Leipzig Connection*,
> 1988, pp. 55–56)

This expressed the educational ideology of the corporate elites who were donating money to support public education, from founding kindergartens to endowing universities. Similar remarks from the ensuing two decades are not hard to find. In 1905, A. J. Russell, head of Columbia State Teacher's College, where John Dewey would soon be located, asked, "How can we justify our practice in schooling the masses in precisely the same manner as we do those who are to be their leaders?" None other than Woodrow Wilson, just before the first world war, told businessmen in a speech:

> We want one class to have a liberal education. We want
> another class, a very much larger class of necessity, to
> forego the privilege of a liberal education and fit them-
> selves to perform specific difficult manual tasks. (quoted
> in John Taylor Gatto, *The Underground History of American
> Education*, 2001, p. 38)

In other words, the elites wanted to create *masses* who would work but not think! Their sentiments expressed goals of social control—via a system that would increasingly stress vocation at the expense of academics. This system would transform public schools into social-engineering centers aimed at producing workers and consumers who would neither know nor care about, much less challenge, government and industrial policy— or introduce unwanted competition with the elites. This became the guiding agenda directing public education.

Dewey moved to the Rockefeller-bankrolled Columbia State Teachers College, where he created and began to build the Progressive Education movement. Dewey's philosophy advanced as the goals of education not the transmission of knowledge or the integrated study of those disciplines (history, philosophy, theology, etc.) necessary for an understanding of a Constitutional republic's founding, but rather "adjustment" to a "changing world." With support from other well-funded professional guilds such as the National Education Association (which Dewey helped found and was also supported with Rockefeller dollars), Progressive Education became the Establishment among teachers and administrators. The fledgling behaviorist movement in psychology, the most visible offspring of the Wundtian school, threw its support behind Progressive Education, placing its anti-intellectualism on open display. One of behaviorism's godfathers, Edward Thorndike, openly opined, "Academic subjects are of little value" (quoted in Gatto, p. 39).

None of this is to say the elite ignored, for example, the teaching of history. Simply eradicating such subjects from the curriculum would have been too obvious. What they needed was to ensure their subordination within education designed for a centralized and "scientifically" managed economy that would emasculate personal independence and lead to mental conformity.

In 1911, Andrew Carnegie founded the Carnegie Corporation, along with four other titanic organizations. The Carnegie financial empire worked closely with other tax-exempt foundations (Rockefeller and Guggenheim, for example) to hijack history at the university level. As G. Edward Griffin reports, they sought out graduate students sympathetic to a collectivist view of society, supported them financially, and found them employment at prestigious Ivy League universities:

> They selected twenty candidates at the university level
> who were seeking doctorates in American History. Then

they went to the Guggenheim Foundation and said, "Would you grant fellowships to candidates selected by us, who are of the right frame of mind, those who see the value of collectivism as we do? Would you help them to obtain their doctorates so we can then propel them into positions of prominence and leadership in the academic world?" And the answer was "Yes." So they gathered a list of young men who were seeking their doctorate degrees. They interviewed them, analyzed their attitudes, and chose the twenty they thought were best suited for their purpose. They sent them to London for a briefing. (In a moment I will explain why London is so significant.) At this meeting, they were told what would be expected if and when they win the doctorates they were seeking. They were told they would have to view history, write history, and teach history from the perspective that collectivism was a positive force in the world and was the wave of the future. In other words, in the guise of *analyzing* history, they would *create* history by conditioning future generations to accept collectivism as desirable and inevitable....

Under the orchestrating baton of Nicholas Butler, President of Columbia University and President of the Carnegie Endowment, an organization was formed in 1884 called The American Historical Association. This then created a series of controlled groups, called Committees, each of which focused on a particular segment of the overall educational mission. After these had published their recommendations, the Carnegie Fund created another controlled group in 1929 called The Commission on the Social Studies, which attracted to its membership an impressive list of academic personalities, including the Superintendent of Schools

> in Washington, D.C., the Director of the American
> Geological Society of New York, the President of
> Radcliff College, the Dean of the Graduate School at
> the University of Minnesota, the head of the Institute
> for the Study of Law at Johns Hopkins University, and
> eleven professors of history at such prestigious insti-
> tutions as Columbia University and the Universities of
> Chicago, Michigan, Minnesota, and Wisconsin. Other
> institutions that provided staff services or facilitated its
> work in other ways included Harvard, Stanford, Smith
> College, and the Universities of Iowa, North Carolina,
> and West Virginia. The Commission was funded by a
> $340,000 grant from the Carnegie Corporation—at a
> time when $5,000 was an excellent annual salary for a
> college professor. (G. Edward Griffin, *The Chasm: The
> Future Is Calling (Part One)*, http://www.freedomfor-
> ceinternational.org/pdf/futurecalling1.pdf)

The court historians for elite-created, tax-exempt foundations thus became the core of the American Historical
Association, which became the largest organization of academic
historians in the country. Other academic guilds formed: the
American Philosophical Association in my discipline became
the largest organization of philosophy professors in the country.
Such entities served as gatekeepers of the various academic disciplines, as well as venues where their dominant members could
articulate disciplinary orthodoxy. They sponsored conferences
where scholars could interact, and advanced peer-reviewed journals published at the universities. This ensured the establishment
and protection of specific methodologies and orthodoxies that
would not challenge the growing power system. Token "chal-
lenges" were permitted, such as the faux-radicalism that evolved
over time into the cultural Marxism of the "tenured radicals."

The articles and books of these men and women were laden with academic jargon unintelligible to nonspecialists; this guaranteed a disconnect between them and the problems of real working people. "Academic radicalism" might have been obsessed with capitalism, but would never name nor threaten anyone with real power. Indeed, huge foundations such as Rockefeller and Ford bankrolled much academic leftism as it developed in this country (for details, see René A. Wormser, *Foundations: Their Power and Influence*, 1958, 1977, 1993).

Never again would government schools at any level, from kindergarten through graduate school, be free of social engineering. Collectivism became the social philosophy of public education, as tax-exempt foundations worked out the details of how to implement central economic planning—for example, in such works as the Carnegie Corporation's *Conclusions and Recommendations for the Social Studies* (1934).

As time passed problems emerged, especially after World War II, with growing evidence that children were not learning what they should be learning in school. Diagnoses appeared (e.g., Rudolf Flesch, *Why Johnny Can't Read*, 1955). Such works targeted Progressive Education, which became a dirty word to that portion of the public these diagnoses reached (parents of the emerging troublesome segment of the middle class). These works targeted methodologies, such as whole-language teaching, that had descended from the Gallaudet school.

The educational Establishment contained the emerging dissent from well-qualified writing teachers such as Flesch by consenting to the need for "reforms," which became a mantra that would persist for decades (we hear it today). Progressive Education adapted to more up-to-date fashions that purported to offer solutions to the problems of public education, while keeping the overriding economic and social agenda intact. The newer fashions went by names such as Mastery Learning and eventually Outcome-Based Education. The "outcome" sought was behavioral, not academic. Students were to respond in specific ways on standardized tests; teachers increasingly were required to "teach to the test." Their capacity to do so was itself measurable in terms of student performance that delivered a desired response; this became known as "accountability."

So was public education a failure? This is a complex question. From one standpoint, public education was doing what it had been designed to do: produce consumers who would spend money and employees that would not question their superiors. In this sense, government schools were *not* failures; *they were in fact successes*, at least up to a point. As Thorndike had observed, academic subjects are of little value to the masses that the economic powers wanted. Academic subjects do little to further an emerging globalism. In fact, they do the opposite by encouraging unwanted questions posted to those in authority. The super-elite and those administering their goals in various institutions (corporate as well as governmental) needed workers who would accept instructions and accept team membership in tight collectives (also known as *soviets*). Each generation of graduates exhibited more of the desired behavioral traits, evidence of steadily increasing mind control. Literacy levels and mathematical abilities slowly declined, as did intellectual curiosity. Specialization and a focus on vocation increased. The entertainment industry prospered, as fewer and fewer Americans read good books. What remained of the healthy distrust of concentrations of power on which the American republic was founded was diverted in directions where it couldn't do harm or muster much support. The spirit of individual self-reliance—increasingly dismissed under such rubrics as "rugged individualism"—began to pass away. Intellectuals who defended such notions were marginalized and written out of their disciplines; their works were ignored or dismissed as "outside the mainstream." As this population voted, candidates for public office who did not support what the elites wanted could also be marginalized as "fringe" by controlled media.

III.

Such claims as these will doubtless be met with skepticism and charges of incredulity. But the specifics are now documented— as well as the length of time the slow destruction of the American mind has been underway. Consider the following on how the stage was set (note the involvement of the now well-known superelite-founded Council on Foreign Relations):

> Mr. O. A. Nelson, retired educator, has supplied the vitally important documentation needed to support the link-up between the textbooks and the Council on Foreign Relations. His letter was first printed in "Young Parents Alert" (St. Elmo, Minnesota). His story is self-explanatory.

> "I know from personal experience what I am talking about. In December 1928, I was asked to talk to the American Association for the Advancement of Science. On December 27th, naïve and inexperienced, I agreed. I had done some special work in teaching functional physics in high school. That was to be my topic. The next day, the 28th, a Dr. Ziegler asked me if I would attend a special educational meeting in his room after the AAAS meeting. We met from 10 p.m. until after 2:30 a.m.

> "We were 13 at the meeting. Two things caused Dr. Ziegler, who was Chairman of the Educational Committee of the Council on Foreign Relations, to ask me to attend...my talk on the teaching of functional physics in high school, and the fact that I was a member of Progressive Educators of America, which was nothing

but a Communist front. I thought the word 'progressive' meant progress for better schools. Eleven of those attending the meeting were leaders in education. Drs. John Dewey and Edward Thorndike, from Columbia University, were there, and the others were of equal rank. I checked later and found that *all* were paid members of the Community Party of Russia. *I* was classified as a member of the Party, but I did not know it at the time.

"The sole work of the group was to destroy our schools! We spent one hour and forty-five minutes discussing the so-called 'Modern Math.' At one point I objected because there was too much memory work, and math is reasoning; not memory. Dr. Ziegler turned to me and said, 'Nelson, wake up! That is what we want...a math that the pupils cannot apply to life situations when they get out of school!' That math was not introduced until much later, as those present thought it was too radical a change. A milder course by Dr. Brechner was substituted but it was also worthless, as far as understanding math was concerned. The radical change was introduced in 1952. It was the one we are using now. So, if pupils come out of high school now, not knowing any math, don't blame them. The results are supposed to be worthless," (quoted in Charlotte Thomson Iserbyt, *the deliberate dumbing down of america*, 2000, pp. 14–15)

This, of course, was the origin of the so-called "new math," which left a generation of high-school students unable to multiply and divide, understand fractions, or do other simple arithmetic computations without calculators—or make change at cash registers! The "new math" was just one component of the general attack on the individual's ability to reason his way through matters of crucial importance to his life. Frustrated by the teaching methods, many students decided on their own that they were "no good at math" and gave up. As adults, many lost control over their finances and ended up tens of thousands of dollars in debt. Others, schooled with the destructive, whole-language approach to reading, never become good readers. They gave up on subjects like history and special areas such as the history of our government and its founding, all of which require an ability to read and process information logically.

With each passing generation, students learned less and less about private property and other rights that antecede the authority structures of government. They learned less and less about the ideas of the Founding Fathers or those in the Declaration of Independence and the Constitution. Such notions as natural law became *very hard to grasp,* even for the average college undergraduate. Finally we reached the point where it was possible to focus just on the fact that many of the Founding Fathers owned slaves, among the worst of sins in our present-day politically correct times; some, such as Jefferson, may have even sired children by their slaves! By the 1990s, scene of the emergence of political correctness, such historical gossip loomed larger in the pseudoscholarly portrayal of those who began our republic than any *ideas* they might have had. These portrayals ignored what our founders had said about the need to place limits on government. Academics presented brazenly irrationalist and anti-intellectual approaches in their books, articles, classrooms, and conference performances— and few noticed or cared. Evidence continued to mount that American students were not learning—not even acquiring the technical skills that globalist employers want. The latter eventually turned to Asian and Middle Eastern students who, whatever their drawbacks, had not been tainted by post-Dewey schools or their stepchildren.

How, precisely, did we arrive at this depressing state of affairs? John Taylor Gatto isolates three documents that contributed massively to shaping contemporary government schools and furthering these trends. One was a federal exercise titled *Designing Education for the Future* (1967). This program exemplified the Prussian philosophy by defining education as "a means to achieve important economic and social goals of a national character." It centralized education by imposing directives on state education departments—loss of federal funds was the price tag of noncompliance. In effect, state education departments became "agents of change" and were advised to "lose [their] independent identity as well as [their] authority" in order to "form a partnership with the federal government."

The second document was the *Behavioral Science Teacher Education Project* (also 1967). This project employed Wundtian-behaviorist methods with schoolchildren, under the assumption that in the future "a small elite" would control all important matters. With children who often had nothing in common with one another thrown together into classrooms, schools turned into conformity factories that became laboratories for social control. This environment ensured that the more intelligent children would be social misfits. Some would endure bullying by their peers. Ideally, as these children grew older and burned with resentment, they would conclude on their own that controls over the "Neanderthals" were necessary. As Gatto explains:

> Children are made to see, through school experiences, that their classmates are so cruel and irresponsible, so inadequate to the task of self-discipline, and so ignorant they need to be controlled and regulated for society's

good. Under such a logical regime, school terror can only be regarded as good advertising. It is sobering to think of mass schooling as a vast demonstration of human inadequacy, but that is at least one of its functions. (*Underground History*, p. 41)

The third document was Benjamin Bloom's multivolume *Taxonomy of Educational Objectives* (actually dating back to 1956), which became the textbook for the different ways children and teenagers supposedly learn, as defined within the Wundtian-behaviorist paradigm. The well-known distinction between *cognitive* and *affective* domains has its roots in Bloom's efforts. Bloom's tenets were presupposed, akin to "settled science," by all that came after: Mastery Learning, Outcome-Based Education, Goals 2000, School-To-Work, and Workforce Investment. The last three were built into federal statutes in the 1990s, passed by a Republican Congress and signed by a Democratic president, Bill Clinton, giving them the force of law. Standardized tests soon came to be regarded as essential to determining children's mental states and susceptibility to educational engineering, including how easy or difficult it would be to purge improper feelings and attitudes brought into the school from their parents. Teachers found themselves increasingly circumscribed by regulations; the new educational orthodoxies had to be written into detailed "lesson plans."

But all was not well in paradise. We said above that from one standpoint, public schools were successful. They weren't producing legions of intellectuals who schooled themselves by reading Locke and Jefferson. But social engineers' efforts to prepare a compliant workforce were meeting with very mixed results. By the 1980s, of course, many children and teenagers had actually become uncontrollable. We began to see national conferences devoted to "classroom management," an unwilling recognition that *Wundtian-behaviorist methodology simply does not work*—if only because total control over a child's environment is impossible. Combined with factors outside the control of the social engineers, such as broken homes, absent parents, and other products of general social and cultural decay (reasons for which we will explore in chapter 3), pedagogy designed not to truly educate sometimes resulted in bored, impulsive, and occasionally angry children. When they became teenagers, the situation grew worse. Their noses told them that in most cases their teachers' hands were tied. Thus they did what they could get away with—especially those in "protected groups" who learned they could respond to attempts to control bad behavior with accusations of racism that could ruin a teacher's career! They became disruptive in class, bullied other children and sometimes teachers, brought illegal drugs to school if they were so inclined, weapons if they could, and dyed their hair different colors or wore nose and face piercings as indicators of rebellion against the dull conformism of public education. In a few highly visible cases, their anger exploded into violence (often under the influence of *legal* drugs such as Ritalin).

There's a reason why most inner-city schools eventually had to ban gang regalia and install metal detectors at every entrance to prevent children from bringing handguns to school! This had not yet happened when I was a child! Perhaps the educational elite's first premises, going back to Wundt, about what children are—organic stimulus-response machines to be conditioned and controlled—are untrue, and this is why our culture is producing so many uncontrollable children who then grow into irresponsible adults.

IV.

The superelite believed fully, as we have seen, that most children's future should be to service the global economy. They became increasingly open about it. Consider the infamous Marc Tucker letter to Hillary Clinton dated November 11, 1992—sometimes known as the *Dear Hillary* letter—which found its way into the *Congressional Record*. Tucker is president of the National Center on Education and the Economy, one of the major think tanks behind School-To-Work education, the culmination of subordinating the public school curriculum to national economic planning. Here are some crucial passages from the *Dear Hillary* letter (italics mine). There is no concealment here; Tucker names names openly:

> I still cannot believe that you won. But utter delight that you did pervades all the circles in which I move. I met last Wednesday in David Rockefeller's office with him, John Sculley, Dave Barram and David Haselkorn. It was a great celebration. Both John and David R. were more expansive than I have ever seen them—literally radiating happiness....
>
> The subject we were discussing was what you and Bill should do now about education, training and labor market policy. Following that meeting, I chaired another in Washington on the same topic....
>
> Our purpose in these meetings was to propose concrete actions that the Clinton Administration could take—between now and the inauguration, in the first 100 days and beyond....

We think the great opportunity you have is to *remold the entire American system for human resources development, almost all of the current components of which were put in place before World War II....What is essential is that we create a seamless web of opportunities, to develop one's skills that literally extends from cradle to grave and is the same system for everyone—young and old, poor and rich, worker and full-time student....*The other major proposal we offer has to do with government organization for the human resources agenda.

The letter continued with paragraph after paragraph of this sort of thing. Tucker offered his vision of "An Economic Strategy Based on Skill Development":

- The economy's strength is derived from a whole population as skilled as any in the world, working in workplaces organized to take maximum advantage of the skills those people have to offer.

- A seamless system of unending skill development that begins in the home with the very young and continues through school, postsecondary education and the workplace.

Tucker's suggestions for "reorganizing" education included "national standards of performance in general education" to reward students at the age of sixteen with three more years of "free" education:

All students who meet the new national standards for general education are entitled to the equivalent of three more years of free additional education. We would have the federal and state governments match funds to guarantee one free year of college education to everyone who meets the new national standards for general

> education. So a student who meets the standard at 16
> would be entitled to two free years of high school and
> one of education beyond that.

Tucker was silent on what to do with those who did not meet the new national standards or who refused to cooperate behaviorally. What we see here should be clear: the complete subordination of education to the economy in the spirit of globalism—vocationalism, or what Beverly Eakman calls "education for the New World Order." Note Tucker's suggestion that this should begin in the home." Very young children's first natural teachers are, of course, their parents—making the assumption (admittedly a tall one in this day and age) that the child *has* two loving parents. Was Tucker proposing that his vocational-technocrats commandeer homes?

He offered little in his letter about the exact meaning of "skills," but from the overall context, it should be clear that what Tucker meant were not skills in the traditional sense in spelling, reading, basic grammar, basic arithmetic, critical reasoning, and so on. In fact, there was *nothing* in his agenda calling definitively even for simple literacy! School-To-Work actually follows up the globalist Goals 2000 agenda on which Tucker also worked. Goal 3 of Goals 2000 stated:

> All students will leave grades 4, 8 and 12 having demonstrated competency over challenging subject matter, (math, etc.) and...will insure [*sic*] that all students learn to use their minds well, so that they may be prepared for responsible citizenship, further learning and productive employment.

From the Secretary's Commission on Achieving Necessary Skills (SCANS), we learn that "essential foundation skills...

include a number of cognitive and interpersonal abilities, including the capability to think and solve problems…work effectively alone and in teams, and take personal responsibility for one's own self-development." This includes "exercising leadership, working with diversity, and working well as a team member."

Notice again that there is no mention of academics or of individual merit or excellence. In fact, some School-To-Work apologists have been as open in their disdain for academics as Thorndike was. The SCANS report quoted one "educrat":

> Many companies have moved operations to places with cheap, relatively poorly-educated labor. What may be crucial, they say, is the dependability of a labor force and how well it can be managed and trained, not its general educational level, although a small cadre of highly educated creative people is essential to innovation and growth. Ending discrimination and changing values are probably more important than reading in moving low-income families into the middle class.

Moreover:

> Dramatic changes in the way we will raise our children in the year 2000 are indicated, particularly in terms of schooling….We will need to recognize that the so-called basic skills, which currently represent nearly the total effort in elementary schools, will be taught in one-quarter of the present school day….When this happens—and it's near—the teacher can rise to his true calling. More than just a dispenser of information, the teacher will be a conveyor of values….We will be agents of change.

And:

> The frameworks represent one kind of standards: con-
> tent standards. Now it is time to take the next step and
> develop performance standards…students must meet
> the standards in order to graduate….All students
> need the opportunity to work with business partners
> and see the…ways applied learning competencies can
> enhance learning in academic subjects. To that end
> applied learning—the ability to work in groups…to
> manage one's work…are essential to good citizen-
> ship…as well as for a productive worklife.

An English teacher, who remains unidentified (for obvious
reasons), retorted sarcastically, "Right, and we're going to be
relegated to helping kids write resumes. Of course, they won't
be able to write, spell, or speak intelligently, but they'll have a
decent resume as long as traditional teachers are still available to
write it for them."

Here we have open admissions of the desire for what
amounts to a workforce of conditioned wage slaves—supervised
by "change agents" who have themselves been trained to sabotage the educations of those placed in their charge. Corporations
approve of School-To-Work education because it promises them
compliant labor at a very cheap price. I have been drawing
upon a report titled "School-To-Work: A Formula for Failure"
(Holgate, 1997). This report asks pointedly, "How do you move
low-income families into the middle class by not educating
them?" The goal of School-To-Work and similar movements,
however, is not and never has been an educated middle class. As
School-To-Work advocates and change agents David Hornbeck
and Lester Solomon observe in their *Human Capital and America's
Future* (1991), "*Educated employees have higher turnover rates, lower*

job satisfaction, and poorer promotion records than less educated employees." Another School-To-Work advocate, Lauren Resnick of SCANS, said, "*Most employees under this model need not be educated. It is far more important that they be reliable, steady, and willing to follow directions.*"

School-To-Work, when brought to fruition, requires high-school students to choose a "career path" by the time they reach tenth grade—sometimes earlier. The "integrated curriculum" integrates vocation and political correctness into every subject. It maintains information databases on students to measure their "progress" against "international benchmarks" (i.e., benchmarks designed within the United Nations orbit). It reduces teachers to the status of "facilitators," in accordance with the psychology of stimulus-response.

School-To-Work was sold to business as the solution to one of its primary complaints about employees: they are often so poorly educated they cannot read, comprehend, and follow simple written instructions. The complaints have not diminished, of course, because once you have completely subordinated education to the workplace, *it ceases to be education*. Moreover, the need to quash academics to prepare students for the workplace suggests something seriously amiss with the *workplace*. Ultimately, today's workplace is more the product of elite-directed social engineering than it is free enterprise. The latter has not existed in America on any large scale for well over a hundred years. Thus we have a workplace that does not fit what normal human beings really are—which doubtless explains why corporations (and government agencies) experience high turnover rates among employees with real educations. It also, perhaps, explains many of the problems plaguing government schools today.

V.

Where are we today? Unfortunately, this overview has only scratched the surface. My intent was to demonstrate a Cardinal Error: allowing the formation and building up of an educational system whose premises are not fundamentally American and is thus unable to transmit our founding principles from generation to generation, allowing us to sustain Constitutionalism and individual freedom, correcting our missteps when necessary (e.g., getting rid of chattel slavery) while keeping our fundamental premises intact. The full story of the slow destruction of the American intellect goes beyond the scope of this work. I therefore recommend the three books that in my view do the most to document how this Cardinal Error has worked (and is still working) to destroy real education in the United States: Charlotte Thomson Iserbyt's *the deliberate dumbing down of america* (2000), John Taylor Gatto's *The Underground History of American Education* (2001), and Beverly K. Eakman's *The Cloning of the American Mind* (1998). For shorter treatments, do not miss Allan Quist's books *FedEd: The New Federal Curriculum and How It's Enforced* (2002) and *America's Schools: The Battleground for Freedom* (2005), nor Sheldon Richman's *Separating School and State* (1994), which contains some important history of this problem going back to Horace Mann. Iserbyt's and Gatto's works are readily available online. Iserbyt has compiled a rich collection of downloadable resources related to this problem on her website http://www.americandeception.com. All of these works consider, from various angles, not just the fashions themselves that have destroyed our society's ability to teach critical, logical thinking and transmit accumulated knowledge to its children, but how the effort has come from the upper echelons. The aim for over a hundred years now has been the same: social control.

We ought to note in closing this chapter that the 2000s decade has seen more of the same. Republican President George W. Bush's No Child Left Behind Act of 2002 continued the micromanaging of government schools via "teaching to the test"—standardized tests that are constantly being adjusted and dumbed down. Democratic President Barack Obama, elected in the throes of the Meltdown of 2008, has shown no interest in reversing anything his predecessors put in place. (At this point, the reader should go back to the introduction and reread Carroll Quigley's remark about the essential identity of the two major political parties.) Today's "twentysomething" generation—products of School-To-Work and Workforce Investment education—have little interest in, much less a grasp of, government and economics, and even less of their own limitations. With rare exceptions, they have little knowledge of or interest in the edifice of "global governance" being put in place all around us. New technologies they accept, since these increase convenience. The same will be true of the No Child Left Behind generation to come. Here is investigative journalist Greg Palast's description of the actual purposes of No Child Left Behind; nothing in it should be unfamiliar by now:

> The new world requires highly educated workers, but not too many. We saw how rising productivity created gargantuan wealth worldwide in the past two decades for a few. Maintaining the rise of productivity and riches through new technology requires a skilled, imaginative, highly educated, well trained workforce. In India, very highly skilled workers account for one million

jobs—about 2 percent of the workforce. America can afford to make it 10 percent. But no more. What about the other 90 percent? Someone's got to unload the goods shipped in from China, stock Walmart's shelves and ask you, "Do you want fries with that?" In this flat, tilted new world, we have to adopt the methods used by emperors of Confucian China: test for the best, cull the rest....

No Child Left Behind offers no "options" for those with the test score Mark of Cain—no opportunities, no hope, no plan, no funding. Rather, it is the new social Darwinism, the marketplace jungle brought into the classroom. This is educational eugenics: identify the nation's loser class early on. Trap them, then train them cheap. Someone has to care for the privileged. No society can have winners without lots and lots of losers. And so we have No Child Left Behind—to provide the new worker drones that will clean the toilets at the Yale Alumni Club, punch the cash registers color-coded for illiterates, and pamper the class on the higher floors of the new economic order. (*Armed Madhouse,* 2006, p. 218–19)

Again, neither School-To-Work, No Child Left Behind, nor its likely successor, Marc Tucker's latest brainchild, published under the title *Tough Choices or Tough Times* (2006), have much to say about teenagers who don't meet their "international benchmarks." Perhaps the near-collapse of the nation's financial system during 2008–09 woke up a few people, but not nearly enough; and all too many are being suckered by talk of a "recovery" that simply does not exist outside of government numbers. The latter are confident that all of us can continue living beyond our means if only the central banks can create enough fiat money.

Of course, as America becomes a third-world nation, we can be assured that we will still need young people who can flip hamburgers, serve coffee in the local Starbucks, or sell Chinese-made goods in Walmart or shopping malls.

But should people be relegated to such roles at the age of sixteen? The vocational model of education we have been studying does just that! Most products of this model are interested in making money and being entertained. So long as their checks come every two weeks, they are content. They assume that if there are problems in our world, they will be solved by the "experts." Markets are happy to oblige the sheepletariat's desire for a steady diet of entertainment, meaning that (for example) career athletes are able to sign nine-figure contracts, while those struggling to educate in the traditional way are often compelled to do so for free on the Internet.

In this environment, it became possible for the two major presidential candidates of 2004—George W. Bush and John Kerry—to be members of the same supersecret organization, Skull and Bones; both comment publicly that it is so secret they can't talk about it, *and this not be news!* The superelite, our political class, and its administrators are happy to oblige the sheepletariat's apathy regarding matters of state, or of the economy—although there has been an upsurge of mild unrest over the federal spending spree since 2008, embodied in, for example, the Tea Party movement, whose members are, not unexpectedly, maligned as racist "tea-baggers."

The most sensible immediate antidote for concerned parents is to refuse to allow their children anywhere near a government school. As of this writing, homeschooling is still legal in the United States. It is also the fastest-growing educational movement in the country—a welcome sign of the realization

that something has gone terribly wrong with American education. For a Christian perspective calling for a mass exodus
from government schools, I recommend Rev. E. Ray Moore's
Let My Children Go! (2002) and Bruce Shortt's *The Harsh Truth
about Public Schools* (2004). One does not need to be a Christian,
however, to recognize the anti-intellectualism and dangers to
individual freedom inherent in dominant tendencies such as
School-To-Work and No Child Left Behind. All one need realize is that the merging of education with workplace training
has been a central feature of every totalitarian order, which is
why you can find it as one of the key provisions in Marx's and
Engels's *Communist Manifesto*. Marx and Engels spoke of (tenth
plank of the *Communist Manifesto*): "Free education for all children in public schools. Abolition of children's factory labor in its
present form. Combination of education with industrial production, etc., etc." Independent schooling has already been quashed
in European Union-dominated nations such as Germany. At
present, escape is still possible in America. Every state in the
union has organizations devoted to accumulating resources for
those who homeschool their children. Research shows that on
average, homeschooled children and teenagers are as much as
four years ahead of their peers in every academic subject (see
Bruce Shortt, *The Harsh Truth about Public Schools*, pp. 342-51).

There is a problem, however, and it would be wrong not
to discuss it. Educrats have constructed a largely self-contained
and self-perpetuating system. They permeate federal and state
education agencies and hand down directives, which administrators and teachers have the choice of either following or giving
up their careers. The prevailing fashions control major accredit-
ing agencies. All school administrations do as they are told and
impose central directives on their teachers and faculty, or risk

having their institution's accreditation revoked. The professional guilds and educratic hierarchies have the workaday practitioners by the throat. They would drop the axe on homeschooling in a minute if they believed they could get away with it. In this environment—where those who teach their children at home are still a tiny minority faced with public indifference at best and incredulous rejection at worst—it has proven very difficult for the movement to make the headway required to reverse educational decline in the United States. Given the amount of damage done to multiple generations, it may simply be too late! In the present economic situation, which has given us levels of unemployment unprecedented since the Great Depression, we desperately need as large a percentage as possible of a generation that can think outside the box, as it were, and develop new forms of entrepreneurship. It is encouraging to find a few "millennials" doing this; but the numbers are not enough, and thus far have not extended to members of older generations who have been thrown out of work.

Government schools, meanwhile, continue to graduate students who may have a few job skills but no real learning. Sometimes, to the extent that jobs require reading and understanding complex sequences of instructions, they do not even have those. Students have been exposed to little in the way of deep thought. They can't begin to understand what motivated a Thomas Hobbes or a John Locke or a Thomas Jefferson. If they have any grasp of politics at all, they are followers of one or the other wings of the Washington, D.C., Party. This is encouraged through student organizations and the mainstream media. And we wonder how a Barack Obama can be elected president of the United States on the basis of very good oratory skills and an empty promise of "change" (and let us not pretend that political correctness had nothing to do with the failure of the GOP to mount any kind of credible opposition to the rise of the first black U.S. president).

Is there a solution to this depressing situation? Perhaps if we had not committed Cardinal Error Three, matters might be more promising.

CHAPTER

3

Cardinal Error Three. Americans—intelligentsia first, *consciously*, but eventually our so-called leaders and much of the public *tacitly*—abandoned the native religiosity of most of the Founders and embraced a naturalistic materialism also imported from Europe. The consequences soon began to undermine our civilization. Christian institutions have survived, but in forms not threatening to the worldview and goals of the superelite.

• • •

I.

Early Americans did not see eye to eye on theological specifics, but most had an inherent religiosity, as I will call it. That is, unstated acceptance of a transcendent realm and a transcendent God suffused their lives independently of a specific creed or church doctrine. From this realm and God had come eternal standards of moral truth. Early Americans understood moral truth as built into the fabric of the created order, an idea that formed the basis of British common law. They weren't philosophers given to debating first principles, obviously. But they implicitly realized, as have many wise men and women down through the ages, that life in this world acquires stable meaning only through insight into a world beyond this one, and that this alone can provide the basis for an enduring civic morality based on something more than mere enculturation, or if that fails, intimidation or force. Such notions were the key to a free and responsible people, to the extent such could be had. While Protestants had a different understanding of the relationship between the individual and the church than did Catholics, with unfortunate animosity between them, both could trace the intellectual pedigree of natural-law thinking back to the same philosopher/theologian: St. Thomas Aquinas. And one could trace the idea of the necessity of an overriding check even on responsible government to that of original sin. As John Adams understood the issue facing those who would create and then maintain a free republic: "We have no government armed with the power capable of contending with human passions unbridled by morality and religion.... Our Constitution was made only for a moral and a religious people. It is wholly inadequate to the government of any other" ("Letter to the Officers of the First Brigade of the Third Division of the Militia of Massachusetts," Oct. 11, 1798).

The Founding Fathers also accepted that at least some class stratification was the natural order of things—as opposed to the ideal of a "classless society" promoted by Marxists and those influenced by Marxian thought, who reject on principle the very idea of a "natural order of things." There is, in the Founders' views, at best a benign aristocracy of excellence, which most fully emerges under conditions of personal freedom and economic liberty. Excellence will manifest itself through entrepreneurship and increasing real prosperity if private-property rights are recognized and protected by the state. When natural distinctions are challenged and eroded, the benign aristocracy will be replaced by an oligarchy interested only in wealth and power. A benign aristocracy seeks out and welcomes excellence into itself; an oligarchy is threatened by anyone attempting to operate outside its power structures. What is important, then, is not class stratification, but class mobility: at our best, we make it possible for anyone, through hard work and perseverance, to rise from humble beginnings and join the aristocracy. Sadly, the converse is also true. It must be just as possible for someone to be born into opulence and, through chronic irresponsibility, fall terribly.

Early Americans did not support social innovation as necessarily salutary; nor did they trust those who would alter society as a whole according to some abstract design. Along with major British philosophers from John Locke and David Hume to Edmund Burke, they recognized that custom, convention, and tradition are not arbitrary; rather, these represent organic and largely spontaneous patterns of human action, relationships, and social institutions that prove themselves successful over a long time. The Founders therefore no more trusted human nature than did Hobbes who saw human failings as inevitably requiring powerful central government (a *Leviathan*); otherwise we are ever at risk of falling back into the state of nature (anarchy). What saved our Founders from Hobbesian cynicism was their native religiosity. Man's fallen state explained why human nature needed the checks of "rules of order" supplied by custom and tradition and given expression in the rule of law. A religious people would behave sufficiently well to enable "rules of order" to be kept to a minimum.

It should be clear: this was not an explicit political philosophy and theology; it was implicit and lived from the bottom up, not written down and enforced from the top down by an elite. Yet it gave rise to the most promising civilization in history. There were some monumental blunders, it is true. Chattel slavery stands as the most obvious example, although it should be noted that this institution was hardly invented on North America. The treatment of Native Americans was another mistake—again perpetuating patterns of conquest brought here from elsewhere. We corrected these mistakes in time, at least somewhat; but unfortunately, those who sought to undermine this civilization had already begun using the slavery issue as a means to keep people divided. It is fair to say the United States has paid dearly for blunders Americans did not initiate.

The wisest leaders of early America recognized the indispensability of Christian theology in the body politic, whatever their specific doctrinal differences and despite the fact that they didn't write Christianity explicitly into any of our founding documents. Religion is invariably a contentious subject because it deals with ultimates in ways no other area of human life touches, and because it lies beyond the purview of rational proofs. Thoughtful, well-intentioned people can disagree on details or interpretation or on entire creeds, which is why we have so many Christian denominations. Be this as it may, spiritual convictions have infused ultimate meaning into lives immersed in immense suffering, given their pain significance, and in the end, supplied sufferers with a reason to live (see Victor Frankl, *Man's Search for Meaning*, orig. 1946).

Religion has had its dark side, of course. Religious institutions and those in them are as vulnerable as anyone to the lure of power. Religious leaders are only human. They can impose creeds by force just as easily as any political authority can, and they do so far more effectively because of their implicit claim to sanction by God himself. They can rule by instilling fear of hellfire and damnation. Such men gave us the Spanish Inquisition. They held heads of state in thrall before the rise of dynasties such as the Rothschilds. Governments had long been more than willing to sponsor national churches such as the Church of England. When governments sponsored specific bodies of religious doctrine, as they always had in Europe, it was invariably a recipe for repression. Thus Thomas Jefferson's call, however often misapplied, for a "wall of separation between church and state" in his letter to the Danbury Baptist Association (1802).

So again Americans blazed a different trail, one set out in our First Amendment, which promised "Congress shall make no law respecting an establishment of religion, or prohibiting the free exercise thereof." Oceans of ink have been spilled over what this so-called Establishment Clause means—in recent years, often ignoring everything after the comma. The point is: our republic was of necessity Christianity friendly, but disavowed establishing any specific Christian denomination as a national church akin to the Church of England. There was to be room for many denominations, many ways of worship. These were left up to the people themselves, without interference from the state and without their interfering with the state. The assumption here is that a society *can* be infused with a bottom-up commitment to one or more variations on the Christian worldview without allowing that worldview to be transformed into a top-down theocracy. If society is decentralized, and potential instruments for the abuse of power are dispersed as widely as possible, we can prevent national theocracy, even if local theocracies develop here and there.

So why has the Establishment Clause proven so troublesome? Why have numerous Supreme Court decisions, one by one, forced Christianity out of education and out of the public square, typically on Establishment Clause grounds? The most obvious reason is that never in their wildest imaginings did the Adamses and Jeffersons think that one day the federal government would overwhelm the states and that federal power would be everywhere, dictating terms to every institution, often as part of an arrangement established by their acceptance of federal dollars. Since federal entanglements with any institution that openly acknowledged a Creator would be subject to legal challenge as "establishing" religion, and since by the middle of the twentieth century, that encompassed nearly all legal and educational institutions, those institutions found themselves unable to acknowledge a Creator without entering a legal minefield.

II.

Other factors were emanating from the European intelligent-sia, working very slowly to curtail the influence of Christianity, which in America was rendered more vulnerable by the absence of an explicit and unified body of doctrine or any significant interest in such. Christianity had lost the allegiance of many European intellectuals before the American founding. In the skilled hands of authors such as Voltaire, to cite an obvious example, the Church became an object of ridicule. The bank-ers, whose "religion" was essentially materialism, as we noted in chapter 1, moved in to fill the vacuum.

What went wrong? Historians and other scholars again disa-gree, as a *huge* body of literature testifies. Moreover, the prob-lem has many dimensions and is capable of being explored from within many disciplines; much of it therefore goes outside the scope of what we can offer here. Please allow me to offer a few of my own humble thoughts—on how Western philosophical theology set itself up for a fall.

In a nutshell: major voices in medieval philosophy/philo-sophical theology opened the door themselves to skepticism, and thence to humanism, by articulating what they believed to be logically rigorous and ultimately decisive proofs for the existence of the God of Christianity—implying that such proofs were both possible and desirable. St. Anselm of Canterbury, St. Thomas Aquinas, and René Descartes developed the best-known attempts at proving God's existence. These are the classical argu-ments philosophy students still study—the ontological, cosmo-logical, and teleological or design arguments. First, these proofs implicitly embed the Platonist presupposition that logical form is ontologically prior to God and is therefore the tool to use in proving that he exists. They also presuppose that precise, absolute proof is necessary for intellectual acceptability—despite Aristotle's wise warning in the *Nicomachean Ethics* that "precision is not to be sought for alike in all discussions, any more than in all the products of the crafts" (Book I).

As the products of fallible, finite minds employing Platonist tools to grasp an infinite Being, the Creator of all things, including logical form, the classical arguments turned out to have insurmountable weaknesses. In time, those who identified rational belief with rigorous proof, or who saw decisive worldly, empirical evidence as their standard of credibility, found themselves forced to conclude that belief in God was not rational or credible. This attitude was exemplified in manifestations of emerging Enlightenment humanism—for example, Baron D'Holbach's rejection of theism in his *System of Nature* (1770) and David Hume's character Philo undermining "natural religion" in *Dialogues Concerning Natural Religion* (1781). In the face of formulations of, say, the "problem of evil and suffering," moreover (also in Hume's more-than-capable hands), Christianity's problems seemed to mount.

Given these human-centered criteria, belief in the Christian God seemed no more credible to the enlightened mind than belief in the gods of the ancient Romans, Greeks, or Egyptians; the enlightened mind, therefore, no longer sought freedom *of* religion but freedom *from* religion. Early Enlightenment writers (Denis Diderot, Jean le Rond d'Alembert, and others) produced their *l'Encyclopedie* in France during 1751–1772, with later supplements, revised editions, and translations. This work openly urged skepticism toward belief in God: "to change the way people think," as Diderot stated (quoted in *The Making of the West: People's and Cultures, A Concise History, Vol. II*, 2007, p. 611). One could "wager" that an "infinitely incomprehensible" being exists, as had Blaise Pascal over a century before, as if in anticipation of what was to come, but this seemed an act of desperation—almost an admission of defeat.

The other alternative was to embrace some form of Christian existentialism, pursued, for example, by the Danish philosopher Søren Kierkegaard, whose subjectivism about religious truth fully decoupled it from rational understanding. Most modern theologians have, in one way or another, followed in Kierkegaard's wake by maintaining his separation between faith and rational understanding of truths existing apart from the believer (Martin Buber, Paul Tillich, Rudolph Bultmann, Gabriel Marcel, and others).

What was—is—*Enlightenment humanism*? The phrase does not refer to a unified, fully articulated school of thought any more than does *Christian theology*; but in all its forms, it represents a human-centered view of existence with roots going back to the ancient Greeks instead of the ancient Hebrews. Its ancestor is without a doubt the vision of the ideal society drawn by Plato in the *Republic*. An important step toward humanism can be seen in the autonomous Cartesian mind of the *Meditations* (1641). Humanism drew heavily on the writings of social philosophers such as Jean-Jacques Rousseau in *Du Contrat Social* (1762). Its followers set out to transcend the "self-imposed immaturity" label Immanuel Kant gave it in the opening paragraph of his famous essay "What Is Enlightenment?" (1784). Enlightenment humanism was optimistic and idealistic. Its primary tenets: (1) human nature is inherently rational and morally good, but has been corrupted; (2) what has corrupted human nature are society's institutions—especially religious ones, but also monarchies that claim divine sanction (the "divine right of kings")—and the implied need for a person to depend on authorities, whether religious or political, instead of on autonomous reason; (3) we therefore need to abolish these institutions and work for the transformation of society *en toto* to bring it more into alignment with our rationally developed ideals; (4) doing so will bring about indefinite social improvement and one day perhaps even the perfection of that "paragon of animals":

> What a piece of work is a man! how noble in reason! how infinite in faculty! in form and moving how express and admirable! in action how like an angel! in apprehension how like a god! the beauty of the world! the paragon of animals! (*Hamlet*, Act 2, Scene 2)

In any event, Enlightenment humanism stands in sharp contrast to the implicit philosophy of early Americans sketched above.

It dawned on some observers (Edmund Burke being the obvious example) that something had gone terribly wrong when the instigators of the French Revolution, having adopted *Liberté! Egalité! Fraternité!* as their humanist, optimist rallying cry, turned France into a bloodbath. What went wrong? Christians, of course, believe in original sin, that human nature is *not* inherently good (Romans 3:23; Job 5:7; Isaiah 64:6, etc.), which explains the corruption of institutions that are, after all, products of human beings. They conclude that (1) above is false. Every transformational agenda therefore rests on a false premise, that our human "default setting" is innocence. This also tells them that attempts by an intelligentsia to force real societies onto a path of universal melioration and progress toward Utopia are bound to leave nations in ruins when human nature refuses to cooperate. Original sin, for the Christian, explains the lust for power itself—including when manifested in supposedly Christian institutions. All of us recall Lord Acton's adage that "power tends to corrupt, and absolute power corrupts absolutely." According to a Christian worldview, that statement doesn't get things quite right. Human nature is already corrupted by sin; concentrations of power just play to this corruption and make it worse.

This worldview explains why humanism, in the hands of those who knew how to exploit it, eventually gave us tyrannies whose thirst for blood made 1790s France look like a cakewalk by comparison: the Soviet Union under Lenin and Stalin, Nazi Germany under Hitler, China under Mao, Cambodia under Pol Pot, and so on. Utopia looks great to the Platonist intellectual with a holistic vision of a perfect world—but actual flesh-and-blood human beings never fit into this vision. At best, they become cogwheels in massive state machinery. Those who resist or who otherwise do not fit the plan are crushed like insects by its policing mechanisms. Dissent, after all, cannot be tolerated.

There are, of course, more "modest" forms of humanism, as we've seen. These "modest" forms of humanism are what has guided state-sponsored education. They are not openly totalitarian and can tolerate dissent on the margins. Their purveyors would prefer to avoid open coercion, using behavior modification instead of brute force. What humanist systems all have in common, though, is that in practice, individuals are never an end in themselves, to be respected as having intrinsic worth, owned only by oneself and one's God. Rather, the individual becomes a subject of the state, if not to tyrants, then to the money powers that come to own the political classes as they bend capitalism into their service.

Libertarianism may seem to be an exception to this. According to much libertarian political philosophy, individuals own their own lives and the fruits of their labors. No one is anyone else's master; no one is anyone else's slave. No one has a moral claim on the labors of another, or on their fruits (see John Hospers, *Libertarianism*, 1973; or Tibor R. Machan, ed., *The Libertarian Alternative*, 1974). Libertarianism, moreover, may appear to be firmly outside the Platonist mold by taking its cue from Aristotle. Where we arrive, however, is again at the view that man is the "rational animal" and again, therefore, innocent—but corrupted by Platonist collectivism and statism. A few authors who describe themselves as Christian libertarians agree with the bulk of libertarian economic arguments, but reject the assumption that enlightened self-interest alone can build a just and humane society. Surely this last idea is dubious when viewed against recent history and has failed to resonate with the majority of thoughtful persons who see unrestrained corporate activity as no less potentially dangerous than unrestrained government. Economics as a science requires a larger worldview—just as an economic system is only one part, however central and crucial, of a larger civilization. The belief that corporate giants seek competition in a *laissez-faire* economy illustrates, in the end, the fundamental naïveté of the secular libertarian alternative.

It is one of history's ironies that Enlightenment humanism has led to so many forms of suppression of the individual human being, since, again, Enlightenment philosophy took its cue from the individualistic epistemology that began with the Cartesian method of doubt as a means of establishing certainty ("I think; therefore, I am"—emphasis on the *I*). Real flesh-and-blood persons, including intellectuals, are simply not suited psychologically for complete autonomy and self-sufficiency, especially in a moral sense. The Cartesian individual is, in fact, an intellectual myth—a construct of modern philosophy. Real persons have a multitude of complex relations to "the other": other persons, from family members outward, and a multitude of objects in the world behaving according to the laws governing them, posing problems to be solved. To be sure, the Rousseauian collective—the "general will"—is also an intellectual fiction descended from Platonism. Society is built up by fallible persons with a multitude of relations, attempting both individual and collective solutions to the problems of survival and advancement in the course of living—a process that can no more happen without rules for living, moral and practical, than can we understand the physical universe without appealing to laws governing physical objects.

These rules do not enforce themselves; the only available means of enforcement has been the state. Those claiming that "society" can generate another enforcement mechanism have only to produce examples and show their capability of operating on a large scale in a mass society of millions of human beings who do not know one another. No examples have been forthcoming. The absence of the state is not an anarchist utopia, but Hobbes's state of nature where life is "solitary, poor, brutish, nasty, and short." This explains why, if you place forty teenagers together in a confined area, you will get *Lord of the Flies*; for that matter, there is no guarantee that forty adults who do not know each other will figure out how to get along. (Just read online forums!)

Underlying Enlightenment humanism was not merely rebellion against Christianity in the name of autonomous reason, but a developing alternative, an equally comprehensive view of the universe we will call *materialism*. (It could also be called *naturalism*, or *naturalistic materialism*, although *naturalism* is more easily understood as a *method* originating within this view of nature, rather than the view of nature itself.)

What, precisely, is materialism? Before Voltaire, D'Holbach, Hume, and Kant, physician and philosopher Julien Offray de la Mettrie penned *L'Homme Machine* (*Man, A Machine*) (1748). With belief in the Christian God substantially weakened by the demand for a Platonist-premised proof that could never provide a credible "exit visa" outside the world of space and time, the stage was set for the rise of a philosophy that added to the above: (5) the universe is self-existent and not created; (6) it is comprised exclusively of entities that obey the laws of physics and chemistry, or entities whose behaviors can be explained ultimately in terms of physical causality alone; and therefore (7) the totality of humanity—human nature, action, society, morality—is ultimately subject to physical causality and biological explanation.

The originators of the scientific revolution had been essentially Christian, even if also influenced by ancient Greek schools (Pythagoras, for example). That is to say, they believed with Aquinas that a rational, law-governed natural order had been created by a rational God, and thus was capable of being apprehended by beings who possessed the power of rationality because they had been created in God's image. If the leading minds within a culture do not believe, *a priori*, that the universe is intelligible to human minds, then that culture will not develop science. Most ancient cultures never developed any sciences because they believed that nature was an arena controlled (or perhaps embodied) by whimsical, irrational deities or other entities, not the law-governed Providence of the Christian God.

But as an increasingly radical empiricism took over European thought, whatever could not be observed through the senses or their extensions (scientific instruments), or measured and quantified, was dismissed as unreal. This included "school metaphysics," which Hume dismissed at the end of his famous

Inquiry Concerning Human Understanding as "sophistry and illusion" (also in 1748). This is essentially the view Wilhelm Wundt would apply to children. His descendents, the behaviorists, would extend radical empiricism to human beings. All that we saw in the preceding chapter on education follows naturally; we need only add (8): *what is subject to physical causality, measurement, and biological explanation can be brought under conscious control if the right techniques can be discovered and utilized.* A technology of behavior, pursued through governance by technocrats, follows naturally from the materialist conception of the human person, which in turn was inferred from the realization that no one had ever seen a human soul (*psyche*), measured it, or otherwise studied it in the laboratory. It probably didn't exist; and neither did a transcendent God. As for Jesus Christ dying on the cross in payment for our sins and then rising from the dead? Forget it!

In the final analysis, Enlightenment humanism—particularly as its commitment to materialism becomes explicit—leaves us on our own, not just scientifically/technologically, but morally: not answerable, that is, to any Higher Power defining good and evil outside of human culture and its contingencies.

III.

By the early 1800s, other things being equal, a clash between the two worldviews, the Christian and the materialist, seemed inevitable in the scientific and other intellectual communities. In the middle of that century, however, a new development changed the rules of the game, making it difficult to talk about worldviews at all, or how philosophy affects culture in a broad sense. Hume's specific dismissal of "school metaphysics" in his *Inquiry* foreshadowed the new development. Here is the full statement, at the very end of the work:

> If we take in our hand any volume; of divinity or school metaphysics, for instance; let us ask, *Does it contain any abstract reasoning concerning quantity or number?* No. *Does it contain any experimental reasoning concerning matter of fact and existence?* No. Commit it then to the flames: for it can contain nothing but sophistry and illusion. (David Hume, *An Inquiry Concerning Human Understanding*, 1955 ed., p. 173; italics in original.)

These remarks offered a prelude to a new mode of thought that emerged gradually over the next few decades. The pivotal figure was the thinker credited as the father of sociology: Auguste Comte. Comte's writings, culminating in the multivolume *Philosophy and Positive Polity* (1850), unleashed the doctrine known as *positivism*. Positivism formalized the idea that scientific/empirical methods alone held the key to knowledge of all factual truth; that all religion, including Christianity, was by nature superstition; and that modern philosophy could also be discarded as the pointless building of intellectual air-castles—as useless as its own caricature of medieval scholastics' debating how many angels could stand on the head of a pin.

Comte argued that a civilization underwent three stages of development, or existed in three conditions, as he also called them. He called this the "law of the three stages." He didn't invent this idea; an early version can be found in Giambattista Vico's writings a century earlier. But Comte gave it its clearest articulation. The stages weren't historical, but rather levels of a culture's intellectual maturity. During the *first* stage or condition, the religious one, supernatural explanations of the world prevail. Since gods, spirits, demons, and so forth are whimsical at best, irrational and malevolent at worst when they act in the world to generate its phenomena (storms, eclipses, etc.), no *explanation* of these in any scientific sense is possible. Comte granted that Christian monotheism is the highest form of the first stage. One fickle deity makes for a far more orderly universe than a legion of them! But one fickle deity still doesn't open the door to scientific explanation.

During the *second* stage or condition, the metaphysical one, philosophers spin grand systems out of their imaginations and, perhaps, personal experience or education to explain the world—examples range from Aristotle's cosmology, Aquinas and his effort to synthesize Aristotelian thought and Christianity, and the dualism of Descartes, the "father of modern philosophy," down through Kant's transcendental turn and Hegel's absolute idealism. At this stage or condition, the political philosophers may speak of such notions as natural law and natural rights. Or they may speak of categories of the understanding or the requirements of duty. The point is to have a grand intellectual system that accounts for everything. Since none of these systems' main claims are empirically testable, we are left with a "strife of systems," each philosopher crossing out his predecessor's (or opponent's) prejudices and substituting his own. Philosophical explanations of the world are more rational than supernatural ones, Comte granted, but because of their essentially *a priori* methodology and their epistemological individualism, they, too, hold out little hope for genuine cognitive progress.

During the *third* stage or condition, the scientific one, rarely, if ever, achieved in the past, but now emerging in the Enlightenment consensus, scholars turn to empirical science: phenomena are observed and patterns discerned running through them; hypotheses are put forth and tested step-by-step against further observation. According to this image of science, a specific method has appeared: scientists attempt to replicate results of experiments; they collect and tabulate data sets; they refine hypotheses into *theories* that they work steadily at improving. They ascertain what a given theory predicts we should observe, as part of further testing. Refinement continues, as theory is further compared with observation. Science, in this image, embraces an empirical, not an *a priori* method; it is, moreover, a community endeavor, not one performed by isolated individuals. It seeks workable solutions to specific problems in terms of revisable lawlike generalizations about phenomena in the empirical world. It does not entertain notions of timeless absolutes suggesting an exit visa to another world. Those developed theories that solve the most pressing problems of the time and continue to survive the best empirical tests, perhaps also suggesting new lines of inquiry and promising continuing development, deserve to be called *knowledge*. This necessarily excludes the supernatural and the metaphysical.

The idea caught on. Emile Littré, French lexicographer and philosopher, founded *La Revue de philosophie positive (The Positivist*

Review) in 1867. This was the first periodical devoted to the discussion and advancement of Comte's ideas, as well as those of predecessors such as Saint-Simon. British sociologist Harriet Martineau translated Comte's works into English, introducing his thought to a variety of scholars and activists, some of whom we will encounter in the next chapter. The reception was mixed. Comte's views about science and the three stages were welcomed, but not so much another notion of his, that of a "religion of humanity." It was clear that science was advancing by leaps and bounds. Newton had given us the model science in physics, unifying celestial and terrestrial mechanics. Antoine Lavoisier had begun the revolution in chemistry with his theory of combustion; this revolution progressed to John Dalton's atomic theory. Other scientists were investigating the fossil record. Georges Cuvier noted for the first time that many species in the past had become extinct and proposed the idea, now called *catastrophism*, that a series of worldwide catastrophic events— floods, for example—explained what was observed. The biblical flood in Genesis was but the latest. Sir Charles Lyell rejected this approach and applied basic physical concepts to geology. He rejected catastrophism, especially the idea of a universal flood, in favor of *uniformitarianism*, the idea that "the present is the key to the past." That is, Lyell concluded in *Principles of Geology* (1830–33), we should observe processes at work today and *infer* that these processes can explain the totality of geologic history, given sufficient time. The only obstacle to the notion that the vast stretches of time necessary for this view of the world really existed was the biblical model, which was rapidly losing ground.

The stage was set for Charles Darwin, who studied Lyell closely, as well as making a multitude of observations of his own on board the *Beagle*. Darwin also encountered Thomas

Malthus's work on population biology, which held that population growth necessarily led to a struggle for existence amid insufficient resources. With its hypothesis of natural selection, *The Origin of Species* (1859) changed the world as few volumes have either before or since. Biological evolution was not a new idea, of course; but until Darwin, no one had been able to suggest a mechanism to explain speciation, the development of new species from old ones through a natural process; nor had there been any basis for thinking the Earth to be old enough for gradual evolution in the Darwinian sense to have generated the panorama of life biologists can observe. This, however, was changing throughout physical science: decades before, the Kant-LaPlace hypothesis had offered a solar system of planets of both natural origin and of great age, now on the order of hundreds of millions of years. Just as astronomers were developing a naturalistic theory of the origin of planets, biology began to coalesce around Darwin's naturalistic theory of evolution— that accidents of birth gave certain members of any population a natural advantage in the sense of better adaptation to their environment, that those individuals were the ones who tended to survive and breed, passing their advantages to their offspring, and that this explains the panorama of all life. Darwinian biology thus offered a materialistic theory of the origin of life and of all species, including humanity. With the support of Thomas Henry Huxley, "Darwin's bulldog," and other younger biologists enthusiastic over the new view of life then emerging, Darwinism soon dominated biological science. Evidence that a materialist worldview—not empirical evidence—explained the show of support for Darwinian evolution can be found, surprisingly, in textbooks themselves. Paleontologist J. Marvin Weller's text *The Course of Evolution* states openly: "Darwin was particularly fortunate in his timing because the intellectual atmosphere in England was favorable for the consideration of a new materialistic theory of evolution, and he promptly gained the active support of several able and aggressive young biologists" (1969, p. 2).

There can be little doubt that many contributions to knowledge have indeed grown out of the sciences. They will last if our civilization lasts. I mention this for any readers who suspect an antiscience "ambush" coming. No such ambush is waiting. Scientific progress, measured as genuine through solved problems and technological applications, is surely a true gauge of knowledge. Contributions to knowledge are one thing, however; philosophical ideologies are another, and positivism did not render them meaningless. Moreover, a false philosophical premise will not thwart definitive results if enough other premises are true. Science, as we stated earlier, was founded upon and has always operated under the assumption that the universe is a place of order and that its order is intelligible to the human mind—premises accepted by both Christians and materialists. Science, moreover, was specific and problem-focused; accordingly, it employed a range of specific methods often tailored to the occasion. Have the sciences made mistakes along the way? Of course they have. Many are well documented (examples: the phlogiston theory of combustion, the Piltdown hoax). The uniformitarian idea in geology has been modified considerably due to the recent realization (1980s) that the dinosaurs were killed off by a catastrophic, extinction-level event of some kind. Very likely the realization of other mistakes will come regarding human origins, more recent catastrophes, the true age of civilization, and other knowledge. For example, we have ancient maps that are unquestionably compilations from still older maps, showing an Antarctica and Greenland free of ice (see Charles Hapgood, *Maps of the Ancient Sea Kings*, 1966). We have other fragments of evidence that civilization may be much older than is generally accepted, including objects clearly of human origin excavated from quarries of solid rock ostensibly millions of years old (the other possibility being that the rock is much younger and that our dating methods determining the ages of the rocks are wrong). My point: such errors are normal and to be expected from a fallible enterprise.

Positivists turned science into an ideology. They tried to superimpose their ideology on science and make use of the sciences to advance a multitude of questionable causes. Like previous forms of humanism, positivism was optimistic about human nature, focusing on the possibilities of science and technique. It was, in a word, *positive* about these possibilities (as Comte had been). Its advocates soon combined it with powerful analytic tools developed by nineteenth-century logicians, and in the early decades of the twentieth century, transformed it into *logical* positivism. Logical positivism relied on an idea going back to Kant (earlier versions of the same idea are found in Leibniz and Hume), that of a cleavage between two kinds of propositions— *analytic* and *synthetic*. The former were matters of logical truth, mathematical truth, or definition, devoid of empirical content (that is, they said nothing about the world). The latter were matters of empirical truth (or falsity), because they could be tested against experience and experiment and would either meet or fail such tests. For the logical positivist, the cognitive meaning or significance of an empirical claim is in its verification. The propositions of religion (also ethics) seemed to be neither analytic nor empirically verifiable; so, to the logical positivist, they weren't "real" propositions at all. Perhaps they had *emotive* significance. In the legal realm, this translated into "legal positivism," first given voice by utilitarian thinkers such as Jeremy Bentham, who dismissed all talk of natural rights as "nonsense upon stilts." Legal positivists saw rights as legal constructs only. You have the rights that the legal system, a creation of the state and its authority structure, says you have. No more, no less.

In this view, propositions about worldviews became as meaningless as those of religion since they cannot be tested and validated by the logical positivist method of verification. The practical consequence of this was that a specific worldview such as naturalistic materialism could win the allegiance of intellectuals without much in the way of criticism or opposition from within the intellectual community. Would-be critics could not formulate their objections in acceptable language! Useful treatises and schools of thought that drew attention to the metaphysical commitments of modern science did exist, but they failed to gain any traction as logical positivism soon dominated the philosophical conversation, especially in the English-speaking world.

With Comte the positivist founder of sociology, Wundt and Freud dominant in psychology, and Darwin in biology, by the early twentieth century, naturalistic materialism had won the day in Europe. It would soon make inroads in the United States, working through the educational networks being set up and funded by the Rockefeller and Carnegie financial empires. The latter did not argue for it; they presumed it. Naturalistic materialism would enter American psychology through J. B. Watson and Thorndike, and philosophy through John Dewey. American culture was pragmatic and business-oriented, as was clear from the emphasis in education on "agricultural and engineering" training before the Rockefellers came along. Despite the significant body of ideas that went into the founding of the American republic, later generations by and large did not have much interest in intellectual conversation. This made America vulnerable. The enemy you don't notice or care about will soon overwhelm you. The positivist-materialist mind-set overwhelmed American culture, unnoticed until it was too late. It served superelite purposes perfectly!

IV.

What would happen with Western ethics once Christendom had lost its grip on the intelligentsia and soon began to lose its grip on the public mind generally, first in Europe and then in the United States? The ethical ideas that seemed to make the most sense in a secular world were those of the nineteenth-century utilitarians: Bentham, his associate James Mill's genius son John Stuart Mill, and their numerous followers. Utilitarianism held that we ought to pursue the greatest amount of good for the greatest number of those our actions can affect, and that the good is *pleasure* and a relative absence of pain. In other words, according to the utilitarians the good life for a human being is a life pursuing pleasure and avoiding pain, and not just for oneself but for all whom our actions may affect. (Mill does speak of *happiness*, by which, he tells us in his major work *Utilitarianism* [1863], he means pleasure and the absence of pain).

This kind of morality faced a problem of some magnitude that its adherents never took seriously enough: pursuing the greatest amount of good for the greatest number was quite compatible with sacrificing some on the altar of the greater good. In fact, there was little basis in this perspective for valuing the life of individual persons at all, if those who identified with power believed they saw a greater good achieved by disregarding their interests. We learned this the hard way with the infamous Tuskegee experiments, in which 399 black men in Macon County, Alabama, were literally sacrificed so the public health community could study the progress of untreated syphilis over nearly forty years. This may be an extreme case, but there are countless modest ones; for there is nothing in the tacit utilitarianism that U.S. culture embraced to bar the subtle manipulation of the public by those with the resources to do so—especially if said manipulations made the lives of the masses more pleasurable!

There are many examples of how the American public mind was manipulated and led in a desired direction. Interestingly, one of the most significant of these efforts began in Great Britain, as did the utilitarian philosophy itself. Consider the Tavistock Institute of Medical Psychology, founded in 1920 and renamed the Tavistock Clinic. Very little is known about its early years; its records were kept strictly private. It is clear, however, that Tavistock researchers were acutely interested in how extreme conditions affected the malleability of human behavior. In 1940, then Director John Rawling Rees gave a speech titled "Strategic Planning for Mental Health." He stated:

> We have made a useful attack upon a number of professions. The two easiest of them naturally are the teaching profession and the Church; the two most difficult are law and medicine....Public life, politics and industry should all of them be within our sphere of influence.... If we are to infiltrate the professional and social activities of other people, I think we must imitate the Totalitarians and organize some kind of fifth column activity! If better ideas on mental health are to progress and spread we, as the salesmen, must lose our identity....Let us all, therefore, very secretly be fifth columnists. (*Mental Health*, 1940, pp. 103–06)

Tax-exempt foundations such as the Rockefellers began to bankroll studies on the social effects of radio, mass media generally, and later, applied psychology. Several large grants were made by around 1937 and included, for example, the Radio Project (also supported by the Institute for Social Research at Columbia University), which included Theodor Adorno of the Frankfurt School, Gordon Allport of Tavistock, and Frank Stanton, who went on to become president of CBS. The purpose of the Radio Project was to study the effects of mass media on mass culture. Among its first projects was to study how women tended to become addicted to daytime dramas—"soap operas" (originally "radio dramas")—and investigate how radio could be used to influence women's mind-sets and lead them to a greater willingness to accept infidelity and casual sex. (For details see Eakman, *The Cloning of the American Mind*, pp. 143–46). Another Radio Project effort focused on the possibilities of mass suggestion as revealed through a close study of the infamous Orson Welles broadcast of H. G. Wells's *The War of the Worlds* in 1938: 25 percent of an estimated 6 million listeners believed the reports to be real. Many of these, in fairness, believed Germans were invading, not Martians; this was due to an earlier broadcast from Munich. The full scope of such investigations was large, ranging across newer communication media (magazine and book publishing, advertising, Hollywood entertainment and the growing celebrity culture, eventually television) that grew to maturity during the first two-thirds of the twentieth century.

Yet another Rockefeller Foundation grant was made in 1947, enabling the creation of the Tavistock Institute of Human Relations. It began to explore mind-control techniques, including propaganda, isolation, hypnosis, psychotherapy, the effects of drugs both legal and illegal on consciousness, and suggestibility. Some of this research came to the attention of the CIA when it was created, and eventually made its way into the hands of the clandestine investigators such as the architects of MK-Ultra, the most infamous "black ops" investigation into the use of drugs, sensory deprivation, and the like, as methods of mind control. The Tavistock network became a bridge between British and American covert intelligence. They picked up where the Radio Project left off, analyzing the effects on the public of radio, television, popular music, popular movies, and other forms of mass entertainment. We cannot begin to canvass all these efforts here. One thing became clear, however: it was not especially difficult to lead men *and* women of the rising middle class by their noses if the right stimuli were supplied. Whatever was wrong with behaviorism, it wasn't entirely ineffective in societies whose economies gave rise to mostly anonymous masses of nuclear families, most of whose members had been "educated" in public schools.

We come now to what may be the most important example of all of human mass manipulation. By the middle of the twentieth century, its academic guilds fully immersed in logical positivism and its educational system in the hands of progressive educators, the larger culture especially in the growing cities and suburbs was very slowly embracing materialism in a bottom-up fashion not unlike that of the religiosity of its ancestor as an unstated worldview. America was ready for "sexologist" Alfred C. Kinsey's decoupling of sexual activity from morality.

Kinsey began his career as an entomologist—a biologist specializing in insect behavior. More importantly for our purposes, he, too, was a materialist whose early interest in the sexual behavior of insects was generalized into an interest in all sexuality, especially that of humans. His ideas also came to the attention of the Rockefeller Foundation, which bankrolled his Institute for Research in Sex, Gender, and Reproduction at Indiana University. Kinsey assembled a team of "researchers" whose thinking was the same as his. The result was two volumes that caused the greatest stir since Darwin's *The Origin of Species* was published: *Sexual Behavior in the Human Male* (1948) and *Sexual Behavior in the Human Female* (1953).

Arguably, the seismic cultural shift precipitated by Kinsey's work over ensuing decades was greater than that of Darwin. The main claim made by Kinsey and his team was that the predominance of sexual monogamy in middle-class America was a myth, and any morality surrounding it, hypocrisy. A key Kinsey thesis was that children were sexual from infancy. Kinsey and his team claimed to base their results on data-driven empirical studies, like any other social science. At the time, no one seemed overly curious about how they had obtained their data sets. In fact, they were most likely conducting torturous experiments on children and even infants that would have been considered criminal offenses had anyone known about them. But the Institute for Research in Sex, Gender, and Reproduction was very secretive, and Kinsey would not allow anyone on his team who was not properly "objective" about sex; to him, "objectivity" meant not just data-driven empiricism, but amorality. Kinsey also obtained data from interviews with imprisoned sexual criminals; several of his "researchers" were almost certainly pedophiles. (See Judith Reisman, *Kinsey: Crimes and Consequences: The Red Queen and the Grand Scheme*, 1998.)

After the publication of *Sexual Behavior in the Human Male*, Kinsey became an academic celebrity. His ideas began to filter into the cultural mainstream. However shocking and out of accord they seemed with "middle-class values" (still derived essentially from Christianity), they fit with the implicit utilitarian outlook that had crept into European-American culture. They emerged as unbridled hedonism. There can be no doubt that the sex drive is one of our most powerful, and entirely nonrational in the intellectual's sense of rationality—which is why cultures either keep it on a short leash or perish. The first highly visible disciple of Kinseyite hedonism was Hugh Hefner, founder of the *Playboy* empire. Hefner discovered how well open sexuality sells. The sexual revolution followed in the 1960s and literally overwhelmed American culture through the marketplace. Hedonism (whether specifically sexual or not) become America's reigning personal ethic, especially among youth, as implicit utilitarianism had become its reigning social ethic among their elders.

Organized Christianity still had a great deal of influence, of course. Enlightenment agnosticism and atheism had not taken hold in the United States, even among much of the American intelligentsia. But in the long run Christianity was less and less able to withstand these powerful new cultural forces. This is a long story going outside the scope of this book. To sketch very briefly: Christian theology had begun to go off course decades before with the appearance of the dispensationalist theologies of J. N. Darby and especially Cyrus I. Scofield (for a useful account see Joseph M. Canfield, *The Incredible Scofield and His Book*, 1988). Many dispensationalist doctrines as they appeared, e.g, the popular claim that a "rapture of the saints" would remove all Christians from this world prior to seven years of "tribulation," reduced the interest of many believers in the immediate problems of this world. The neutering of American Christianity had gotten underway with the founding of organizations such as the Federal Council of Churches. Originally formed in 1908, the Council would come to represent twenty-five Protestant denominations encompassing over 140,000 congregations of more than 27 million professed Christians. The FCC, like many of these other organizations and personalities we have been considering, also thrived courtesy of Rockefeller dollars. In 1932, it published a credo that openly called for a "cooperative world order" along the lines of European socialism. By this time, its board of directors included a number of avowed communists who had begun preaching a "social gospel" that attempted to marry Jesus with Karl Marx. (The idea, heard among some "liberals" today, that Jesus was the first socialist, has its origins here.)

In the 1940s, the FCC openly endorsed the creation of the United Nations. On March 16, 1942, the very mainstream *Time Magazine* published an article about the FCC's relationship to the "New World Order crowd." Later, the FCC changed its name to the National Council of Churches, which in turn came under the UN umbrella as the World Council of Churches and began to work for the harmonizing of all world religions. Its "missionaries" spent more time on the "social gospel" than on the real Gospel—meaning that large percentages of the generations of Christians to come would not understand the basis of their own Christianity. Many would believe, for example, that salvation comes through works and not through trusting in Jesus Christ as one's personal Savior (Eph. 2: 8–9). Many Christians who believed this last had been fully captured by the "rapture cult."

Through the insidious actions of such clandestine groups within Church hierarchies themselves, Christianity would be left unable to defend itself. The Supreme Court began to remove it from public schools and soon forced it out of all government buildings. The first major decision was *McCollum v. Board of Education Dist. 71* (1948), which ended religious instruction in schools as a violation of the establishment clause in the First Amendment. Then, in *Engel v. Vitale* (1962), the Court ruled that any kind of prayer, even a nondenominational one, violated the principle of separation of church and state if it originated with the school district. In *Stone v. Graham* (1980), the Court found that posting the Ten Commandments in a public school is unconstitutional. Five years later, with *Wallace v. Jaffree* (1985), the Court opined that holding a moment of silence at a state-sponsored event is unconstitutional if the motivation for that moment is silent prayer by members of an audience. Next, in *Allegheny Co. v. ACLU* (1989), the Court found that a nativity scene in a government building violated the Establishment Clause. In *Lee v. Weisman* (1992), the Court reasoned that the appointment of clergy by a school district to read a nondenominational prayer at a graduation function constituted unconstitutional state sponsorship of worship; amazingly, the Court also held that such sponsorship might constitute *psychological coercion* against *children* (as opposed to adults), who might find that the prayer violated their personal beliefs (i.e., the subjectivism the educrats had been quietly working to instill!). Finally, in 2003, Judge Roy Moore, one-time chief justice of the Supreme Court of Alabama, found himself forced from his position following his refusal to recognize the legitimacy of a federal court's order to remove a monument engraved with the Ten Commandments from his own courtroom—the culmination of a legal battle that had begun with an ACLU lawsuit in 1995. In other words, by the turn of the millennium, the U.S. Supreme Court had single-handedly turned the Establishment Clause on its head!

This forced organized Christianity to retreat to Sunday events, decreasing its effect on an urban, secularized, and increasingly controlled culture that began to bypass religion entirely in its search for morality and meaning (see Harvey Cox, *The Secular City*, 1965). The extended family had already been replaced by the nuclear family as members of the World War II generation moved around the country in search of employment.

Now the nuclear family was jeopardized as these cultural forces, facing increasingly impotent religiously grounded moral instruction, set hormone-driven teenagers against their more traditional parents. Nuclear-family parents, largely isolated in cities or suburbs, where impersonal interactions were the norm, found themselves unable to transmit their values to their children. They received no help from public schools, which by this time were teaching Values Clarification. By the 1970s, American culture was fully sexualized. The idea that sexual morality was personal and subjective soon pervaded the youth culture of a middle class that appeared reasonably prosperous economically, but was under siege from multiple fronts. Sexuality education had entered the schools by storm. The basic idea was that kids are going to have sex whether we, the adults, like it or not. Morality is not a factor. We might as well show them how to prevent unwanted pregnancies and protect themselves from sexually transmitted diseases. Our best bet is to give kids condoms and instructions in how to use them.

Some would argue that the "religious right" began to restore "traditional values," at least in part, during the 1980s. One thinks of the Moral Majority and the Christian Coalition, the two most visible groups. This movement, in retrospect, barely scratched the surface. Neither political nor popular cultures were much swayed by the pretenses of the "religious right"; not helping matters was the penchant many of its supposed leaders had to shoot themselves in the foot with their own sexual misdeeds, resulting in their being openly ridiculed by the new cultural mainstream. By the 1990s, the homosexual movement was in ascendance as the latest appendage of the civil-rights movement. By the time the 2000s arrived, it had achieved fascinated acceptance among the majority of young people. Much of this was accomplished through mass media. While most of their elders vehemently rejected such proposals as "gay marriage," youth culture's overall acceptance of homosexuality testifies to the long-term impotence of the "religious right" and its various offshoots, largely consigned to Sunday morning sermons and the cultural oblivion of "right-wing" talk radio. We have not even mentioned the "church growth movement," which is more about feelings than substance, or those "contemporary" church services aimed at youth but which can only leave neutral observers wondering whether they are at a religious service or a rock concert.

V.

We should note that by this time, Western philosophy had also been effectively neutered. Trained philosophers were invariably warehoused in academic departments as professors (if they could find work at all). In a pragmatic, business-oriented civilization built on bankers' fractional money and taken in a specific direction, a trained philosopher had few viable alternatives (other than, perhaps, law school, computer programming, or tending bar). There have been, of course, enormous quantities of philosophical activity in the academic arena—nearly all of it highly specialized, technical, and unintelligible to outsiders—in a word, irrelevant to the larger culture.

Logical positivism faded from influence under the weight of technical criticism, but not before doing its work. It had been the perfect vehicle for building up a professional guild that would not threaten the rapidly growing alliances of government bureaucracies, globalist bankers, and industrial capitalists that dominated the economy, or the cultural forces we have been discussing, or the educational tendencies supported by the huge tax-exempt foundations. None of these were even on most professional philosophers' radar. Logical positivism was really more of an *antiphilosophy*—suited for intellectual life inside an oligarchic system that could pose as a democracy without being seriously challenged. The discipline whose ancestor had set out the premises on which Western civilization—and ultimately the natural philosophical and moral bases for the founding of the American republic—was built, was now *incapable* of producing *effective* critiques of power. It had quietly and almost ashamedly retreated into the recesses of academic decoration behind athletic programs, colleges of business, and centers for technical/vocational training that the land-grant system had originally established. Much of what remains in these recesses is now unable to speak clearly and cogently of objectively knowable truth at all.

Especially embarrassing are the so-called academic radicals spread across philosophy, history, comparative literature, sociology, and cultural studies. As radical students in the 1960s, they had proven useful by effectively weakening traditional scholarship even more. Their continued existence as career academics would be permitted, since they drew dissent and potential unrest in directions where it couldn't pose any real threat. Academic radicals, many of whom had never actually had to read Marx, would apply a kind of baby Marxism to the production of tomes that were just as specialized as the works of logical positivism and analysis, but less well reasoned (or written), less intelligible, and just as oblivious to the superelite at the center of the hated capitalist system.

In the 1980s and 1990s, academic radicals would go crackers over race and ethnicity, gender (radical feminism), homosexuality, and so on, advancing various forms of political correctness, almost as if those with real power cared about women's issues or those of minority groups, or were interested in homosexuality beyond its potential to further disrupt "traditional morality," undermine the nuclear family, and serve as a form of population control. For this same reason, the superelite would also ensure that "abortion rights" were perhaps limited from time to time but not touched at their core, which is the "right" to end a human life before it can be born.

Political correctness was most useful, however, as a form of thought control. "Sensitivity training" inculcated guilt into white men and forced them into self-censorship. They could observe the lives and careers of nonconformists disrupted or destroyed—including the lives of supposedly powerful politicians who slipped up (witness, for example, Mississippi Senator Trent Lott's fall from grace in 2002 following a remark interpreted as supporting segregation). Occasionally we saw lives disrupted by allegations of misconduct that turned out to be bogus, as happened to three members of the lacrosse team at Duke University in 2006. One of the most interesting features of that case is that the vast majority of the faculty at Duke University fell for a bogus complaint based on the skimpiest of evidence, and thus contributed to the vendetta against the three students—they did not ask questions because the students were white and their supposed victim was black. This case generated distrust that remains to this day. In the guise of achieving and celebrating "diversity," the politically correct both sought and achieved racial and other sorts of division. They focused on numbers, ratios, and measured "underrepresentation" of minorities, contentions that logically presuppose an abstract "correct" representation that has never existed anywhere.

The net result: members of different classes and ethnic groups focused suspiciously on each other, not on what was occurring in America's upper echelons, where utilitarian hedonism was developing into a culture of fiscal irresponsibility and unbridled greed. Of course, our financial system nearly collapsed with the Meltdown of 2008. Even this would not shake the grip of the cult of "diversity" in higher education with a sense that this society had much worse problems than too few women and blacks on university faculties.

This, then, is academia in the early 2000s: divided into dozens of micro-specialties, feminized, vocationalized, politically correct, *and mostly unaware of the real power system in Western civilization—much less able to affect it.* Students who do not cooperate are sometimes unable to obtain desired advanced degrees; those able to obtain degrees are refused stable employment. Such individuals—with way too much education for today's marketplace—pay a steep price. The academic job market collapsed in the early 1970s. A member of the "lost generation," I have survived, but I know of individuals with doctorates whose "careers" consist of caring for elderly parents at home. Others struggle daily to pay the bills since neither government nor corporations will make use of their skills. A situation where there are more jobseekers than jobs always invites abuse: conformists are hired; dissidents are weeded out. A system actually unable to affect real power thus perpetuates itself in multiple academic guilds through the intellectual inbreeding of ideologues hiring their own in the name of "diversity." Today, of course, the job system has just about collapsed for everyone else except for those with very specific skills in nursing, health care, or some brand of hands-on technology services (sales, face-to-face customer support, repair, etc.).

There have been a few exceptions to the rule that a philosopher must be a professor. I would be remiss not to mention Ayn Rand. A self-taught Russian immigrant, she gained a substantial following in the 1950s and 1960s, first with her novels and then her essays, especially among college students (much to the chagrin of their philosophy professors). She supplied a counterpoint to the prevailing leftism of most academics. Sadly, Rand, too, was essentially a materialist who accepted the Enlightenment view of human nature and made autonomous Reason into the equivalent of a deity capable of solving all human problems. Rand's "unknown ideal" was (what else?) capitalism. Her life work was an effort, she says, to supply capitalism the philosophical foundation she maintained it never had. Eventually, though, one had to notice that the gallant capitalist heroes of her novels, such as Howard Roark of *The Fountainhead* (1943) or John Galt and Hank Reardon in *Atlas Shrugged* (1957), simply have no real-world counterparts. Ultimately, Objectivism rests on the same false premise about human nature, and doubtless this was clear to those in power who had no problem with thousands of people being diverted in a direction even less effective than academic radicalism. Likewise, Misesians in economics, members of other free-market schools, and libertarians generally tending (with a few exceptions) to rest their views on the same Enlightenment premises, were allowed to believe that capitalists really do want competition in self-regulating markets, rather than market dominance achieved with the help of the state.

To show the short-sightedness of almost all intellectual defenses of capitalism today, all one has to do is look at the rise of the multibillion-dollar pharmaceutical industry (Big Pharma), the insurance industry (think AIG), the food industry (think Monsanto), or any of a dozen other industries where corporate behemoths grew to dominance *with the help of government regulation they embraced because it limited competition*. One need only realize, moreover, that the various corporations represented by phrases like *Big Pharma*—like their predecessor, *Big Tobacco*—grew prosperous manufacturing and distributing dubious products: either clearly unsafe (think of the Vioxx fiasco) or whose safety can reasonably be questioned since we have no means of ascertaining their *long-term* effects.

Fundamental irresponsibility in multiple endeavors (including irrational decisions by those who bought houses they couldn't afford) led to the financial debacle of 2008. Capitalism and materialism make for an unstable and potentially destructive mixture! In a materialist culture, profit will invariably take precedence over human life and well-being; rather than transactions being voluntary, the wealthy will eventually dictate terms within the economy. Rationalization will take precedence over truth. The rule of the day in the secular city: *caveat emptor!* Let the buyer beware! (For a source and additional thoughts along these lines—despite the absence of the metaphysical element emphasized here—see David C. Korten, *When Corporations Rule the World*, 1995.)

The time is ripe for a sustained criticism of materialism and of materialist culture. You are unlikely to get such criticism from any professional intellectual today who is a loyal member of his/her academic guild.

VI.

Some will retort that no one is suppressing Christian institutions or ideas. There is no "church of materialism," they will scoff. No one has a gun to anyone's head forcing them to subscribe to Darwinian evolution or the Kinseyite view of sexuality or attend "contemporary" church services. Christians in Western societies freely attend the religious services and other events of their choosing. Christian holidays continue to be celebrated (although with time one has seen more *Seasons Greetings* or *Happy Holidays* than *Merry Christmases*). Christians *can* send their children to Christian schools instead of public schools. There is an abundance of Christian seminaries. Christians have their own publishing networks and radio stations; they can distribute ideas freely. While it is true that open expressions of Christianity are forbidden in federal court houses, and teachers cannot openly teach Christianity as the one true faith in public schools, no one is prevented from praying anywhere, including in public. On the other hand, those who are openly agnostic and atheist sometimes *do* find themselves stigmatized. A person running for office who says he or she is Christian will obviously get more votes than a professed atheist. In light of all this, how seriously can it be taken that Christianity as a worldview has been largely supplanted by another worldview, unrelievedly hostile to it, capable of being labeled *materialism*?

Perhaps the best answer is already implied in the discussion above about how Christian denominations have been neutered. Those in positions to get things done—serving the superelite through its various appendages, and through alliances spread across wealthy foundations, global corporations, and prestigious universities—don't find the Christianity of our time to be a threat, in *any* of its guises, any more than they find philosophical radicalism or the conservative populism of movements like the Tea Party to be a threat. It has been sufficient for the elites to believe Christianity's claim to epistemic authority has been discredited, that both theirs and the majority of the public's practical values are elsewhere. They see Christian doctrines as all but irrelevant outside churches and seminaries, so that their role in society today is little more than providing comfort and existential security in troubled times. "Megachurches" and the "church-growth movement" can do that. The superelite, and those close to them, thus see no need to deprive the masses of their cherished beliefs. They may be quietly contemptuous of what they consider a crutch based on myths, but they see it as harmless—and not an obstruction to their goals for the world. Seminaries prepare their students for work in churches, not political activity, after all. Churches are preoccupied with increasing membership and improving appearances, so they spend money on plush new sanctuaries. The 501(c)3 tax-exempt status accorded most churches prevents their endorsing candidates for public office or other significant involvement in the political process. Many Christian pastors, finally, read passages like Romans 13: 1–3 and I Peter 2: 13–16 as instructions directly from God to be obedient to governing authorities!

Thus, because of the prevalence of "Sunday Christianity" in a culture where professed Christian and non-Christian alike spend enormous sums chasing material possessions, the superelite does not *care* if the majority of the population claims to be Christian. Besides, there are plenty of ordinary working people who want nothing to do with "religious fundamentalism" or established Christian denominations. They aren't necessarily atheists; they just can't stand the fear mongering and hypocrisy of much organized religion. They see the "rapture cult," for example, as stupid, and as an effort to lead the easily-swayed by their noses (sometimes persuading them to hand over their entire life savings!). Some of those who reject Christianity today sense that at least some highly visible Christian leaders haven't been especially honest and have been as greedy and as motivated by power as any secular elite. There is some evidence to support this. Think of the scandals that brought down the Bakkers, for instance, or Jimmy Swaggert's ministry. The reality, though, is that not one Christian leader in America is in a position to establish a theocracy on American soil or even make significant inroads toward one as part of, for example, a national "third party." Such an effort would be opposed at once, not by the elites or the government, but by significant factions in the public itself—and by many Christians. Not only is there no need to suppress Christianity openly, but any attempt to do so would raise red flags and cause many more problems than it would solve.

In sum, Christian philosophy at its best offers a metaphysics, epistemology, ethics, political philosophy, and a direction to one's life if one chooses to pursue it. Its apex was expressed in the philosophical theology of St. Thomas Aquinas. Aquinas, despite his error in believing that God's existence could be "demonstrated," believed that a perfectly rational and benevolent God had created a rational world order, and that those created in God's image had been "imprinted" with a finite version of the Divine Reason (*Logos*). God's infinite and nonspatiotemperal perception of the Creation was that of Eternal Law; our finite perception was of Natural Law, made possible by that "imprint" of Eternal Law in us. Divine Law then consisted of God's direct commands to humanity; Human

Law consisted of laws passed by governments, intended as subordinate to the first three. The point: God's *cosmos* is "governed" by providential patterns inherent in all created things, and these patterns are intelligible (perhaps up to a point) by rational beings applying correct methods of inquiry. Hence the old idea of Providence. One of the most interesting twentieth-century theologians and epistemologists of Christianity espousing this kind of doctrine and laying out its foundations was Cornelius Van Til, whose Christian presuppositionalism contends that God's existence and creative nature is an ultimate presupposition, or given, and not the result of a proof; God as *Logos* is, in fact, presupposed in the very idea of proof, in a sense analogous to Aristotle's contention (*Metaphysics, Book IV*) that one cannot provide a proof of the principle of noncontradiction because the principle is presupposed by any intelligible discourse, including that of supplying a proof of something.

What matters for us is that Western science and American culture both originally presupposed an essentially Christian worldview. This worldview was lived by ordinary people, whatever the intellectual conversation did—although what went on in this conversation eventually affected them. Neither science nor freedom arose elsewhere precisely because the god or deities of other faiths was/were not perceived as rational or as having created rational beings capable of grasping a comprehensible world. Only the West could have given rise to "government by consent of the governed." The only foundations that freedom ever really had began to be abandoned when Enlightenment philosophers embraced radical empiricism in the 1700s, when science embraced materialism in the 1800s, when intellectuals forgot how to talk about worldviews, also in the 1800s, and eventually when Western culture embraced utilitarian hedonism and legislated its Christian roots into irrelevance in the 1900s.

We are now in the 2000s and paying a very steep price! We are surrounded by technology, but the scientific view of the universe no longer commands confidence even among intellectuals, much less the public. Many of the former no longer grasp how we can speak of a world that is intelligible outside our linguistic and cultural constructs. Their schools of thought go by such names as post-structuralism, deconstructionism, neopragmatism, and so on. Members of these and other new schools argue that assertions of truth conceal efforts at domination (usually by straight white men over everyone else). They understandably see evidence of authoritarianism and domination everywhere. They fail to trace it to the *real* sources of hegemony: the superelite, the international banking cartel at its core, and the semisecret organizations—especially the Fabians—that have grown up alongside and around it, behind the more visible political and corporate elites. Thus is the fate of Western civilization, having committed the Third Cardinal Error.

One of Auguste Comte's core interests was the future of secular humanity. Among the visions that would sweep the intellectual wing of the superelite was the possibility of a "scientifically" planned society ruled over by a world government that had swept Christianity aside, including from the public mind itself. Such visions would capture the imaginations of major writers of the 1900s. Examples include H. G. Wells and Bertrand Russell. Both, at different times, were members of the British Fabian Society, which we have mentioned several times already. It is time to turn our full attention to this group, its role in the decline of the American republic, and how it came to exist in a kind of symbiotic relation of interpenetration and mutual permeation with the globalist banking cartel. It would be within the world of Fabian activity, after all, that the Western superelite would rise to full maturity and power.

4

Cardinal Error Four. Americans did not recognize the British Fabian Society for what it was and remained blind as the Fabian mind-set "penetrated and permeated" all major institutions in this country. Fabians exploited the structural weaknesses and moral culpabilities inherent in the capitalism that the banks had created, and in American institutions generally. America's "leftward" drift has been guided by the Fabians for over a century—as has capitalism itself.

• • •

I.

Surprisingly few scholars and writers working to expose super-elite and world-government movements have mentioned the British Fabian Society. Carroll Quigley, of all people, appears to dismiss them out of hand without even naming them by name. He refers only to "wild-eyed and bushy-haired theoreticians of Socialist Harvard and the London School of Economics" (*Tragedy and Hope*, p. 949). Nor does he discuss the Fabians in his post-humous *The Anglo-American Establishment* (1981), though he does mention several individual Fabians by name. Quigley, for whatever reason, left the impression that the Fabians are insignificant. This is wrong and must be corrected. Their influence on left-wing, or "progressive," politics, first in Great Britain and then in the United States, was enormous and only grew with time as the policies they originated spread and became entrenched. Major economist and economic historian Joseph Schumpeter recognized their importance (see his *Capitalism, Socialism and Democracy*, 1942); and it is significant that arch-capitalist Alan Greenspan also pays them homage at strategic points in his autobiography (*The Age of Turbulence*, 2007). Anne Fremantle provided a firsthand account of the early years of the Fabian Society and the dramatic changes it brought about in British politics (*This Little Band of Prophets: The British Fabians*, 1959). Margaret Cole, herself a Fabian, gave a lucid perspective on the patience the Fabians exercised in transforming the English-speaking world (*The Story of Fabian Socialism*, 1961). Philip Crane, who went on to serve in Congress, identified them as the major force in the capture of the Democratic Party (*The Democrats' Dilemma*,

1964). Finally, Rose L. Martin saw them as instrumental in having moved America leftward from the last turn of the century up to the 1960s (*Fabian Freeway: The High Road to Socialism in the U.S.A.*, 1968). Martin's work received the most attention; however, given that Quigley's far more visible work had failed to mention the Fabians, her discussion had no staying power, and interest in them disappeared.

We already noted how collectivist views of society had been advancing since the days of Rousseau and Saint-Simon. Ultimately, these views go back to Plato and his philosophical vision of a perfect social order, in which individual persons are not ends in themselves, but a means to the harmony and well-being of the whole. Significant elements of Enlightenment thought would integrate this vision into the materialist view of the universe. Having rejected the idea of original sin, the Enlightenment embraced a meliorism about the human condition that we could improve ourselves *morally* by our own means indefinitely. This was not a "scientific" meliorism, however. Marx dismissed Saint-Simon (for example) as a "utopian" socialist, as opposed to a "scientific" socialist such as himself. Classical Marxism viewed the bourgeoisie (capitalist owners of the means of production) and the proletariat (workers owning only their own labor) as, by historical necessity, on a collision course that could only result in violent revolution. Capitalism would be ended and replaced by socialism—the dictatorship of the proletariat. Iron laws of economic change guiding history assured this. The Marxian phrase became, significantly, the *materialist conception of history*. Once the dictatorship of the proletariat had eradicated the last vestiges of capitalism, its control would diminish and the system would evolve into communism.

Marx labored to produce a systematic and very detailed analysis and critique of capitalism (*Das Kapital*), which ran to multiple volumes and which he did not live to complete. He was largely silent about socialism *per se*, although it was a given that the proletariat would be better off. By the 1880s—near the end of his life—it was dawning on some observers, including Marx himself, that violence was no more necessary than it was desirable. Gradualism, as in biological evolution, had begun to influence socialist thought. Perhaps one could work toward the kind of society one wanted through *penetration and permeation*. For the Fabians, penetration involved infiltrating existing institutions by members of their society. Once those institutions were captured, permeation would involve furthering Fabian goals by non-Fabians. But who were the Fabians?

The mid-1800s witnessed an upsurge of interest in socialism in England. Robert Owen's ideas and communal experiments had attracted attention. In the early 1880s, an organization of young, idealistic professionals called the Fellowship of the New Life began to meet in London. In January 1884, a splinter group was officially organized as the Fabian Society. Their first meeting was in the home of Edward Pease, historian and member of the London Stock Exchange. Their credo stated explicitly, "The Fabian Society consists of socialists." But they had decided not to hurry the job: it was more important to establish socialism *properly* than establish it *quickly*. They thus took their name from Quintus Fabius Maximus, the Roman general also known as the Cunctator or Delayer, who specialized in delaying tactics. *Fabian Tract No. 1*, a four-page leaflet, stated, "For the right moment you must wait, as Fabius did most patiently when warring against Hannibal, though many censured his delays; but when the time comes you must strike hard, as Fabius did, or your waiting will be in vain, and fruitless." The Fabians' symbol was the tortoise—striding slowly forward; inoffensively; quietly, quietly; but always on the move. They never "struck hard" as such. As it turned out, they didn't have to.

The early Fabians spent their first years studying and learning. Their sources ranged from Owen to Darwinian evolution to Comtean positivism. Of Comte, Edward Pease wrote in his *History of the Fabian Society* (1918), "His philosophy accepted science, future as well as past." They thus supported separating economics from philosophy and studying society empirically. The Fabians also drew on John Stuart Mill's *Utilitarianism* (1863) and Henry George's *Progress and Poverty* (1879), in addition, obviously, to Karl Marx, who had just died in 1883. Though they were more interested in behind-the-scenes activity than in philosophy or ideology, the Fabians fit nicely into the shift from Christianity to materialism and the meliorism of Enlightenment humanism, since they believed that much human suffering was caused by capitalist institutions and could be alleviated only by transforming the economic system.

The most famous early Fabians were Sydney and Beatrice Webb and playwright George Bernard Shaw. Other members included classical scholar Graham Wallas, psychologist and sexual-liberationist Havelock Ellis, theosophist Annie Besant, artist Walter Crane, the above-mentioned Edward Pease, author Israel Zangwill, and Marx's daughter Eleanor.

The Fabians met and strategized—and expanded. They were excellent networkers. Their influence grew during the late 1880s and early 1890s, especially after the publication of *Fabian Essays* (1890). This collection promoted socialism in language anyone could read—as opposed to Marx's turgid prose. Yet they did not seek ideological purity. *Fabian Tract No. 70* advised,

"The Fabian Society, far from holding aloof from other bodies, urges its members to lose no opportunity of joining them and permeating them with Fabian ideas as far as possible. Almost all organizations and movements contain elements making for Socialism....The Fabians are, therefore, encouraged to join all other organizations, Socialist or non-Socialist, on which Fabian work can be done." *Fabian Tract No. 41* advised members "to join the Liberal and Radical Associations of their district, or, if they preferred it, the Conservative Associations...."

Penetration and permeation *worked*! The Fabian Society grew and its influence spread! Joseph Schumpeter wrote of the Fabians:

> They set out to persuade whoever would listen. They lectured to working-class and bourgeois crowds. They pamphleteered ably and extensively. They recommended or fought particular policies, plans and bills. The most important of all their avenues to influence, however, was their contact with individual "keymen," or rather with individuals in the entourage of political, industrial and labor leaders. Their country and their own social and political location in their country offered a unique opportunity for establishing and exploiting such contacts....
>
> A few were able to avail themselves of connections formed in Oxford and Cambridge students' unions and common rooms. They were not living, morally speaking, on another planet. Most of them were not straight enemies of the established order. All of them stressed willingness to cooperate much more than hostility. They were not out to found a party and greatly disliked the phraseology of class war and revolution. Whenever

possible they preferred making themselves useful to making themselves a nuisance. And they had something to offer to the parliamentarian or administrator who often welcomed suggestions as to what should be done and how to do it....

The civil service accepted this. And not only that: being to a considerable extent in sympathy with at least the immediate aims of the Fabians, it allowed itself to be educated by them. The Fabians in turn also accepted this role of unofficial public servants. In fact, it suited them perfectly. They were not personally ambitious. They liked to serve behind the scene. Action through the bureaucracy whose growth in numbers and in power they foresaw and approved fitted in very well with the general scheme of their democratic state socialism. (*Capitalism, Socialism and Democracy*, pp. 322–23)

The Fabians were successful because the time for them was right:

Socialist endeavor of the Fabian type would not have amounted to anything at any other time. But it did amount to much during the three decades preceding 1914, because things and souls were ready for that kind of message and neither for a less nor for a more radical one. Formulation and organization of existing opinion were all that was needed in order to turn possibilities into articulate policy, and this "organization formulation" the Fabians provided in a most workmanlike manner. They were reformers. The spirit of the times made socialists of them. They were genuine socialists because they aimed at helping in a fundamental reconstruction of society which in the end was to make economic care a public affair. They were voluntarist socialists and therefore

> they would at any earlier stage have come within the
> Marxian concept of utopists. (pp. 323–24)

The Fabians, Schumpeter concluded, were more effective at bringing about socialism than Marx or his followers had ever been:

> better Marxists than Marx was himself. To concentrate
> on the problems that are within practical politics, to
> move in step with the evolution of things social, and to
> let the ultimate goal take care of itself is really more in
> accord with Marx's fundamental doctrine than the revo-
> lutionary ideology he himself grafted upon it. (p. 324)

That is, they worked piecemeal, focusing on the problems before them, rather than with a comprehensive Platonistic vision; though not scientists as such, they were Comtean "stage three" operators. They successfully negotiated potentially treacherous waters by moving their agenda forward while avoiding the kind of attention that leads to confrontation. They sought to be *helpers*, not *troublemakers*; quiet doers, not vocal prima donnas. Since as the saying goes, one can attract more flies with honey than with vinegar, the kindly Fabians succeeded where angry Marxists failed.

II.

Close inspection of not-usually-cited but nevertheless crucial documents makes it clear that the Fabians hijacked Cecil Rhodes's plans—known from passages in his multiple wills—for a secret society that would expand British control around the world. In his "Confession of Faith" (1877), Rhodes asked:

> Why should we not form a secret society with but one object the furtherance of the British Empire and the bringing of the whole uncivilized world under British rule for the recovery of the United States for making the Anglo-Saxon race but one Empire.

Rhodes went on to advocate seeking out the "best and the brightest":

> Take...the younger son with high thoughts, high aspirations, endowed by nature with all the faculties to make a great man, and with the sole wish in life to serve his Country but he lacks two things, the means and the opportunity; ever troubled by a sort of inward deity urging him on to high and noble deeds, he is compelled to pass his time in some occupation which furnishes him with mere existence, he lives unhappily and dies miserably. Such men as these the Society should search out and use for the furtherance of their object. (*The Last Will and Testament of Cecil John Rhodes*, 1902)

Rhodes was no socialist, of course, but as we just saw, this need not bother a Fabian. Like many ambitious capitalists with a taste for empire building, Rhodes had ideas the Fabians found useful. And he had money! Assisted in his start by Lord "Natty"

Rothschild, he made a fortune mining diamonds in South Africa. The money from the Rhodes fortune established the Rhodes Scholarship program at Oxford University in accordance with his will. The Fabians were instrumental, however, in arranging Rhodes's main contacts. According to William H. McIlhany's *The Tax-Exempt Foundations* (1980), William T. Stead—who compiled the materials that went into the volume cited above—was a Fabian. In 1891, he had introduced Rhodes to future Round Tablers Alfred Milner, Arthur Balfour, and others. In other words, behind the "Anglophile network" Carroll Quigley credits in *Tragedy and Hope* (p. 950) were the Fabians!

In 1895, a large grant from the estate of Henry Hunt Hutchison, also a Fabian, enabled Sidney and Beatrice Webb to found the London School of Economics (LSE), which would become a part of the prestigious University of London system in 1900, while building its identity as the world's leading social-science research institution. Also in 1900, Fabians were instrumental in helping organize the British Labour Party, with George Bernard Shaw writing its constitution. By this time, the Fabian Society claimed 861 members. In 1913, one group of members began publishing *The New Statesman*, not officially a Fabian publication, but featuring writings of leading Fabians in each issue. The Fabian turtle moved steadily forward and never looked back! The Fabian Society, though not a political party and with no ambitions of becoming one, was on its way to controlling British politics. The Crown and residing money powers looked on with approval. It was clear: the Fabians knew what they were doing.

Fabian thought also appeared on American shores. Authors from Henry George to Edward Bellamy (author of *Looking Backward: 2000–1887*, 1888) had paved the way. An American edition of *Fabian Essays* appeared in 1891. Later that decade, a publication titled *The American Fabian* put out several issues. Shortly after the turn of the century, major writers such as Upton Sinclair and Jack London were attracted to socialism, as was famed defense attorney Clarence Darrow. They and a few others organized the Intercollegiate Socialist Society (ISS), which formed study groups in several prestigious American universities, including Harvard and Princeton. Thus came the first incursion of leftists into American academia. It is probable that Franklin Delano Roosevelt was exposed to their ideas while an undergraduate at Harvard. Though welcomed in academia and with growing support within organized labor, the Fabians clearly knew that few Americans would warm to socialism under that name. The Webbs began using the term *industrial democracy*. Eventually, the ISS changed its name to the League for Industrial Democracy.

The Fabians surrounded Dr. Woodrow Wilson, then president of Princeton, as a kindred spirit with a collectivist view of society. In "Colonel" House, whom we met briefly in chapter 1, they found a permanent link to the banking elite and to their attempt to establish the Federal Reserve. After the engineered Panic of 1907, the bankers were ready to move. The Fabians saw only advantages to the coming centralization. The alliance between them, with House the lynchpin figure, grew into the twentieth-century superelite! House anonymously authored *Philip Dru: Administrator* (1910), which promoted a central bank, a graduated income tax, control over both political parties, and "socialism as dreamt of by Karl Marx." He became Wilson's right-hand man as the bankers engineered his ascension to the presidency.

In chapter 1 we discussed how the year 1913 was pivotal in the ruination of the American republic. Control over monetary policy was again placed in the hands of a state-sponsored central bank controlled by the superelite, including, obviously, N. M. Rothschild and Sons. That year also saw the first incarnation of the Internal Revenue Service and the creation of the Anti-Defamation League. The IRS created the first direct, unapportioned tax on workers' incomes. Such a tax had been ruled unconstitutional by the Supreme Court (*Pollock v. Farmers Loan & Trust Co.*, 1895). The response was to change the Constitution by adding the Sixteenth Amendment. Today, shadows hang over that effort. Was the Sixteenth Amendment really ratified in the way the Constitution requires? Independent researcher William J. Benson contends it wasn't (see his *The Law That Never Was*, 1985). Arguments of this sort are routinely rejected by the courts as "frivolous," and it is hazardous not to file tax returns; some who have refused very visibly, such as Irwin A. Schiff (author of *The Biggest Con: How the Government Is Fleecing You*, 1977, and *The Federal Mafia: How the Government Illegally Imposes and Unlawfully Collects Income Taxes*, 1990), have ended up in prison. The Anti-Defamation League later branded criticism of the Federal Reserve and other manifestations of superelite influence as "anti-Semitic." Their attacks all but destroyed the reputation of Eustace Mullins following his publishing *Secrets of the Federal Reserve* (1952).

It is also worth noting that 1913 was the year Columbia University's Charles A. Beard published *An Economic Interpretation of the Constitution*, advancing the thesis that the Founding Fathers' primary motive in writing the Constitution was to protect their interests as wealthy landowners. Beard was also a Fabian.

During the winter of 1917–18, "Colonel" House, a master organizer with a huge network, assembled a small, trusted group of scholars and diplomats into what he called the Inquiry.

It is revealing that he would use this term, in light of what we learned about "commissions of inquiry" when investigating the Jay Treaty; the Fabians were still operating from Great Britain, after all. After a meeting at the Hotel Majestic on May 30, 1919, House's Inquiry became the parent of the Royal Institute of International Affairs in the City of London and the Council on Foreign Relations in New York. The CFR was formally organized on July 29, 1921; by November 1922, it had nearly three hundred "carefully chosen" members and had begun publishing a journal, *Foreign Affairs*. These organizations began laying the foundations for the rise of a globalist mind-set. Globalists had suffered a setback when the U.S. Senate torpedoed U.S. participation in the League of Nations, dooming to irrelevance one of their first major efforts, even though it survived in Europe for a time. The United States would, of course, join its stepchild, the United Nations, organized in 1945 after the bloodiest war in world history.

How far did Fabian penetration and permeation reach into international banking? It is probably fair to say that the relationship evolved into one of *inter*penetration and *mutual* permeation. Their goals were the same: control. New international institutions resulted. The first appeared in 1930. The Bank for International Settlements (BIS) was established in Basel, Switzerland, through the Hague Agreements, ostensibly set up to oversee Germany's remaining obligations from the first world war. Its two founders were Hjalmar Schacht, a Rhodes Round Tabler who later became Hitler's *Reich* minister of economics; and Montagu Norman, governor of the Bank of England and a Fabian. The BIS was thus Fabian-permeated from the start and became the central bankers' central bank, a power center that answered neither to any national government nor to any market, only to superelite bankers. The Federal Reserve became one of its leading members. About the BIS, Carroll Quigley writes:

> The powers of financial capitalism had another far reaching aim, nothing less than to create a world system of financial control in private hands able to dominate the political system of each country and the economy of the world as a whole. This system was to be controlled in a feudalist fashion by the central banks of the world acting in concert, by secret agreements, arrived at in frequent private meetings and conferences. The apex of the system was the Bank for International Settlements in Basle [sic.], Switzerland, a private bank owned and controlled by the world's central banks which were themselves private corporations. The growth of financial capitalism made possible a centralization of world economic control and use of this power for the direct benefit of financiers and the indirect injury of all other economic groups. (*Tragedy and Hope*, p. 324)

Member central banks of the BIS also included all those of Western European nations, as well as those of rising Eastern powers such as Japan.

David Rockefeller Sr., fifth grandson of John D. Rockefeller Sr., and who became arguably one of the most powerful and well-connected of today's superelitists, went to the City of London in the 1930s and studied at the LSE. He graduated, having written a senior thesis titled "Destitution through Fabian Eyes," recounted in his *Memoirs* (2002, p. 75–76). Rockefeller's vision of a globalized world led him to the helm of the Council on Foreign Relations in 1949 and to assist in founding the European Bilderberg Group in 1954. He has regularly attended the Bilderberg Group's top-secret annual meetings, which for several days transform plush hotels into armed enclaves with carefully selected staff members sworn to secrecy, though there is evidence of a mole in the organization (see Daniel Estulin, *The True Story of the Bilderberg Group*, 2007). Operating from the helm of the huge Chase-Manhattan Bank, Rockefeller was also instrumental in founding the Council of the Americas in 1965.

By the mid-1940s, more visible organizations had become components of the growing "global governance" landscape. The crucial meeting was held in Bretton Woods, New Hampshire, in July 1944. During that meeting, a new monetary system was devised that pegged all major currencies to the dollar as the world's reserve currency and pegged the dollar to gold, fixing the relationship at $35 per ounce of gold. Out of that meeting came two key organizations: the International Monetary Fund and the World Bank, both formally organized in 1945. The United Nations was also founded in 1945. The phrase *United Nations* had been coined by Franklin Delano Roosevelt, who gave the idea of a world body his enthusiastic support. The land on which its headquarters was built was donated by the Rockefellers, who also lent the organization their full support. The UN General Assembly convened for the first time in 1946.

One of the most important steps taken over the ensuing three years was the creation and implementation of a General Agreement on Tariffs and Trade (GATT), negotiated during the UN Conference on Trade and Employment and taking effect in 1949. It would remain in effect until 1995, when the World Trade Organization replaced it. A special brand of British-American capitalism was being developed. It was not the *laissez-faire* capitalism of Ayn Rand and her disciples, or of libertarian philosophers; it was a capitalism that could be steered in the direction globalists wanted it to go.

III.

At this point we must digress, hopefully for a good reason. Didn't I say the Fabians were socialists, not capitalists of *any* sort? This elicits a crucial question: were the two systems really alternatives, as nearly everyone has always assumed, or were they parts of a single historical process?

According to a strict reading of Marx, capitalism and socialism are parts of a single process. Capitalism would self-destruct because of the rising antagonism between the bourgeois and proletariat classes and be replaced by socialism as a matter of historical necessity. The Marxian complaint, echoed by the early Fabians, was that capitalism could produce wealth but not distribute it fairly, that is, equitably. The wealth retained by the bourgeois class exceeded what went into producing it: profit equals surplus value. In that case, capitalism left to its own devices would yield worsening extremes of wealth and poverty. It would generate a class antagonism that would grow until it exploded. The impoverished proletariat would attack the bourgeoisie and destroy their economic dominance. Socialism, led by the dictatorship of the proletariat, would replace capitalism and then dissolve all material bases for class antagonism. When that occurred, socialism would evolve into communism.

In other words, even during the so-called Cold War, *communism didn't really exist!* Bolshevism wasn't really communism, despite the term! Communism hadn't happened yet!

By the mid-twentieth century, circumstances had changed considerably, and Marx's views were proving inadequate. Capitalism *as practiced* did not seem about to self-destruct. Marx never foresaw the system's resilience and adaptability. He had no concept of entrepreneurship. He did not foresee that capitalism would raise the living standards of all who participated in it, bourgeois or proletariat. His model being the factory system as it had existed in nineteenth-century Europe, he did not imagine the economic diversity that would characterize twentieth-century capitalism. Where practiced, however far it diverged from the philosophers' *laissez-faire* image, it made everyone better off— and continued to do so, despite the attacks and sabotage coming from various quarters.

Capitalism *as practiced* gave rise to the largest middle class in history. Science, technology (transportation, communications, etc.), and medicine all made tremendous advances. As these advances spread through society, they put refrigerators in kitchens and automobiles in garages. They put radios in bedrooms, televisions in family rooms (and then added color), and microwave ovens in kitchens. In the 1980s computers began appearing. They moved from large businesses to smaller offices and then to homes as miniaturization set in. Advances in medical science had already lengthened the human life span. Not just the rich, but those in the middle class who had saved, could enjoy a retirement—something few of their parents could have done. The proletariat could see this. Thus, contrary to Marxian prophesy, they did not want to *overthrow* the bourgeoisie, they wanted to *join* the bourgeoisie! For a time, many members of the working class did just that—or their children did. The more adventurous became the next generation's entrepreneurs.

In most respects, capitalism is the most natural system in the world for human beings who are free to take the actions that will improve their lives. Capitalism is manifested when ownership of the means of production is private, *even if conditional on licensing and taxation*, and owners can accrue capital: man-made, reproducible wealth. Systems of production and distribution develop, divisions of labor appear, wages are established, and so forth, all in that economic space known as the marketplace. Capitalism is not a system of anarchy; property rights and free transactions are protected by—and, if need be, constrained by—a legal system. A minority of individuals owns the engines of production, of course; the majority of those who work in the private sector do not. This was the system we spoke of earlier that began to develop in the 1800s, and even more so in the 1900s.

One more ingredient factored into the development of the capitalism that matured on U.S. soil: fractional-reserve lending. While small endeavors could rely on their own resources to get started, the larger concerns needed capital up front. They went for it to the banks, which would loan in accordance with the system we sketched in chapter 1. Thus the temptation to devalue the currency was built into British-American capitalism from the start. Problems arise especially if banks that make bad loans are not allowed to fail. This can happen only when government protects them, which happened with central banks as they developed. It is difficult to know what would have developed had central banking and fractional-reserve lending been repudiated. Loans would have allowed the gradual rise of large concerns, but the process would have occurred more slowly and been constrained far more by what common people wanted and were willing to pay for. Most enterprises would have remained small. Perhaps no one would have developed the means to destroy competitors. There may well have been no vast fortunes accrued, such as that of the Rockefellers.

Sadly, though, this latter scenario is not what took root in the West. British-American capitalism, which embraced both fractional lending and central banking, was already being steered in a direction that would benefit the bankers and those close to them—in ever-larger corporations. The result was a system already fundamentally collectivist and statist, answering to the privileged more and more and to the common people less and less. It was therefore vulnerable to further steering from the inside without the need for revolutionary ferment.

The Fabians thus modified their playbook. They surmised that they could best have socialism by engineering a specific form of capitalism—a form of capitalism corporatized and collectivized, increasingly government friendly, capable not just of giving the common people what they wanted, but subtly encouraging various forms of dependency, and with a rising commitment to globalism in scope (or as close to that as was achievable). "Fabianized" capitalism *would* evolve smoothly into socialism!

The progressive era instigated by the Fabians began to expand the size and reach of the federal government, supposedly to prevent monopolies and cartels by regulating industry. It should be clear by now that a consolidation of power was occurring behind the scenes in the United States, its primary institution being the Federal Reserve created in the Coup of 1913, as we called it above. In the 1920s, the Federal Reserve caused the artificial boom that empowered the "Roaring '20s," and the meltdown of that period occurred in October 1929. In the 1930s, with the country in the grip of the Great Depression caused by the Fed's sudden credit contraction (see Murray N. Rothbard, *America's Great Depression*, 1963), government expanded further when Franklin Delano Roosevelt established the Social Security system.

Perhaps the most important intellectual development during this period was John Maynard Keynes's *General Theory of Employment, Interest and Money* (1936). Keynes argued that government intervention into the economy was necessary, especially during economic downturns, to supply stimulus money and create jobs in case the economy stabilized with a high rate of unemployment. Keynes—a Fabian who had lectured at the LSE in 1911—has been the dominant voice among professional economists ever since. Many of his recommendations seemed to work. We climbed out of the Great Depression (courtesy also of World War II). The economy recovered—although the term *welfare capitalism* better describes what settled into place during the post-war era. By this time, *laissez-faire* was, as far as professional economists were concerned, a museum piece.

Americans as a whole accepted this system. By the late 1950s, it seemed better than *everything* that had gone before. It allowed business expansion and entrepreneurship—and with *safety nets*. Expanded government, moreover, was able to undertake immense projects of its own, such as the interstate highway system, which served to connect different regions of the country as never before. Additional road and highway building, coupled with advances in automotive technology, created suburbia and, with it, more jobs. The GI bill, the federal government's then-largest direct involvement in education, made it possible for those returning from World War II and Korea to enter college. Higher education expanded—increasing (and tenuring) a kind of academic class perfectly suited for the already-created academic guild system we encountered in a previous chapter. Both business and government, however, wanted newly degreed college graduates. The tacit conviction that everyone should go to college made higher education a goal for more and more young people.

Overall, the growing system gave rise to an enlarging and mostly satisfied middle class whose members worked in business institutions of all sizes and at all levels (small and big business; upper management, middle management, etc.), as well as in government. Throughout the burgeoning suburbs, all manner of small businesses proliferated to service the desires of those who had money to spend.

Neither wealthy nor poor, but somewhere in between, many in the middle class soon had enough leisure that if they chose to do so, they could think issues through for themselves. A few who had attained higher education's loftiest achievements were growing uneasy. They had stumbled on the incentive system that encircled everyone and encouraged a mass-consumption culture. They questioned the ambience of conformity that, rightly or not, is thought to have characterized the period beginning shortly after 1946 and ending around 1964. They began to analyze it, question it, and write down their thoughts.

Sociologist C. Wright Mills became the first to write openly of *The Power Elite* (1956). William Whyte pondered the mind-set of *The Organization Man* (1957); Vance Packard worked to expose *The Hidden Persuaders* (1957) and *The Status Seekers* (1960); Alan Harrington questioned the authenticity of *Life in the Crystal Palace* (1960). Sometimes the restless wrote fiction instead of nonfiction analyses. In influential novels such as *On the Road* (1957, though written a number of years earlier), Jack Kerouac portrayed characters whose lives of unstructured rebellion in nihilism contrasted sharply with middle-class life. Such works defined the lifestyle and outlook of the so-called Beat Generation, that group of cultural rebels who presaged the Hippies of the following decade. Did the welfare-capitalism of this period—for all its apparent strengths and creature comforts—conceal a visceral nihilism behind the spreading array of consumer products and creature comforts? Consider also that the most influential novel by an American to come out of this decade actually preceded all of the above: J. D. Salinger's *The Catcher in the Rye* (1951), a then-shocking excursion into teenage alienation and angst whose main character is a product of an upright, upper-middle-class home.

Did any of this material encourage the adult middle class, in aggregate, to question capitalism? Of course not. The capitalism of the day had done well by them and they were satisfied. Unease was therefore limited to a handful of intellectuals and to fringes of the population such as the Beats. Much of that era's middle class had been born in the 1920s and grown up during the Great Depression, or born during the Depression and grown up during the war years. Many of their number were familiar with poverty and knew what work was, since they had had to work in their early years. They had developed an ethic that work—not a sense of entitlement—was the key to escaping poverty and achieving success. The "greatest generation," having experienced the hardships of the 1930s, fought and won World War II. Some of them saw people they were close to die suddenly and horribly. They had a sense of the precariousness of life, which could be mitigated (though not eradicated) by diligent work and the building up of financial security. They did not buy the idea that anyone was owed a living; nor did they believe society could function without properly enforced rules. Thus their response to authors like those above was impatience or indifference.

Yet the seeds of intergenerational collectivism had been sown in the 1930s with that first entitlement: Social Security. This program set the stage for attaching nonsalary compensations called *benefits* to employment. In 1943, a new law enabled the federal government to begin withholding taxes from wages.

The amount of taxes collected nearly doubled, which paid for the expansions and interventions of the federal government mentioned above. The "greatest generation" did not object. They saw the GI Bill as beneficial, since without it, many of them could not have attended college. Most people took no issue with government intervention, especially if it directly benefited them. Magnificent new federal programs kept coming, moreover! We experienced our first "Sputnik moment" in 1957 when the Soviets launched the craft bearing that name. The Russians were getting ahead of us! The space program begun in response culminated in the Apollo moon landings in the late 1960s. The advantages of these technological successes surely outweighed their disadvantages. Later, also in the 1960s, when Medicare and Medicaid arrived, the "greatest generation" again approved. Some of them now had to care for their elderly parents, living longer due to advances in medical science and technology. They also knew *they* were not getting any younger, and their turn would come. Automatic extraction of income and Social Security taxes from their paychecks—with a "refund" of the former the following spring!—seemed a small price to pay for what were now regarded as essential government services, even if these services (in true Fabian fashion) were expanding government's reach a little at a time.

In sum, "adjusted" Americans (cf. Snell and Gail Putney, *The Adjusted American*, 1964, 1972) accepted the system surrounding them, whatever its compromises. They had all the evidence they needed that hard work, persistence, and an eye-to-business frame of mind paid off. Unfortunately, they did not pay attention to matters that needed their attention.

There is one thing readers should keep in mind when reading what is to come: whatever its successes and however easily most of the middle class can be guided, *the superelite did not trust the idea of a financially independent middle class.* Controls over it may have existed, but they were too tenuous and uncertain. Moreover, *to the extent capitalism is left unhampered or unmanaged, it gives rise to such a population; therefore, capitalism can be built up to achieve globalism but must be discarded once it has served its purposes.* Keeping these firmly in mind explains a great deal of the disaster that came later.

IV.

With the children of the "greatest generation," the situation was different. A substantial fraction of the baby-boom generation, which began to be born in 1946, grew up without having to face the struggles that had shaped their parents' outlook. From their earliest days, their basic needs were met. They could take their parents' achievements for granted! The suburbs were safe and protected. Most did not have to begin work in their childhood or even in their teens. They therefore had hours of leisure time, and courtesy of "allowances" given by their parents, they had disposable income they had done nothing to earn. They were soon more inclined to spend than save, and so began the national spending spree to come. Let us note four more aspects of the developing culture that would shape the mind-set of the largest cohort in history, the generation born during the period 1946–1964 and best known as the baby boomers.

(1) Baby boomers' role in society as children was ambiguous from the start. On family farms, there had been work for everyone, including children; but in the capitalist world, which called for years of education and specialization, children were potentially just underfoot. Child-labor laws forbade employers from hiring children to begin training them early. So what was to be done with them? They were warehoused in public schools for twelve years. Thus baby boomers became victims of the Second Cardinal Error, for Progressive Education was coming into its own. Teaching was more about socialization than transmission of knowledge. Instruction in right versus wrong came down to the subjectivism of Values Clarification and similar fashions. The

"values" that mattered were those of the group. Independent-minded children had their thinking subordinated to and overwhelmed by group activities; nonconformists were ostracized and often bullied, which sometimes made their nonconformity more radical.

There was also little or no instruction in personal finance or other matters of economics at all, nor about property rights, which had long ago become conditional upon payment of one's property taxes to one's county government. If baby boomers did not learn from their parents where wealth came from, that it had to be produced and distributed through specific courses of coordinated human actions, they would usually not learn it at all—and their parents turned out to be generally poor communicators of what they were doing (see my essay "The Dangers of Growing Up Comfortable," *The Freeman*, 2000). As a result, many baby boomers did not learn economics. Rather, as they grew up comfortably they developed a sense of entitlement that followed them into adulthood and left them even more vulnerable to Fabian permeation than their parents had been. Their sense of entitlement was only reinforced as they learned about Social Security and Medicare through aging grandparents—and eventually, aging parents. These programs, in fact, were becoming the federal government's largest expenditures—and politically untouchable.

(2) The Kinseyite revolution in sexuality began to take hold in the 1950s with the Beats. Almost unnoticed at first, it exploded into popular culture and became a dominant influence by the late 1960s, courtesy of Hugh Hefner's *Playboy* empire. The birth-control pill (which is more than fifty years old as this manuscript nears completion) made it possible for men and women—and teenage boys and girls—to have sex without significant risk of

pregnancy. In 1973, *Roe v. Wade* legalized abortion as the "solution" to unwanted pregnancies. A scourge began that would kill more than 50 million unborn babies by the time of this writing. Condoms were introduced to further prevent pregnancies and sexually transmitted diseases, and reduce the perceived "need" for abortions. A great deal of generally well-intended effort went into persuading teenagers and young adults to use condoms, sometimes admonishing them that out-of-wedlock sex was a bad idea: a mixed message ("we'd prefer you didn't, but here's how to do it safely"). Ethical subjectivism, after all, allowed no foothold, or even a toehold, for a convincing argument about why kids *shouldn't* have sex if they can do so safely and avoid unwanted pregnancies (ethical subjectivism averred that "everybody has their own morality," after all—complete with the grammar mistake).

The revolution in sexuality entered the rock-music mainstream with Elvis Presley, and its influence only spread with that medium. As did drug use and abuse. Recreational drugs had been around for decades, of course, but the 1960s saw them spread into the mainstream. Drug use became acceptable to middle-class youth, most of whom lost respect for prohibition laws that didn't work and for moral admonishments that struck them as silly. With their sense of entitlement and large amounts of leisure time leading to just plain *boredom*, all without any guiding worldview or moral compass, teenage boomers saw no reason *not* to experiment.

Naturally, their loud music and recreational drug use brought them into conflict with their elders. From a superelite standpoint, this was good. It destabilized the nuclear family, just as guided capitalist development had destabilized the extended family before it; and, along with the rising divorce rate (also a product of a cultural ethos that placed exclusively utilitarian value on marriage), it left an increasing number of children dependent on the good graces of the state. All this preceded the homosexual movement's rise to visibility in the 1990s and its acceptance within the American cultural mainstream during the 2000s.

(3) In the late 1960s, with the leading edge of the baby boomers swelling university admissions, a doctrine sometimes called *cultural Marxism* began working its way into higher education. It appeared in an environment already sympathetic to hard-leftism because of earlier Fabian permeation. Cultural Marxism had developed in the 1920s in Europe independently of the Fabian movement, but its architects employed the same techniques and doubtless saw the Fabians as comrades in arms. It began with Antonio Gramsci and George Lukacs, who also observed that economic Marxism had failed because the proletariat wanted to join instead of overthrow the bourgeoisie. In accordance with their own power motivations, they concluded that what was needed was a "long march through the institutions" to "capture the culture" (Gramsci's phrases), eradicating Christianity, as well as every vestige of economic individualism and free enterprise.

In the 1930s, Gramsci and Lukacs founded the Frankfurt School, which soon included luminaries such as Max Horkeimer and Theodor Adorno, whose star students were Erich Fromm and Herbert Marcuse. Several members of the Frankfurt School including Marcuse came to the United States having fled the Nazis. They found a welcome environment at the Fabian-created New School for Social Research in New York City and established the Graduate Faculty of Political and Social Science. Marcuse became the most visible leftist social philosopher in America.

He wrote works with names like *Eros and Civilization* (1955), which combined notions taken from Marx and Freud (and, by default, the Kinseyite mind-set) and argued for the elimination of Christianity and capitalism. The following decade, Marcuse's *One-Dimensional Man* (1964) became a key text of the New Left, the intellectual wing of the Hippie movement. Marcuse also authored the landmark essay "Repressive Tolerance" (1965), which provided the foundation for differential treatment based on race, as well as a rejection of free speech in discussing the subject: the root of political correctness.

The baby-boomer protégés of the Frankfurt School hard-leftists stayed in universities (their "educations" having left them unqualified to do anything else). They either won tenure as faculty members or stepped into administrative roles. Either way, they began reshaping their institutions. Faculties at major universities moved leftward as they embraced affirmative-action programs and, for example, the radical "gender feminist" movement. Political correctness ("PC") developed in major universities and law schools in the late 1980s, a major impetus being the perceived need to protect such programs and movements from the criticism they were increasingly receiving (see Nicholas Capaldi, *Out of Order: Affirmative Action and the Crisis of Doctrinaire Liberalism*, 1985; Frederick R. Lynch, *Invisible Victims: White Males and the Crisis of Affirmative Action*, 1989; Thomas Sowell, *Preferential Policies: An International Perspective*, 1990; Steven Yates, *Civil Wrongs: What Went Wrong With Affirmative Action*, 1994; for "gender feminism" see Christina Hoff Sommers, *Who Stole Feminism? How Women Have Betrayed Women*, 1994).

"PC" soon spread outward from campuses, as some of us predicted it would. By 2000, it dominated corporate media, the military (which had embraced "women in combat"), and even professional sports. (Think of the relentless media perse-cution of Atlanta Braves reliever John Rocker the year follow-ing his frank assessment of New York subway riders, until he couldn't perform on the mound and his career was destroyed.) Corporations embraced political correctness. In Columbia, South Carolina, in 2000, a thriving multimillion-dollar barbe-cue business whose owner, Maurice Bessinger, had flown the Confederate Battle Flag over his stores was largely wiped out in a few weeks as the result of a single unsubstantiated allega-tion by one city reporter, based on religious tracts found on a table in his main store, that Bessinger believed in slavery. Such was the world "PC" had created, in which baseless allegations are taken uncritically as fact, and the accused are guilty until proven innocent. Food distributors, intimidated by the bad publicity, refused to carry Bessinger's products. (Bessinger tells his story in *Defending My Heritage*, 2001.) As a result of these irresponsible attacks, Bessinger had to shut down his facilities. The majority of those who lost their jobs were African Americans.

Along with far more visible examples, such as Senate Minority Leader Trent Lott's remarks in 2002 that were inter-preted as racist, by the middle of that decade, most Americans were censoring themselves. It was clear that open opposition to what the PC crowd wanted could end careers even among the powerful, sometimes at the hands not of hard-leftists, but of their own. (Trent Lott's fall into oblivion was orchestrated, after all, not by "liberal" Democrats but "conservative" Republicans!) There have been many attempts to thwart political correctness and expose its roots. The list of books and articles is too long to name them individually. None have proven successful. They are up against, among other things, a culture that has indeed been "captured": a capture completed with the mainstreaming of homosexuality and growing calls for the legalization of marriage (as opposed to "civil unions") between homosexuals.

(4) A larger moral universe, having little to do with the politics of the left as such, settled into place as "Generation X" (born between 1964 and 1984) came of age, rendering it more pliable than the baby-boomers' worldview. It combined the essences of (1), (2), and (3), largely unnoticed by baffled elders who were unable to examine or question the materialism of their "secular city." The older generations were vulnerable because their eye-to-business mind-set, which also enveloped those baby boomers who became Yuppies (Young and Upwardly Mobile), doesn't view such issues as important. Many of the latter described themselves as "economically conservative" but "socially liberal." If others were Christians, their "Sunday Christianity" was as helpless against the highly sophisticated, well-orchestrated attacks of the Frankfurt School's intellectual descendents as their brand of capitalism would be—as we will soon see. Materialism, as noted earlier, promotes a hedonistic lifestyle in which the good life is a life of personal gratification, comfort, and noninvolvement: "whatever floats your boat" became a catchphrase for youth in the 1990s and 2000s. In this case, of course, "values" were not all "subjective." Those regarding the fundamental goodness of personal pleasure, spending, and the moral equivalence of all lifestyles certainly stand out as central to the "ethic" of our present reality.

There is now, however, every reason to believe that such an "ethic" will slowly destroy the moral compass of an individual, a generation, or an economic system—especially a capitalist one. Hedonism of the moment is ultimately at odds with the needs of capitalist civilization over the long run. These needs include self-discipline, a capacity to plan amid changing conditions, long-term thinking, and finally—an element usually not paid attention to by economists—a sense of the difference between practices and products that improve, or at least maintain, civilization, and those that undermine it by enabling its members to destroy themselves a little at a time. Capitalism, as Ludwig von Mises observed acutely, does not service one's own personal whims or self-indulgences (see his *The Anti-Capitalistic Mentality*, 1956). But it will service the whims and self-indulgences of consumers *en masse*. Capitalism provides the majority of consumers with what they want. What consumers want, however, is not chosen *ex nihilo*, in a cultural or philosophical vacuum.

As the twentieth century came to a close, what America's consumers wanted was whatever would maximize their entertainment and, if possible, bring immediate pleasure: the instant-gratification culture. Kinseyite hedonism had become a driving force in the marketplace, as the multibillion-dollar-a-year online pornography business abundantly shows. Capitalism, in whatever guise, rewards those who satisfy the immediate desires of the consuming masses, and withholds support from the insufficiently enterprising—or those with different values. The capitalist engine passes no judgment on whether what the buying public wants is *good*—ethically or even in the sense of bringing long-term benefits, as opposed to harm; think of cigarettes, junk food, and drugs (legal as well as illegal), in addition to pornography.

Capitalism thus can lead to the enriching of those supplying not just pointless, but dangerous and *evil,* products (see David Kupelian, *The Marketing of Evil*, 2005). In other words, contrary to Mises and, in general, the Austrian school's "subjective theory of value," not all values—not even economic ones—exist exclusively in the minds of consumers. Reality dictates that some consumers' values are objectively superior to others. Some are life-enhancing and civilization-enhancing; others are destructive. In a universe governed by cause and effect, where actions have consequences, matters could not be otherwise. Austrian school economists correctly distinguish between what is seen and what is not seen. What was not seen by many economists is that in the absence of a moral compass, capitalism will begin to destroy itself quite independently of what any cultural Marxist is doing!

V.

Ultimately, therefore, however natural capitalism might be, it can be made to act as its own destroyer. How is this possible? It begins with marketing, which had long been of interest to the superelite. The Rockefeller Foundation had bankrolled Tavistock and similar institutes that investigated how to control human behavior. What they learned could be applied to buying patterns. What did the masses want? What would causally affect their wants and desires? Those in corporations had learned that there was no need for open coercion or confrontation when propaganda, infiltration, subterfuge, and the subtle conditioning of malleable populations would do the job. Independent developments served their purposes.

Edward Louis Bernays—nephew of Sigmund Freud—had appeared on the scene as the boy genius who founded advertising and public relations. Influenced by both his uncle and French sociologist Gustav le Bon, who held that crowds are by nature irrational and need to be controlled, Bernays had authored a slim tract titled *Propaganda* (1928). The book's opening paragraph stated very succinctly:

> The conscious and intelligent manipulation of the organized habits and opinions of the masses is an important element in democratic society. Those who manipulate this unseen mechanism of society constitute an invisible government which is the true ruling power of our country. We are governed, our minds are molded, our tastes formed, our ideas suggested, largely by men we have never heard of. This is a logical result of the way in

which our democratic society is organized. Vast numbers of human beings must cooperate in this manner if they are to live together as a smoothly functioning society....

Whatever attitude one chooses toward this condition, it remains a fact that in almost every act of our daily lives, whether in the sphere of politics or business, in our social conduct or our ethical thinking, we are dominated by the relatively small number of persons...who understand the mental processes and social patterns of the masses. It is they who pull the wires which control the public mind, who harness old social forces and contrive new ways to bind and guide the world. (*Propaganda*, pp. 1–2)

This matter-of-fact tone of the managerial thinker permeates Bernays' writing. He was no more a revolutionary than the Fabians. He clearly did see himself as one who "understood the mental processes and social patterns of the masses." Bernays believed his description of modern society was inevitable; he accepted it and went to work in his corner of the capitalist world. His role, as he saw matters, was to use what he understood of mass psychology to design advertising and public-relations campaigns that would encourage the masses to buy what capitalists produced.

Why was this necessary? With society advancing, with standards of living rising and people's leisure time increasing, more and more of their immediate needs were satisfied. *Capitalists could not cease producing, however.* If they did, their own wealth and living standards would cease to grow; the economy itself would stop growing. Employees would be laid off; a crisis would hit. Thus arose the need to ensure that what was produced was *wanted,* even if it wasn't *needed.* The increasing expansion of the world of suburbia was more than mere consumer choice: *it was a necessary dynamic of the system itself.* New spending habits had to be inculcated in consumers, and then reinforced.

From this dynamic emerged the professional advertiser, whose aim was to convince buyers to *want* what someone had produced. Those who study the advertising and marketing process closely realize the truth: unless their education includes a heavy dose of critical thinking, *most people buy on emotion and then rationalize (if at all) their emotional decisions with after-the-fact logic.* The successful advertiser and marketer therefore appeals to emotion. Bernays was very good at what he did. For successful advertising campaigns on behalf of numerous corporations Bernays was compensated quite well; he became a multimillionaire.

Economists such as Joseph Schumpeter anticipated some of this. Schumpeter's major work, *Capitalism, Socialism and Democracy* (1942), was decades ahead of its time in pinpointing long-term threats to capitalism, especially from its own dynamic within the specific cultural ambience that had been built up. Originally studying under Austrian school economist Eugen Böhm-Bawerk (under whom Mises also studied), Schumpeter broke from the main line of Austrian thought by describing capitalism as a *process* that was continually revolutionizing itself from within, rather than moving toward the equilibrium theorized by classical economists and Keynesians, or exemplifying a *laissez-faire* ideal. We should note that Schumpeter was in no sense an opponent of capitalism. He had written the definitive work describing entrepreneurship as central to the capitalist engine (*The Theory of Economic Development*, 1911). Nevertheless, he concluded with Marx that capitalism could not survive. His reasons were not Marx's reasons. Capitalism would be undermined not by *failure,* but by its *success,* which "undermines the social institutions which protect it, and 'inevitably' creates conditions in which it will not be able to live and which strongly point to socialism as the heir apparent" (p. 61). His ensuing discussion prophetically points to the essential feature of British-American capitalism *as practiced*:

> The essential point to grasp is that in dealing with capitalism we are dealing with an evolutionary process.... Capitalism...is by nature a form or method of economic change and not only never is but never can be stationary. And this evolutionary character of the capitalist process is not merely due to the fact that economic life goes on in a social and natural environment which changes and by its change alters the data of economic action; this fact is important and these changes (wars, revolutions, and so on) often condition industrial change, but they are not its prime movers. Nor is this evolutionary character due to a quasi-automatic increase in population and capital or to the vagaries of monetary systems of which exactly the same thing holds true. The fundamental impulse that sets and keeps the capitalist engine in motion comes from the new consumers' goods, the new methods or production or transportation, the new markets, the new forms of industrial organization that capitalist enterprise creates. (p. 82)

The history of the capitalist productive apparatus, Schumpeter goes on to say:

> is a history of revolutions....The opening up of new markets, foreign or domestic, and the organizational development from the craft shop and factory to such concerns as U.S. Steel illustrate the same process of industrial mutation—if I may use that biological term— that incessantly revolutionizes the economic structure

> from within, incessantly destroying the old one, incessantly creating a new one. This process of Creative Destruction is the essential fact about capitalism. It is what capitalism consists in and what every capitalist concern has got to live in. (p.82–83)

Schumpeter used this phrase—*creative destruction*—to put his finger on what he took to be the essence of the capitalist process—always eliminating the old as it introduced the new. The idea that markets move toward equilibrium is just wrong. The capitalist engine tends to *disrupt* equilibrium. This feature tends to shorten time horizons by rewarding those who focus on the here and now, maximizing profits for the next quarterly report, possibly at the expense of long-term tendencies that also need to be attended to.

Schumpeter also concluded that British-American capitalism would accentuate tendencies brought into it from the Enlightenment mind-set: the tendency to approach the world critically and rationalistically. If one can avoid committing our Third Cardinal Error, of course, such a tendency might be beyond reproach. Regardless of worldview, the surrounding world presents a person with problems to solve. Action via critical reason—often through trial and error—solves the problems, while magical beliefs and incantations do not. Thus, to the intelligent Christian, prayer is not simply asking God to grant your wishes and solve your problems by divine fiat. The Christian worldview, developed properly, maintains that God created an orderly universe that is governed by cause and effect and is intelligible to the human mind. Hence, rational, strategic action is possible. I see that whenever I do x, y results; I infer that if I want y as the solution to some problem, I should always do x; and if y is something I want to avoid, I shouldn't do x. I might find a way to build this pattern into a machine that will accomplish the desired result much faster and more efficiently than I could ever do with my hands. The aggregate efforts at finding *better* solutions to the problems of living—making workaday tasks easier, cleaner, safer, and more efficient—yields progressively more advanced technology. Self-interest is definitely a factor; if I invent something new, I will want credit for it. If I can mass-produce it to exchange with others, I expect to be paid. Others, of course, will purchase what I offer only if they believe it will improve their lives. One of my needs is to persuade them that it will—or hire someone to do the persuading for me (e.g., an Edward Bernays if I can find him!). A system of exchanges develops; a new corner in the marketplace emerges.

Schumpeter notes, however, that eventually someone will design and build a better or more efficient device than mine, which, if it catches on, will render my operation obsolete. This is creative destruction, which ensures that capitalism *left to itself* will lead to some dislocation. *If extensive enough*, these dislocations will lead some to question the process that gave rise to them and urge restrictions be placed on it. Meanwhile, the critical and rationalistic culture that capitalism enables and encourages will eventually be applied not just in those practical and technical arenas where it is most effective, but in *all* arenas. Some of those whose lives are disrupted by the creative-destruction process will question capitalism itself—especially if they see more destruction than creation, and perceive themselves as being in the grip of something they have no control over. Those who have been enriched by the process will, on the other hand, question all limits on pure economic activity, including national borders, which will be seen as obstacles serving no purpose.

Schumpeter's observations become more troubling given the emergence, noted above, of generations that inherit the benefits of capitalism without having participated in attaining them. We raised the issue of the critical rationalism that capitalism encourages. The explicit development of critical rationalism is the province of intellectuals. Capitalism, by raising the standard of living and creating conditions for leisure, gave rise to a larger population of intellectuals—an intellectual class, if you will—than was ever possible before. This class, the adult version of those intelligent children and teenagers who grew up pursuing hobbies freely in suburban leisure and went to college to pursue the "life of the mind," takes the excitement of the free play of ideas for granted as another entitlement. *Even if they never so much as heard of cultural Marxism, they will not be satisfied with much of what capitalism has to offer, careerwise.* Compared to what they experienced as students, life in capitalist society is dull, often inauthentic because of "office politics" (cf. M. M. Kennedy, *Office Politics*, 1980), and definitely not "free." Perhaps it was this that troubled those writers of the 1950s (Whyte, Harrington, etc.) and united them with the Beats, whose means of finding freedom, such as it was, was to drop out and take to the roads.

Expansionist government's commitment to higher education gave the intellectual class somewhere to go, at least for a time—into professorships hopefully leading to tenure—but its members could never rid themselves of the sense of existing in a kind of bubble. After all, as faculty members, they frequently confronted students who saw little of value in their subjects, which were far removed from the students' own academic majors, aimed as they were at securing them viable employment somewhere in the capitalist hierarchy. The bottom line for the intellectual class: its role in capitalist civilization is profoundly ambiguous. This pushed them leftward—before "PC."

Capitalism, it should be clear, is profoundly unheroic (*anti-heroic* is Schumpeter's term). There are a few exceptions to this, in their own capitalistic way, such as Microsoft founder Bill Gates or Apple's Steve Jobs or Facebook's Mark Zuckerberg, but capitalism only leaves room for a few such individuals who are in the right place at the right time, have the right skills, and take the right actions (often having the right connections). Many other highly intelligent, creative people are consigned to anonymity. Unsuited for business, they pursue life in the intellectual class.

If too large an intellectual class develops, however, its surplus members have nowhere to go; the market for professors is limited, just as is the market for anyone else, leaving many intellectuals with no personally meaningful or satisfying way of earning a living. (Journalism will not do; it is too controlled. Freelance writing is typically not an option; one freelance writer in ten thousand can earn a living at it.) Some intellectuals will blame capitalism for their plight and turn against it with a vengeance—especially if they *do* discover cultural Marxism. They will align themselves with and fall directly under the sway of the Fabian mind-set without having heard of the Fabian Society. Call them selfish or self-indulgent or narcissistic if you will, they will often be more articulate as speakers and writers than most of capitalism's would-be defenders, who are generally too busy engaging in capitalist activities to defend capitalism. Some will network their way into government positions where they can influence policy. They will work to undermine capitalism by strangling it with regulations and taxing it to pay for them.

In other words, by creating the conditions for a substantial intellectual class but leaving its fate uncertain, capitalism encourages hostility from those who wield the power of the pen, one might call it. Few capitalists have been trained to defend their economic space. Thus the capitalist engine ends up largely defenseless against a group ironically made possible by its successes, and becomes more so as this class's influence on subsequent generations grows. The intellectual class can draw attention to real problems, such as poverty, a rising disparity between rich and poor, stagnant wages, the growing cost of health care, the possible effects of industrial activity on climate, and so on. Defenders of capitalism will seem to argue that the solution to problems created by capitalism is more capitalism, and this will not sound convincing to a public not sufficiently educated to examine fundamentals. Their alternative is to embrace ideas and policies that place limits on the capitalist engine—adopting "social responsibilities," as it were (think of sustainable development, to be discussed below). These ideas will be popular, and will aid the capitalist organization in adapting to the changing culture. Capitalism is thus socialized from within, slowly and quietly, unlabeled as such, the process unnoticed until it is irreversible.

We noted above the Marxian complaint, which was also the Fabian complaint, that capitalism creates huge gaps between wealth and poverty. We also noted that capitalism has the means of overcoming, or at least minimizing, these gaps over time. Capitalism created the largest middle class in history—as well as a legion of thinkers who were uneasy about many of its features in one way or another. Schumpeter wrote back in the 1930s and 1940s; one could doubt that he is any more relevant today than Marx. This would be a mistake!

Schumpeter's genius is that he predicted with amazing accuracy the vast creative destruction of changing technology that characterized the entire half-century following his death in 1950! It was as if he'd peered into a crystal ball! He foresaw, in outline at least, many of the results of automation and other manifestations of the technological revolution—long before computers appeared outside highly specialized research-and-development facilities and early science fiction. Not only was his analysis of capitalism on target, it is arguable that he barely scratched the surface. For it seems clear: something eventually *does* go terribly wrong; capitalism *as practiced* does appear to have re-created a divide between the haves and have-nots. The problem is globalization and the emergence of globalism as a superelite ideology. As national borders are rendered increasingly irrelevant by global corporate activity, and technology makes it possible to move operations to locations where labor is cheapest and regulations by governing authorities are lax, the process begins to erode those gains made by the middle class in just one generation! (Let us recall that by nature the superelite do not trust the middle class!)

VI.

Given the strong tendency toward globalism, is it a feature of the capitalist process, or a product of capitalism hijacked? This question is extremely urgent! Currently, we have the capitalist minority, which owns or works within the upper echelons of global corporations, and a much larger population, those harmed by creative destruction in the context of globalization or who have observed and written about harm done to others. The latter's more articulate members have questioned core elements of capitalism itself, such as the belief in the applicability and ultimate benefits of Ricardan free trade. David Ricardo argued in the early 1800s that free trade was justified by comparative advantage: different nations producing different goods both gain through the free exchange of each other's surplus, because, other things being equal, in the absence of trade they have higher costs for producing the same goods. Marx came out in support of free trade for different reasons:

> What is free trade...? It is freedom of capital. When you have overthrown the few national barriers which still restrict the progress of capital, you will merely have given it complete freedom of action. So long as you let the relation of wage labor to capital exist, it does not matter how favorable the conditions under which the exchange of commodities takes place, there will always be a class which will exploit and a class which will be exploited. It is really difficult to understand the claim of free-traders who imagine that the more advantageous application of capital will abolish the antagonism between industrial capitalists and wage workers. On the

contrary, the only result will be that the antagonism of these two classes will stand out still more clearly....All the destructive phenomena which unlimited competition gives rise to within one country are reproduced in more gigantic proportions on the world market....Do not imagine, gentlemen, that in criticizing freedom of trade we have the least intention of defending the system of protection. One may declare oneself an enemy of the constitutional regime without declaring oneself a friend of the ancient regime....But in general, the protective system of our day is conservative, while the free trade system is destructive. It breaks up old nationalities and pushes the antagonism of the proletariat and the bourgeoisie to the extreme point. In a word, the free trade system hastens the social revolution. It is in this revolutionary sense alone, gentlemen, that I vote in favor of free trade. (Karl Marx, "On the Question of Free Trade," speech to the Democratic Association of Brussels, January 9, 1848)

"Free trade" as it actually developed—in a form having so *little* to do with David Ricardo's model that we probably shouldn't even be calling it that—surely has some of the characteristics Marx mentioned. Some corporations, by operating globally, reap huge benefits from creative destruction and see more profit ahead; thus they work to circumvent whatever appears to limit their activity, almost as if confirming Marx's words. They ignore national borders and pay lip service at best to loyalty to their nation's principles, including the rule of law. The results are difficult to predict. What will happen will depend in great measure on what, if any, actions are taken by those harmed. If they demand protective measures, then this will work against global capitalism. But will such demands amount to anything?

Colossal resources have been poured into building up a global network controlled by corporations that use governments to obtain specific policy goals. Schumpeter concluded that what he had observed in his time would mean the dissolution of capitalism and the advent of socialism. He spent an entire section of his work examining how socialism might work.

Some writers today see key policies, especially in the Democratic Party (e.g., health-care reform, or "Obamacare"), as instituting socialism. *We need to think outside this box*, because what will most likely be instituted is not so much a replacement of capitalism with socialism, as a radical strengthening of those capitalist institutions that long-term creative destruction has empowered, leading to even greater degrees of centralization of, and control over, the economy by the superelite—if it can finance the process! The term I use for the resulting system is *techno-feudalism*. Recall that Carroll Quigley used the term *feudalism* for what the bankers wanted. Why our term is superior to *socialism* will become clear in discussions that follow.

To sum up our lengthy digression from the Fabians themselves at this point: the British-American world has built up a specific form of globalist capitalism. We have been calling it British-American capitalism. It should be clear that capitalism in whatever form involves some creative destruction: it is in our nature—or at least in the nature of many of us—to figure out better ways of doing things. These will invariably replace the older and less-efficient ways. Under the financial power of the international bankers and the surreptitious guidance of the Fabians, *actually existing capitalism* has had little in common with the *laissez-faire* image presented by capitalism's most able defenders (e.g., the Austrian school). These defenders, also from the intellectual class, it is worth noting, have had surprisingly little influence: an intellectual defense of capitalism has seemed unimportant to most capitalists! The intellectual defenders of capitalism generally reject government intervention into the economy, for example; but most practicing capitalists long ago made peace with expansionist government, centralization, and an oligarchic political system. The resulting system has raised up a citizenry through many generations that, despite stirrings of unrest on the margins, accepts much governmental machinery (Social Security, Medicare, public schools, foreign military interventions, etc.) without question—and actually rebels at any sign this machinery might be disrupted. Long-term effects of capitalism in the British-American mode have weakened the family unit, long considered essential to raising healthy children, if only by compelling children, as they grew up, to leave the nest for good and move all over the country in search of work. Moreover, since children lack the skills to contribute usefully to capitalist endeavors, they are warehoused in public schools, hijacked by Progressive Education and its more recent permutations, where they acquire values that conflict with those of their parents. Capitalism as practiced has allowed the production of much that undermines public health (both mental and physical) because of how poorly educated consumers choose to spend their money. It has provided havens to intellectuals devoted to its destruction—who sometimes write of *late* capitalism to indicate a theoretical perspective in which capitalism is about to implode.

The question for us, then, boils down to: is Schumpeter right about the "inevitable" self-destruction of capitalism, a victim of its own successes via the mechanism of creative destruction? Or has the capitalist engine been hijacked? My hypothesis, it should be clear by now, is that the capitalist engine has been hijacked. This answer, which presupposes the possibility of a more pristine capitalism freed from central banking and within a society freed of the Four Cardinal Errors, may trouble some readers; for if I am correct, we really have no way of knowing what an "un-hijacked" capitalism would look like. It hasn't happened. Can it even exist outside theory? Even the deductive reasoning of the Misesians are, at best, speculations, since among their working premises is the Enlightenment one about the fundamental rationality of human nature ("Human action is necessarily always rational," says Mises in *Human Action*, p. 19).

All we can do is point to the international investment bankers and the Fabians who comprise the core of what I call the superelite. We can draw attention to their manipulations. Then we can look at where those manipulations have brought us today. *We the people* of the United States of America then have a choice: either we take the system back and work toward an "un-hijacked" capitalism, creatively imagining its features or creating the conditions for their emerging as we go along, by destroying, piece by piece, the edifices of central planning; or we will find that our middle-class heritage is history. For unless we are very, very fortunate (perhaps from having invested wisely or luckily), our new economic reality will be serfdom and impoverishment. (There may be places in the world where matters will be more hopeful, of course.) To see why, let us return to our exploration of the Fourth Cardinal Error, our failure to recognize the importance of the Fabian Society.

5

Putting it all together: with the Four Cardinal Errors having been committed, global capitalism has been taken in a specific direction. We the people have dangerously embraced a system based on entitlements that have expanded uncontrollably, on the idea that wealth can be created out of thin air, and that we can live beyond our means indefinitely. In 2008, this system nearly collapsed.

• • •

I.

We digressed from our discussion of the Fabians to consider separate developments, including Schumpeter's disquieting thesis about the fate of capitalism. Let us review. In chapter 1, I contended that our First Cardinal Error was failing to free ourselves from the activities of British bankers based in the City of London, seat of the Crown, and remaining essentially under their thumb. We became addicted to fractional-reserve lending as a means of building up large enterprises, until the bankers finally centralized our economic system with the Federal Reserve System. In chapter 2, we observed how we embraced a school system alien to our founding principles, according to which persons own themselves and answer to their communities and to their God, replacing it with a system in which ultimately persons are owned by and answer to the state—or the state in alliance with corporations. This was our Second Cardinal Error. Schools systematically abandoned the goal of transmitting the achievements of past generations and replaced it with social engineering.

In chapter 3, we charted the replacement of Christendom and its worldview and moral compass with that of naturalistic materialism—our Third Cardinal Error—and saw how this enabled many of the above changes. For when man does away with God, he tends to replace God not with *nothing,* but with the *state*—or the *state* in *alliance* with the *corporation.* In a word, God is replaced by Secular Power, which becomes an end in itself. With the loss of Christianity, we do not have a viable ethics with teeth in it, the utilitarians notwithstanding. Thus Secular Power has had an essentially free reign in reshaping the world according to the will of a globalist superelite. In chapter 4, we ferreted out one specific organization that has directed and guided the rise of Secular Power: the British Fabian Society, also ensconced in the City of London, where it has allied with the Rothschilds and other globalist banking houses. Our Fourth Cardinal Error was our failure to recognize the Fabian Society for what it was, leading to its penetration and permeation first of universities and then other large institutions, eventually creating new globalist ones—until we arrived at the realization that our present reality is that of a specific British-American capitalism, in its Schumpeterian creative-destructive ferment (or permanent revolution from within): hijacked, to enable a small group of dominant men (and women) to ascend to a *de facto* throne of world power *still* based in the City of London!

We can single out specific turning points—or pivotal years (sometimes ranges of years). For example, in 1791 came Alexander Hamilton's first Bank of the United States, created over Thomas Jefferson's explicit objections. Three years later, in 1794, came the Jay Treaty, which was *proclaimed* before being accorded legitimacy, despite the extra-Constitutional nature of a monarchical proclamation. This treaty also created the basis for "commissions" or "inquiries" that would be international in scope and thus operate outside of Constitutional controls. This happened before the ink had dried on our Constitution, which— it should have been clear—would work only if it was adhered to. In the 1840s, came the first state-sponsored schools. In the 1860s, came the scrapping of true federalism with federal-state dual sovereignty. In the 1890s (possibly sooner), the first Fabians appeared on U.S. soil and began the "progressive" movement. The Rhodes-supported movement appeared soon after.

The next major turning point came with the Coup of 1913, when the Federal Reserve System was created. Private banking interests seized control over our money system, and hence our economy. While the Rockefellers of the late nineteenth-century capitalist world had already begun to hijack the system, the Federal Reserve provided the most important vehicle anyone could have wanted for hijacking the money system and achieving a centralized economy. Then, when Federal Reserve policy—supported by the federal government—brought on the Great Depression in the 1930s, we saw the rise of the first entitlements (Social Security) and of Keynesian economics. These have dominated the political and economic landscapes ever since, notwithstanding the contrary momentum achieved briefly by Milton Friedman's monetarism. Alternatives, such as those presented by the Austrian school, were mostly marginalized as "outside the mainstream" and have had to fight an uphill struggle to have their criticisms of the Federal Reserve heard—although they are being heard today via more visible figures such as Congressman Ron Paul (see his *End the Fed,* 2009).

It should be clear, finally, that by the time we get to the middle of the twentieth century, the Four Cardinal Errors are converging—however loose the convergence (with some players unaware of others and total coordination far from achieved). We see additional pivotal years. In the last chapter, we encountered the many events of the 1940s that placed us firmly on the globalist path the superelite wanted (the UN, the IMF, etc.). In the mid-1960s, under Lyndon Johnson, government expanded to further civil rights goals, establish Medicare and Medicaid, among other rising federal programs and projects not excluding fighting a war in Southeast Asia. Spending rose rapidly beyond the government's means to pay.

In 1971, Richard Nixon "closed the gold window" so the federal government could deal with the rise in spending that was continuing unabated. Our money became fiat money exclusively—backed only by legal-tender laws and the public's willingness to use it. The Federal Reserve could now print as much money as was needed, but that meant the national debt had to rise. Our government entered an era of spending beyond its means with little thought to long term consequences. (One of Keynes's adages *had* been, "In the long run we are all dead.") Ronald Reagan held down taxes, but not federal spending, which continued to accelerate; as a result, the national debt shot past $1 trillion for the first time under his watch. His vice president, George H. W. Bush, who was far closer to the superelite than was Reagan, pursued the latter's goals behind the scenes. During 1992–93, the superelite forced the North American Free Trade Agreement (NAFTA) on the country—the culmination of earlier agreements dating back into the 1980s. Businesses had already started moving overseas to escape a regulatory environment growing increasingly hostile, and this accelerated a process that would cost Americans more than 27 million jobs by the end of 2010.

The American middle class, however much a product of capitalism, was now under a direct, concerted, and very well-organized attack—*precisely what the superelite wanted*. Wages began to stagnate in the 1970s, and were unable to keep up with inflation caused by the increased money supply. The public was not told this, of course. The public was supplied with a "core" inflation rate that ignored food and fuel costs as "too volatile." This cooked statistic was the product of Nixon and then Federal Reserve Chair Arthur Burns. Food and fuel costs were where inflation had its most visible effects. The situation would get worse with time, as would the deceptions via government numbers (the unemployment rate being another prime example).

The era of fiat money led to still more spending—by government at all levels, by corporations, by individuals. When Nixon ended the gold standard, the national debt was around $400 billion. As we noted, under Reagan's watch it crossed the $1 trillion threshold. At the end of the first Bush administration, it was pushing $6 trillion. During the second Bush presidency, the figure reached $10 trillion. As of this writing, just over two years into the Obama presidency, the national debt has surpassed $14 trillion! Few of us can imagine figures this high!

A kind of tacit mind-set had developed in many Americans, especially the younger middle class, the children we encountered above, whose relatively affluent parents would have known better. This tacit mind-set took hold in the 1980s and tightened its grip on the public consciousness even more in the 1990s. It may be seen as the direct descendent of the entitlement mind-set, a product of those who received the benefits of wealth they had done nothing to produce. This mind-set, if made explicit, would have to aver: *wealth need not be earned; it can be created out of thin air via credit expansion—money printing, or the electronic equivalent, entering zeros into a database; we both can and are entitled to live beyond our means indefinitely by borrowing and spending, or merely by spending on credit and going into debt.*

Empowered by this assumption, with most of the public following what everyone *else* was doing, the entire nation went on the biggest spending spree ever. It turned out to be unsustainable. It was steeped in *fantasy*, however real it seemed at the time with the Dow's meteoric rise during the 1990s and then its new all-time high in 2007. We did reap seeming benefits, with dozens of new gadgets—smaller and more powerful personal computers in the 1990s as the Internet became a mainstay of modern life, and then cell phones, flash drives, Blackberries, iPods, iPhones, and so on—and we continue to do so. No one denies the amazing technological advances we have seen over the past quarter century. But in 2008, the financial system nearly collapsed. The details involving the subprime-lending fiasco, mortgage-backed securities, hedge funds, credit-default swaps, other derivatives, and so on, are extremely complex, and we need not probe those specifics here, as they would take us even further afield. But we *will* ask: how did this happen? Let's back up and take things one at a time. Let's go back, that is, to the Fabians.

II.

Where were we? We were charting the course of the "Fabianizing" of America. Covering all who pursued Fabian goals is impossible. There are too many such people. We can, however, survey the most important, even if some operated from Great Britain. John Dewey, we observed, was not just the Rockefeller-sponsored founder of Progressive Education, but also a Fabian. John Maynard Keynes was a Fabian, as we noted. Other Fabians worth consulting are author H. G. Wells, historian Arnold Toynbee, philosopher and mathematical logician Bertrand Russell, and later, the American guru of community organizing Saul Alinsky—who would mentor both Hillary Rodham Clinton and Barack Obama (though he would not be Obama's only mentor).

We have already examined Dewey's rise to prominence and the agenda that became Progressive Education, which we now see as an instance of Fabian permeation; Dewey would also take the reins of the Fabian-directed League for Industrial Democracy, which soon permeated organized labor in America, just as the Labour Party in Great Britain was Fabian-controlled from the outset. Dewey's activities also encompassed the rise of the American Humanist Association; he was a lead author of its *Humanist Manifesto* (the first of four such documents), which worked out the key propositions of an explicitly secular-materialist worldview to accompany the Comtean third stage, "scientific society"—one of the few, but very revealing, such efforts. Earlier, in *Democracy and Education* (1916), Dewey had written of "an education [that] could be given which would sift individuals, discovering what they were good for, and supplying a method of assigning each to the work in life for which his nature fits him" (p. 85). Who supplies this method? Educrats, of course. Commoners learn to do as they are told. Dewey had said earlier:

> There is always a danger that increased personal independence will decrease the social capacity of an individual. In making him self-reliant, it may make him more self-sufficient; it may lead to an aloofness and indifference. It often makes an individual so insensitive in his relations to others as to develop an illusion of being really able to stand and act alone—an unnamed form of insanity which is responsible for a large part of the remediable suffering of the world. (*Democracy and Education,* p. 42)

In other words, according to Dewey, self-sufficiency is bad news; the noncollectivists who pursue self-sufficiency are suffering from an "unnamed" form of mental illness—for which Progressive Education and the long-term Fabian agenda are the cure!

John Maynard Keynes believed he had uncovered a different method for destroying the free-enterprise system. He had already examined (along with Lenin) the possibilities of just debauching the currency and making it pointless for commoners to save. In his book *The Economic Consequences of Peace* (1920), the then-mostly-unknown Keynes stated frankly:

> Lenin is said to have declared that the best way to destroy the Capitalist System was to debauch the currency. By a continuing process of inflation, government can confiscate, secretly and unobserved, an important part of the wealth of their citizens. By this method they not only confiscate, but they confiscate arbitrarily; and while the process impoverishes many, it actually

enriches some. The sight of this arbitrary rearrangement of riches strikes not only at security, but at confidence in the equity of the existing distribution of wealth. Those to whom the system brings windfalls, beyond their deserts and even beyond their expectations or desires, become "profiteers," who are the object of the hatred of the bourgeoisie, whom the inflationism has impoverished, not less than of the proletariat. As the inflation proceeds and the real value of the currency fluctuates wildly from month to month, all permanent relations between debtors and creditors, which form the ultimate foundation of capitalism, become so utterly disordered as to be almost meaningless, and the process of wealth-getting degenerates into a gamble and a lottery.

Lenin was certainly right. There is no subtler, no surer method of overturning the existing basis of society than to debauch the currency. The process engages all the hidden forces of economic law on the side of destruction, and does it in a manner which not one man in a million is able to diagnose. (pp. 235–36)

Keynes's *General Theory* became the economic bible of the Roosevelt/WWII era, and remained such for decades afterward. Everyone who believes that the federal government can spend a society into prosperity indefinitely, or that printing-press money can generate more than pseudo-prosperity, is under the long-term spell of Keynes. Eventually this included Alan Greenspan, despite his initial defense of the gold standard under Ayn Rand's temporary and very superficial influence. It currently includes Ben Bernanke, as well as Henry Paulson (one time chairman and CEO of Goldman Sachs and U.S. Treasury secretary under George W. Bush), and Timothy Geithner (son of former Ford Foundation President Peter F. Geithner, former chair of the New York Federal

Reserve, and U.S. Treasury Secretary under Barack Obama, whose economic views are almost pure Keynes). The monetarists following Milton Friedman, who claimed to have an alternative to Keynes, had their day, but their association, justly or not, with the spending spree and the recklessness and corruption that characterized Wall Street of the 2000s decade may have doomed them. The embrace of Keynesian economics in the 1930s was rooted in the first, as well as fourth of the Four Cardinal Errors: failure to free ourselves from British bankers ensconced in the City of London, and failure to recognize the Fabian Society for what it was. Keynes, as both Fabian and globalist, would play a lead role in the design of the Bretton Woods meeting, as well as the building up of the International Monetary Fund and the World Bank, ensuring their Fabian permeation and furtherance of Fabian goals.

The same was true of historian Arnold Toynbee. Toynbee was an original Rhodes Round Tabler and an early Fabian who later became official historian for the Royal Institute of International Affairs. In 1931, he gave an address to fellow globalists at the Conference of Institutions for the Scientific Study of International Affairs in Copenhagen titled "The Trend of International Affairs Since the War." He defended the use of secrecy in the assault on national sovereignty:

> If we are frank with ourselves, we shall admit that we are engaged on a deliberate and sustained and concentrated effort to impose limitations upon the sovereignty and independence of the fifty or sixty local sovereign independent States which at present partition the habitable surface of the earth and divide the political allegiance of mankind.
>
> It is just because we are really attacking the principle of local sovereignty that we keep on protesting our

loyalty to it so loudly. The harder we press our attack
upon the idol, the more pains we take to keep its priests
and devotees in a fool's paradise—lapped in a false sense
of security which will inhibit them from taking up arms
in their idol's defense. The local national state, invested
with the attributes of sovereignty—is an abomination of
desolation standing in the place where it ought not. It
has stood in that place now—demanding and receiving
human sacrifices from its poor deluded votaries—for
four or five centuries. Our political task in our generation is to cast the abomination out, to cleanse the temple and to restore the worship of the divinity to whom
the temple rightfully belongs. In plain terms, we have
to re-transfer the prestige and the prerogatives of sovereignty from the fifty or sixty fragments of contemporary
society to the whole of contemporary society—from
the local national states by which sovereignty has been
usurped, with disastrous consequences, for half a millennium, to some institution embodying our society as
a whole.

Toynbee knew of the plan to re-create the League of Nations in
the form of the United Nations and to work gradually through
it and its satellite institutions to erode national sovereignty.
He spoke of the kind of institution the superelite wanted and
concluded:

In the world as it is today, this institution can hardly be
a universal Church. It is more likely to be something
like a League of Nations. I will not prophesy. *I will merely
repeat that we are at present working, discreetly but with all our
might, to wrest this mysterious political force called sovereignty
out of the clutches of the local national states of our world. And
all the time we are denying with our lips what we are doing*

with our hands. ("The Trend of International Affairs Since the War," *International Affairs*, November 1931, p. 809; all italics mine)

H. G. Wells would author not just those early and much-beloved science-fiction tales such as *The Time Machine* (1895) and *War of the Worlds* (1898), but also, much later, nonfiction works such as *The Open Conspiracy* (1928), *The Shape of Things To Come* (1938), and *The New World Order* (1940). Once a Fabian, he broke with them to pursue an even more radical vision of a socialist world-state encompassing Comte's notion of a "religion of humanity," in which Christianity is a thing of the past and it is "no longer possible for an ordinary young man to get a living as a minister of any Church" (*The Shape of Things To Come*, p. 146). Wells believed that world government—or a world state, as he called it—would solve humankind's problems. In *The Shape of Things To Come*, an imagined future social scientist, Gustave De Windt (Wundt?), provides the ideas that guide the development of the socially engineered state. We catch a glimpse of how the superelite, seen through Wellsian spectacles, view democracy:

> "It is no good asking people what they want," wrote De Windt. "That is the error of democracy. You have first to think out what they ought to want if society is to be saved. Then you have to tell them what they want and see that they get it." (p. 269)

In other words, ordinary people must be led like sheep into a "world state" based on principles of total control by technocratic means. In *The New World Order*, Wells spoke chillingly of the fate of those who would oppose the goals of those seeking to build this "world state":

> Countless people…will hate the new world order, be
> rendered unhappy by frustration of their passions and
> ambitions through its advent *and will die protesting against
> it*. When we attempt to estimate its promise we have to
> bear in mind *the distress of a generation or so of malcontents*,
> many of them quite gallant and graceful-looking people.
> (p. 129; emphasis mine)

As we see, he used the phrase *new world order* openly, not con-
spiratorially. Are we still supposed to believe all this can be dismissed as a "conspiracy theory"?

Finally, Bertrand Russell also developed key consequences of
the Comtean "scientific society," writing openly in *The Scientific
Outlook* (1931) and *The Impact of Science on Society* (1952). The
focus is on education, picks up where Rockefeller's General
Education Board and the Carnegie Corporation leave off, and
brings us full circle. Russell proposed that in the "scientific society," the elite would receive one kind of education, while the
masses would receive another:

> The scientific rulers will provide one kind of educa-
> tion for ordinary men and women, and another for
> those who are to become holders of scientific power.
> Ordinary men and women will be expected to be docile,
> industrious, punctual, thoughtless and contented. Of
> these qualities contentment will be considered the most
> important. In order to produce it, all the researches into
> psycho-analysis, behaviorism, and biochemistry will be
> brought into play. (*The Scientific Outlook*, p. 243)

Later, Russell would set out the role of mass psychology in social
engineering in a fashion going beyond Bernays:

> I think the subject which will be of most importance
> politically is mass psychology….What is essential in

mass psychology is the art of persuasion. If you compare a speech of Hitler's with a speech of (say) Edmund Burke, you will see what strides have been made in the art since the eighteenth century. What went wrong formerly was that people had read in books that man is a rational animal, and framed their arguments on this hypothesis. We now know that limelight and a brass band do more to persuade than can be done by the most elegant train of syllogisms. It may be hoped that in time anybody will be able to persuade anybody of anything if he can catch the patient young and is provided by the State with money and equipment.

This subject will make great strides when it is taken up by scientists under a scientific dictatorship....The social psychologists of the future will have a number of classes of school children on whom they will try different methods of producing an unshakable conviction that snow is black. Various results will soon be arrived at. First, that the influence of the home is obstructive. Second, that not much can be done unless indoctrination begins before the age of ten. Third, that verses set to music and repeatedly intoned are very effective. Fourth, that the opinion that snow is white must be held to show a morbid taste for eccentricity....It is for future scientists to make these maxims precise and discover exactly how much it costs per head to make children believe that snow is black, and how much less it would cost to make them believe it is dark gray.

Although this science will be diligently studied, *it will be rigidly confined to the governing class. The populace will not be allowed to know how its convictions were generated*. When the technique has been perfected, every government that has been in charge of education will be able to control its subjects securely without the need of armies or policemen. (*The Impact of Science on Society*, pp. 29–30; emphasis mine)

Such views mirror chapter 2. The upshot is that in the Comtean-Russellian "scientific society"—its masses educated according to methods first proposed by Dewey, in accordance with desires articulated originally by Rockefeller's General Education Board—science and technology become not instruments of liberation, but instruments of control. Back in the 1930s, the notion went by the name *technocracy*.

This was for the future, and authors such as Wells and Russell envisioned that it would be a glorious future indeed. We would be remiss not to provide a short account of the actual long-term effects of British Fabianism just on Great Britain itself. Cecil Rhodes had wanted to extend the British Empire worldwide. He would almost certainly have been profoundly disappointed.

We already noted that the Fabians were for all intents and purposes the intellectual founders of the British Labour Party, which would come to dominate British domestic politics and economics by the 1940s. The pivotal year in Great Britain was 1945; if there was a time when the Fabians really did "strike hard," it was during the ensuing twenty years. In a crucial election in 1945, the Labour Party gained a majority in the House of Commons. Fabian Clement Attlee was named prime minister. The Labour government nationalized several key industries and professions: utilities and communications, rail, air travel, mining, and medicine (with the creation of the National Health Service). It created a welfare state and raised taxes to support the massive increases in government spending that a welfare state requires. British industry went into a long-term decline from which it has never recovered.

Whatever one thinks of the British Empire that existed until after World War II, the decolonization that ensued hardly helped the many "liberated" peoples. In 1947, British India was partitioned into today's India, dominated by Hindus, and Pakistan, dominated by Muslims. The two nations have been enemies ever since. Now with nuclear weapons, the two still eye one another uneasily as each struggles to control disputed territories in the Kashmir Mountains. Burma was decolonized and became a military dictatorship (now called Myanmar). Much of Africa sank into poverty and remained there. Nations such as Sudan have ended up in genocidal civil wars (think of the situation in Darfur). Rhodesia, named obviously for Cecil Rhodes, eventually became Zimbabwe and saw its standard of living plummet amid hyperinflation under Robert Mugabe's dictatorship—a tragic obvious lesson in the folly of believing that printing fiat money helps one's economy.

By the 1960s, traditional British society was in ruins. Prime Minister Harold Wilson—also a Fabian—decriminalized abortion and homosexuality. He opened the doors to the immigration of large numbers of third-world peoples into Great Britain. The result was ethnic tensions that had been hitherto unknown. The election of Conservative prime minister Margaret Thatcher did little to roll back the effects of over thirty years of leftist policy. Today's Great Britain verges on dysfunction, with high rates of welfare dependency, illegitimate births, racial tension, and crime. Materialism is, of course, the prevailing worldview; by 2008, only 10 percent of the population attended church services regularly, while the illegitimate birthrate reached 50 percent.

In other words, the Fabian Society wrecked its home country. It did so while remaining almost unknown, "penetrating and permeating" from behind the scenes, where Fabians have remained comfortable. Sadly, the Fabians have remained in control of British politics, operating from their safe havens in prestigious institutions such as the London School of Economics, housed within the City of London. The damage they have done throughout the world is incalculable. It remains to be seen whether Americans will wake up to them or continue to commit the Fourth Cardinal Error.

III.

The superelite—globalist bankers, Fabians, and their many protégés—had begun working toward an economic, political, and educational climate in which globalist economics and world government would be seen as inevitable. But they realized this might not happen for decades. David Rockefeller Sr., having studied at the LSE in the late 1930s, had been at the helm of the Council on Foreign Relations since the late 1940s and had helped build up other international organizations, such as the Bilderberg Group, which began in 1954. In 1970, he read fellow globalist Zbigniew Brzezinski's *Between Two Ages: America's Role in the Technetronic Era* (1970). At the time, Brzezinski was a professor at Fabian-permeated Columbia University. He had served as an advisor to the Kennedy campaign for the presidency in 1960 and would later advise both the Johnson and Humphrey campaigns. He'd been invited to join the CFR and to attend Bilderberg meetings. His book describes history as a process moving away from "nationalism" (i.e., more or less autonomous nation-states) through Marxism to globalism. Brzezinski reveals the process in great detail:

> The nation-state as a fundamental unit of man's organized life has ceased to be the principal creative force: "international banks and multinational corporations are acting and planning in terms that are far in advance of the political concepts of the nation-state."…
>
> A global human conscience is for the first time beginning to manifest itself. This conscience is a natural extension of the long process of widening man's personal

horizons....Today we are...witnessing the emergence
of transnational elites, but now they are composed of
international businessmen, scholars, professional men,
and public officials. The ties of these new elites cut
across national boundaries, their perspectives are not
confined by national traditions, and their interests are
more functional than national. These global communities are gaining in strength and...it is likely that before
long the social elites of most of the more advanced countries will be highly internationalist or globalist in spirit
and outlook. (*Between Two Ages*, pp. 56–58)

Brzezinski worried that the populations of the world were not
ready to live in a global society:

The new global consciousness, however, is only beginning to become an influential force. It still lacks identity,
cohesion, and focus. Much of humanity—indeed, the
majority of humanity—still neither shares nor is prepared to support it. Science and technology are still used
to buttress ideological claims, to fortify national aspirations, and to reward narrowly national interests. Most
states are spending more on arms than on social services, and the foreign-aid allotment of the two most powerful states is highly disproportionate to their asserted
global missions. Indeed, it can be argued that in some
respects the divided, isolated, and compartmentalized
world of old had more inner cohesion and enjoyed
greater harmony than the volatile global reality of today.
Established cultures, deeply entrenched traditional religions, and distinctive national identities provided a stable framework and firm moorings; distance and time
were the insulators against excessive friction between
the compartments. Today the framework is disintegrat-
ing and the insulants are dissolving. The new global unity

has yet to find its own structure, consensus, and harmony. (pp. 61–62)

Rockefeller, Brzezinski, and Henry Kissinger organized the
Trilateral Commission in the early 1970s to advance the "new
global consciousness" in three regions: North America, Europe,
and Japan. Its founders' enormous behind-the-scenes influence
in the United States propelled Jimmy Carter into the White
House and would maintain a central presence in all subsequent
administrations, regardless of party affiliation. All these groups
were pursuing Fabian goals, whether the rank and file knew it
or not—and most probably did not. That is, they had become
agents of Fabian permeation.

I should emphasize once more what I said at the very outset, that the preceding—and the material that follows—is not a
"conspiracy theory" no matter how loudly and insistently critics
label it as such. It isn't a *theory*. Recall David Rockefeller Sr.'s
statement, no less candid than Toynbee's:

> For more than a century, ideological extremists at either
> end of the political spectrum have seized upon well-
> publicized incidents…to attack the Rockefeller family
> for the inordinate influence they claim we wield over
> American political and economic institutions. Some
> even believe we are part of a secret cabal working against
> the best interests of the United States, characterizing my
> family and me as "internationalists" and of conspiring
> with others around the world to build a more integrated
> global political and economic structure—one world, if
> you will. *If that's the charge, I stand guilty, and I am proud of
> it. (Memoirs,* 2002, pp. 404–05; emphasis mine)

As writers these superelites aren't conspirators! They couldn't
be more open and straightforward if they tried!

The Democratic Party had been Fabian permeated at least since 1960; John F. Kennedy Jr. had also studied at (where else?) the LSE. The "liberals" built on the collectivism of the Rooseveltian New Deal with programs such as "affirmative action" for women and minorities, which appeared in the late 1960s and gained ground during the 1970s. Also appearing in the 1960s were Medicare and Medicaid, those politically untouchable, major federal expenditures we mentioned above. Environmental pollution was also garnering attention, leading to the creation of the Environmental Protection Agency in 1970. Then there was the ongoing conflict in Vietnam, of course. The federal government needed money, lots of it.

President Richard Nixon and Federal Reserve Chair Arthur Burns—who at Nixon's suggestion had doctored the inflation rate to exclude "volatile" food and fuel costs—chose to print it. We saw above how spending and the national debt began their geometric rise. Never again would the United States live within its means. Eventually, with the ready availability of bank loans and credit cards, neither corporations nor individuals would live within their means. In the 1980s, we went down the road of credit-created pseudo-prosperity. In the 1990s, we shifted into overdrive. There were warnings of trouble ahead. They were ignored. This road would dead-end in 2008. No one could have foreseen this in the 1970s, of course. Even so, these were years of political and economic turmoil. A severe economic downturn plus the Iranian hostage crisis together ruined the Carter presidency.

A false opposition appeared. The federal government, it said, is too large and spends too much money. That much was true: planting truths inside agendas had become a Fabian specialty. As the Carter presidency disintegrated, we began hearing from *neoconservatives*—neocons—educated in New York's City College (also Fabian permeated) and (surprise, surprise) Columbia University. With the idea that "liberalism" had gone too far planted firmly in the public's mind, neocons had instant credibility. In accordance with Fabian support for the specific brand of capitalism that would further their goals, the first wave of neocons penned books with titles such as *Two Cheers For Capitalism* (1978) by Irving Kristol and *Breaking Ranks* (1980) by Norman Podhoretz. What masqueraded as a conservative intellectual and political renaissance began. By the time it had run its course, this movement would ruin the Republican Party. The fact that Republican policies would be saddled with responsibility for the worst economic downturn since the Great Depression would discredit conservatism itself in the eyes of many pundits, none of whom had read real conservative thinkers such as Richard Weaver or Russell Kirk.

The Reaganites spoke of "morning in America"; the truth is, with the rise of the neocons, Fabian permeation captured the Republican Party. One of its mantras would be *free trade*, for which the economists of the day again cited David Ricardo and his theory of comparative advantage. Its new guise began with *enterprise zones*. This latter idea, to all appearances, was the brainchild of one Stuart M. Butler, a policy analyst at the Heritage Foundation, who published two seminal essays on the subject in 1979 and 1980, respectively. The idea was not Butler's, however. Sir Geoffrey Howe, chancellor of the Exchequer of Great Britain, had introduced it in a speech to Parliament in 1978. Howe, in turn, had acquired the idea from Professor Peter Hall, an urban planner based at Reading University. Professor Hall had developed the concept of a "freeport" as a means of developing the depressed inner city—creating unabashedly capitalist enclaves, within which "workers parties" could also be established.

Professor Hall was a Fabian—on the Fabian Society's executive committee.

The idea spread among the new breed of conservative, who assumed it had originated with one of their own. Howe led the way in merging the idea with that of the *free-trade zone*, which, when enlarged to encompass multiple nations, dismantled tariffs, customs, and duties. Managed globalist capitalism was unleashed via so-called *free-trade agreements* (FTAs), the antecedent of which was, of course, GATT. Such agreements in Europe had led to the European Common Market and were gradually eroding national borders all across that continent. A Rockefeller-led conversation had started among the elites to erode borders in the Western Hemisphere, though this was not obvious for several decades.

The neocons saw themselves as the vanguard of a new manifest destiny—especially after the collapse of the Soviet Union left the United States as the one superpower in a unipolar world. Their destiny: to take "liberal democracy" to the rest of the world, echoing what Cecil Rhodes had envisioned for British society almost a century ago. They would form liaisons of convenience with, for example, the so-called Religious Right. Such liaisons enabled them to get many of their people elected to office by masquerading as Christians. Once in office, of course, they paid Christian concerns scant attention; example: abortion. Republicans are constantly running on antiabortion sentiment, yet not one Republican elected to national office has lifted a finger to stop the practice. In fairness, some Republicans have used the courts to end some of its more barbaric variants, such as partial-birth abortions; but abortion in general has continued to be legal as the number of unborn babies killed has soared to around 50 million! What Republicans have done in the mean-time is take money donated by naïve pro-life groups who read the antiabortion plank in the Republican Party platform and assumed it meant something. Leading neocons have furthered globalism, not Christianity. The plain truth is, the neocons who came to control the Republican Party during the Reagan years—finally placing one of their own in the White House with the election of Reagan's vice president, George H. W. Bush, in 1988—have no more interest in spiritual matters than they have in quantum electrodynamics. Their emphasis dovetails with that of the superelite: global political control via encircling economic entanglements.

While we heard a lot of rhetoric about the need for global competitiveness and the evils of "protectionism," the upper-echelon players had no more desire for genuine competition than had the robber barons of the late 1800s. We were approaching a new turning point, where economic coercion would become the norm as entire industries were destroyed and people were forced out of work. The destructive side of creative destruction was in evidence.

The once-thriving U.S. textile industry serves as perhaps the best example. Former textile workers were told, in effect, to "reinvent themselves" for the "jobs of the future." Almost none understood what was happening to them. Where was the creative side? In "knowledge jobs"? These could be done from any-where in the world, and so very soon would not be done in the United States. In health care? In other domestic services? As waiters and waitresses? As greeters in Wal-Mart? None of these jobs paid more than a fraction of what the people doing them had been earning. Our manufacturing base had begun to disap-pear. American workers were too expensive, as were American regulations on business. The ideal participants in this system were multinational and transnational corporations that could locate anywhere and whose only loyalties were to money and power—those whose leadership Brzezinski had lauded back in 1970 in *Between Two Ages*. There were no loyalties to nationality, and this meant the fulfillment of the call by Richard Gardner, former U.S. ambassador to the UN and member of the Council on Foreign Relations and Trilateral Commission, for the slow erosion of national sovereignty:

> The "house of world order" will have to be built from the bottom up rather than from the top down. It will look like a great "booming, buzzing confusion," to use William James' famous description of reality, but an end run around national sovereignty, eroding it piece by piece, will accomplish much more than the old-fashioned frontal assault. ("The Hard Road to World Order," CFR journal *Foreign Affairs*, April 1974, p. 558)

It would shortly be clear to anyone who knew what to look for: *the globalist process furthered by Fabian-permeated corporate elites and all illusions of sovereignty of the United States under our Constitution were on a collision course; also on a collision course were this process and the continuation of a financially independent middle class in America. This was okay: because again, the superelite do not want a financially independent middle class.*

The collision came with Congress's passage of NAFTA in 1993 (actually it was signed by Bush I the year before). The agreement went into effect on January 1, 1994. It had the support of the Bushes and other mainstream Republicans, the Clintons and other mainstream Democrats, and even talk-show host Rush Limbaugh, who otherwise bashed Bill Clinton mercilessly. The incongruity went uncommented on. The superelite wanted it, as was evident when Kissinger called it:

> the single most important decision that Congress would make during Mr. Clinton's first term...the most creative step toward a new world order taken by any group of countries since the end of the Cold War. What Congress will have before it is not a conventional trade agreement but the architecture of a new international system...the first step toward a new world order. (*Los Angeles Times*, July 18, 1993, p. M2)

And again: all this talk about a *new world order* is just "conspiracy theory"? But then, what little public discussion NAFTA received in the fall of 1993 was overshadowed by hysterical mainstream-media coverage of O. J. Simpson's alleged murder of his wife Nicole, and then, as NAFTA was going into effect, by a figure skater whacking another figure skater on the knee. In such ways, America's masses were easily distracted. With NAFTA came an acceleration of the long-term exodus of millions of manufacturing jobs from the United States. Initially these jobs went to Mexico; then, corporations discovered that Chinese labor was even cheaper than Mexican labor. Consequently, mainland China—still a "communist" country—began to emerge as the new globalist order's premier manufacturing center.

Less noticed were NAFTA's effects on Mexico, which were actually worse. Mexico was more vulnerable than America. Mexican farmers could not compete with American "agra-biz," resulting in a mass exodus of newly unemployed Mexicans. Those able to do so came to the United States. They crossed America's open southern border by the millions in search of work—in fields, in construction, in restaurants, for whoever would hire them—and pay them under the table if necessary.

Their willingness to work for lower wages than native-born Americans sent still more Americans to the unemployment lines. Thus our present illegal immigration epidemic, which at its height resulted in almost a tenth of all Mexican citizens residing here, is also an indirect product of Fabian-permeated trade policy.

With the early 1990s economy struggling and the country in a generally sour mood, the Federal Reserve began pumping unprecedented quantities of printing-press money into circulation. Easy credit appeared to turn things around. The Dow began an unprecedented climb, going from 2,800 on January 2, 1990, to a then-incredible 10,000 on March 29, 1999! The mood had not only lightened but been replaced by "irrational exuberance" (Alan Greenspan's infamous term). The Fed's easy-money policy had brought about the boom. Further empowering the boom was the explosion in changing technology, including microcomputers and networks, the World Wide Web, electronic commerce, and so on. "Dot-coms," as they were informally called, appeared everywhere. If you didn't have a six-figure income in the New Economy—the newly emerged, exciting, fast-paced tech sector—it was clearly your own fault! Yet there clearly were people left behind by the New Economy (see Barbara Ehrenreich, *Nickled and Dimed: On (Not) Getting By in America*, 2001).

The New Economy proved unsustainable. It turned out to be what real economists call a *bubble*: a consumer-psychology driven phenomenon of malinvestment resulting in unsustainably high volumes of trade, along with inflated value, created and nurtured for a time by massive credit expansion. While the major innovators (e.g., Apple, Microsoft, Amazon.com) survived, lesser "dot-coms" went out of business by the thousands. The economy sank back into a funk made worse by the 9/11 attacks. Losses in manufacturing jobs, meanwhile, continued apace. These losses were joined by a significant fraction of the new tech sector, a large portion of which went to India. Several writers began calling our trade policies a "race to the bottom" (see Alan Tonelson, *The Race to the Bottom*, 2002). As the 2000s decade continued, however, a housing boom replaced the tech boom. The housing boom, too, turned out to be a bubble— and failed to generate the excitement of its predecessor. It was becoming evident to the observant that millions of people were living beyond their means—as was the country itself.

During the Clinton years, the national debt had stabilized uneasily. Under George W. Bush's watch, it began to rise again, as we noted. The trajectory of federal spending during this period proved that a Republican-controlled Congress and a Republican administration could spend as extravagantly as any group of Democrats—including on two foreign wars—and Bush had cut taxes. Where was the money going to come from? It would be borrowed against the future. The Dow soared again, however, reaching its all-time high, closing at 14,164.53 on October 9, 2007. The corporate elites and their investors were not thinking about the future, for they were doing swimmingly in the present! Interestingly, the Federal Reserve had stopped reporting its M3 aggregate the previous year, on March 23, 2006. The M3 aggregate was the best available measure of the total money supply, including currency in circulation, bank accounts, money market accounts, larger time deposits (over $100,000) and institutional funds. Something was amiss, and the Fed's denizens damned well knew it! The average American's savings rate had gone negative. The housing bubble was about to morph into the next crisis, which has proven to have historic significance. Evidence was mounting of damage done to the economy by loans made to homeowners that the latter could not repay: subprime lending. When people could not pay their debts, they were foreclosed on; foreclosures soon soared to record highs. The spending spree was coming to a dramatic end!

A pivotal event had occurred during the late 1990s. It went all but unnoticed at the time: an item of legislation passed by the Republican-controlled Congress and signed by Bill Clinton, a Democrat, on November 12, 1999. This was the Gramm-Leach-Bliley Act, also called the Financial Services Modernization Act of 1999. It repealed the Glass-Steagall Act of 1933, known for having created the Federal Deposit Insurance Corporation (FDIC) and instituting reforms in banking designed to control speculation. Glass-Steagall had erected walls between commercial banks, investment banks, securities companies, and insurance corporations. Gramm-Leach-Bliley took down these walls.

Almost immediately, we saw mergers such as Citicorp (a commercial bank) with Travelers Group (an insurance company) into Citigroup, which combined banking, securities, and insurance. What emerged in the 2000s decade was called, euphemistically, the "financial services industry." Gramm-Leach-Bliley allowed investment banks to sell high-risk products to traditionally low-risk commercial banks—opening the door to subprime lending, which began to show evidence of trouble on the horizon as early as mid-2007. It also opened the door to unrestrained speculation on Wall Street, which became a high-tech gambling casino!

As noted, we do not need to wade into the details of mortgage-backed securities, credit-default swaps, and so on. All we need emphasize is that the system that generated these oddities nearly collapsed during September 2008. The superelite-owned investment banks and other large corporations (e.g.,

AIG) received bailouts, of course—with an actual threat of total financial meltdown and martial law by none other than Bush's Treasury Secretary, Hank Paulson, if Congress did not immediately pass the Troubled Assets Relief Program (TARP) which spent up to $700 billion to bail out banks and other corporations deemed "too big to fail." It is now known that the Federal Reserve injected $1.2 trillion more, conjured out of thin air, to loan to Wall Street firms. In the spirit of Keynes, President Obama signed the Economic Recovery and Reinvestment Act on February 17, 2009, expropriating $787 billion in taxpayer dollars in what turned out to be a futile effort to stimulate the U.S. economy and promote a recovery. Neither Congress nor the President nor Federal Reserve Chair Ben Bernanke could grasp that the solution to problems created by excess spending and debt is not more spending and more debt. Yet Congress was in a bind of major proportions. Could the American public have tolerated the alternative: a sudden and very sharp depression as the bubble of pseudo-prosperity that had built up since the 1980s deflated all at once?

What happened was a plunging stock market and the loss of hundreds of thousands of jobs per month—and the ruination of George W. Bush's presidency. The 2000s decade ended with this country struggling to extract itself from the worst economy since the 1930s. Job losses, business closings, foreclosures, and abandonments of homes in the real economy turned once-thriving, healthy communities into ghost towns. Tent cities sprang up outside actual cities, where entire neighborhoods stand abandoned. The unemployment rate—the *real* one that counts "discouraged workers" who have given up, those working part-time but seeking full-time work, and so on—remains over 22 percent as of this writing (second quarter 2011)!

Bernanke turned on the money-creation spigot. Perhaps he believed his efforts would duplicate Alan Greenspan's feat. His latest effort began on November 3, 2010; calling it "Quantitative Easing 2" (QE2), he proposed the Fed buy $600 billion in long-term Treasury bonds over the ensuing eight months. He also proposed to reinvest $250 billion to $300 billion in Treasuries with the proceeds from earlier investments, totaling $850 billion to $900 billion more created out of thin air. As of this writing, this herculean effort has been a dismal failure. Unlike the 1990s, when billions of dollars of fractional money was lent by banks to the dot-com start-ups, creating Greenspan's sense of "irrational exuberance," banks have refrained from lending since the Meltdown of 2008 and the ensuing Great Recession (early Greater Depression?). Their restraint is born of desperate attempts to bolster their own finances during a period that has seen more bank failures than any time since the first Great Depression.

There is a sense in which the U.S. economy has become "desensitized" to excesses of liquidity and cheap credit. Consumer demand remains low as of this writing. This has meant a relative absence of business expansion and job creation—a state of affairs that appears likely to continue indefinitely. Our basic point: *all the Barack Obamas and Ben Bernankes in the world cannot create prosperity with stimulus packages and electronic printing-press money, any more than they can by saying a prayer—or for that matter, by snapping their fingers and making a wish*. Our economic problems are far from over. In all probability, we have only seen the first wave of what will be a long and painful decline—a sad state of affairs, if only because it did not have to happen this way.

What is worth noting in closing this section is that the *ideology* of corporate globalism that gave rise to this catastrophe is remarkably close to the *laissez-faire* view of unfettered free-market capitalism that they agree to reject when they speak of the domestic economy. (The *practice* is quite different, of course: instead of allowing real free-market competition, they control governments by forming vast networks of partnerships.) What was rejected when Glass-Steagall was repealed was a regulation designed to control greed, which, given available new technology, was unleashed at an unprecedented level! The rampant greed on Wall Street, combined with mass economic illiteracy brought about by the decline in public education, the mass exodus of jobs out of the United States, and the well-documented widening of the gulf between rich and poor in the United States, all played right into the hands of the academic and journalistic critics of capitalism in the intellectual class—none of whom, at least not before 2008, had looked past the surface of events to see the role of the huge banks, much less the Fabians. Arguably this activity has ruined this country no less than the Fabians ruined Great Britain.

There is much more to be said about Fabian permeation than space permits. We should note that Alan Greenspan references them in *The Age of Turbulence* (2007) and credits them with having had a "tempering effect" (p. 265) on market capitalism that kept the latter politically palatable. The Fabians are still around and still very active, of course. Both Britain's past prime minister, Tony Blair, and its present one, Gordon Brown, are past presidents of the Fabian Society. Brown paid President Obama a visit in March 2009. Obama is a disciple of the Saul Alinsky school of Fabianism, which seeks control over communities in the guise of "organizing" mass action, and has used Alinsky's techniques very effectively. Alinsky's techniques recall Sun Tzu's principles in *The Art of War*, the first of which is: "All warfare is based on deception." Alinsky's rules, which I have annotated, are as follows (*Rules for Radicals*, 1971, p. 127f.):

(1) *Power is not only what you have but what the enemy thinks you have.* This is the first rule; deceive those seen as enemies of change.

(2) *Never go outside the experience of your people.* The result is confusion and retreat.

(3) *Wherever possible, go outside of the experience of the enemy.* This causes confusion in your enemies and forces them to retreat.

(4) *Make the enemy live up to their own book of rules.* No one is absolutely consistent all the time—*no one.* Yet many will assume they are, can be convicted of hypocrisy, and find their credibility damaged.

(5) *Ridicule is man's most potent weapon.* This is extremely potent because ridicule is impossible to answer rationally and can provoke the enemy into a hostile reaction or flustered unreason that further damages his credibility.

(6) *A good tactic is one that your people enjoy.* Obviously, those who enjoy what they are doing will continue doing it.

(7) *A tactic that drags on too long becomes a drag.* This recognizes that foot soldiers have short attention spans, that even fomented crises are of short duration, and that in the absence of definitive results, most will lose interest.

(8) *Keep the pressure on.* The Fabians accomplished much through sheer persistence, improvising where necessary and using everything at hand, including unanticipated crises. "Never allow a good crisis to go to waste."

(9) *The threat is usually more terrifying than the thing itself.* Work to deceive the enemy about what you know, where you are, how many of you there are, and so on.

(10) *The major premise for tactics is the development of operations that will maintain a constant pressure upon the opposition.* Wear down the opposition; provoke reactions where necessary; allow negative responses to those reactions to further wear them down.

(11) *If you push a negative hard and deep enough, it will break through into its counterside.* Negatives are tools to be used and will further frustrate the enemy and cause them to act irrationally. (Alinsky recounts a story of how a corporation under attack by one of his operations responded by sending thugs to burglarize his home.)

(12) *The price of a successful attack is a constructive alternative.* Occasionally the enemy gives in by saying, "You are right. Now tell us what to do about the problem." You better have something constructive to say. The Fabians had thought this through, and usually did.

(13) *Pick the target, freeze it, personalize it, and polarize it.* Consider how former president George W. Bush has been personally demonized for the Meltdown of 2008 despite the easily documented role of laws (e.g., Gramm-Leach-Bliley, which Bill Clinton signed), policies (financial and otherwise), and other factors that predated his administration and over which he had no control. Or ask Sarah Palin whether it is possible to pick a target, personalize it, and polarize it. Or Rush Limbaugh, or Glenn Beck, or the various Tea Party movements that found themselves dragged unwillingly by leftist editorialists into the shooting attack of Congresswoman Gabrielle Giffords on January 9, 2011, although when level heads prevailed, it was clear that the shooter, a troubled man with severe mental problems, had no connections to any of these. These people have their faults and vulnerabilities—like all of us— but well-calculated attacks by their enemies have magnified

them all out of proportion. This, coupled with their failure to muster an effective response—assuming one was possible—and given the fact that conservatives have generally floundered when their views are mechanically associated with unreasoned violence, have all contributed to the erosion of their credibility, and of the credibility of the conservative point of view overall—all at the hands of people none of whom could produce a credible summation of the philosophy calling itself *conservatism* for the purposes of critical evaluation.

These and similar tactics, which surely go outside the experience of those concerned with what is true, have enabled leftists to control much the public conversation in the streets, in the newspapers, in universities, on online forums, and elsewhere—often through intimidation and bullying.

It is quite depressing to have to note that the two dominant forces in American politics right now, the neocons of the Republican Party and the "PC" types who backed either Clinton or Obama in 2008, are both instruments of Fabian permeation. While appearing to lock horns in the mainstream media for public consumption, each has done its part to destroy our republic and undermine its sovereignty. Each is still viewed in partisan terms, although both are controlled by the same entity whose true identity remains almost unknown. Many of those working to make it known are dismissed as "conspiracy nuts" in the mainstream media and by pseudosophisticates who identify with political and intellectual authority.

IV.

Again we are compelled to ask: did the superelite plan the Great Recession, or, perhaps more accurately, create its conditions and allow it to happen? Because of their view of the middle class and the desirability of jettisoning capitalism once its job was done, I believe we can answer this with reasonable certainty: yes, they did. Can they control the results? There are grounds for doubt— and *this* is not good at all for the peoples of the world! What is it the superelite want? In a word (obviously): *power*. In two words: *world domination*. Consider the words of banker James Paul Warburg of the Warburg dynasty, before the U.S. Senate on February 17, 1950: "We shall have a world government, whether or not we like it. The only question is whether world government will be achieved by conquest or consent." But the superelite can sustain it only if their fundamental premise—their own worldview—is substantially correct. I believe it is not. Because of this, the "new world order" is probably doomed from the get-go. But we get ahead of ourselves again!

I am presuming that those who have followed the argument this far realize this isn't the product of "conspiracy nuts." Anyone who still believes that is hopeless. What we see developing today is a system that the superelite have been working toward for decades—much longer, in fact. Money is just a tool. Once materialism dominates your thinking, this is all there is: power for those who have it or are able to obtain it (money leading to power), and maximizing happiness or pleasure and minimizing unhappiness or pain for as many as possible of those who don't have power or want it (utilitarianism).

It is important to note: the scenario to follow does *not* envision socialism replacing capitalism, despite Schumpeter, who appears to have believed socialism could work if it could overcome a number of obstacles. The superelite, however, *never* wanted to eliminate private ownership of capital—as long as *they* are the owners and controllers.

There is no agreed-upon name for the economic system the superelite appear to want. Author Charlotte Thomson Iserbyt describes what is coming, if present efforts remain on track, as a fusion of Soviet-style communism and globalist capitalism. In one widely circulated article, she references the Ford Foundation—which, after the Rockefeller leviathan, is easily the wealthiest of the leftist foundations on U.S. soil—and its involvement in plans to transform this country. In her rendition, the effort goes back at least as far as 1953, the year Rowan Gaither, then president of the Ford Foundation, told Norman Dodd of the Reece Commission:

> Mr. Dodd, all of us here at the policy making level of the foundation have at one time or another served in the [Office of Strategic Services, the forerunner of the CIA] or the European Economic Administration, operating under directives from the White House. We operate under those same directives....The substance of the directives under which we operate is that we shall use our grant making power to so alter life in the United States that we can be comfortably merged with the Soviet Union. (quoted in "United States—Russian Merger: A Done Deal?" http://www.newswithviews.com/iserbyt/iserbyt9.htm, October 16, 2003)

Dodd asked, "Why don't you tell the American people what you just told me and you could save the taxpayers thousands of dollars set aside for this investigation?" Gaither responded, "Mr. Dodd, we wouldn't think of doing that."

The Soviet Union may be gone, of course, but collectivism, central planning, and the desire for power all remain. China, for example, has not only survived but flourished as a tightly controlled society—one which, by the way, was praised back in the 1970s by David Rockefeller, who wrote for the *New York Times*:

> Whatever the price of the Chinese Revolution, it has obviously succeeded not only in producing more efficient and dedicated administration, but also in fostering high morale and community of purpose. The social experiment in China under Chairman Mao's leadership is one of the most important and successful in human history. (August 10, 1973, p. 31)

His use of the phrase "*Whatever the price*" suggests that he knew the price of the Chinese Revolution, which amounted to a mass murder at least ten times greater than that of the Nazi Holocaust, but that he places no more value on the lives of commoners than he would individual members of a herd of cattle—very typical of a superelitist. We will return to this point later.

Regardless of what label we place on it, or which tyrannical governments we regard as antecedents, the kind of system the superelite have wanted for generations is still being brought to fruition. I have been calling it *techno-feudalism* (a term historian Dennis Cuddy has also been using; see his *New World Order: The Rise of Techno-Feudalism*, 2010). This term is superior to *socialism*, which implies abolition of the private sector. We could also reference the phrase the *New International Economic Order,* which appeared in UN documents in the early 1970s for the brand of central planning then being promoted by the Rockefeller-Brzezinski-Kissinger axis. This kind of system would embrace and incorporate capitalist-produced technology, but use it to enslave instead of liberate. It would be a plutocracy: rule by the wealthy. Some, of course, contend that the United States already is a plutocracy and a launching pad for plutocratic rule across as many continents as can be controlled. The primary method of control has been control over economies via control over currency. Even as I write, the dollar—the world's reserve currency since Bretton Woods—is losing its value. It has lost roughly 97 percent of its value since the Federal Reserve was created and 35 percent of its value in just the past ten years.

With Bernanke's QE2, evidence of inflation, which *must* appear eventually following creation of all these fiat dollars out of nothing, has come in the form of soaring food prices, higher fuel and energy costs, and more—ignored by the government's "core inflation" statistic, of course. Other nations have grown uneasy with what is happening to the dollar. Russia and China, for example, signed an agreement in April 2010 to do business with one another in their own currencies. This is not the only such agreement.

Is there an alternative to the dollar? Back in 2009, billionaire financier and superelitist George Soros floated the idea of purposefully weakening the dollar. His scheme involved a tool the International Monetary Fund had been using since 1969: Special Drawing Rights—not a currency as such, but monetary units representing a claim on currencies for which they can be exchanged. SDRs were actually conceived as part of the Bretton Woods system. In March 2009, Zhou Xiaochuan, governor of the People's Bank of China—that nation's equivalent to the Federal Reserve—openly proposed the SDR as a potential alternative to the dollar. Such a transformation would be wrenching and require still more globalist institutions and arrangements allowing SDR banking support. No one is suggesting this could happen immediately. But one thing is certain: the dollar's loss of status as the world's reserve currency would lead to nations such as China unloading the $900-plus billion dollars they have accumulated. Those dollars would come to U.S. shores and bring about unprecedented inflation. If incomes remained stagnant, U.S. citizens would see an unstructured and very painful drop in their standard of living, which could easily provoke social unrest. If the superelite end the dollar's status as the world's reserve currency, they will attempt to do so with sufficient slowness that disruptions and dislocations are kept to a minimum.

We have seen quite a bit of dislocation since the Meltdown of 2008, with the most people dropping out of the official labor force in U.S. history. Unrest has been largely confined to Tea Party groups, which have a certain level of influence among the public but have been largely marginalized by the political class and the mainstream media. The media has kept the public distracted with *American Idol*-type fare and such events as the royal wedding and Lady Gaga's outrageous appearance. The superelite have discovered that they can get away with much, as long as the entertainment machine keeps going! But they shouldn't count on the patience of the American public being infinite—especially if enough people, now online and quite capable of educating themselves, begin to figure out what might be coming.

Under a working techno-feudalism, assuming there could be such, we would have essentially three classes or tiers. At the very top would be, of course, the superelite class: approximately three hundred extended families whose members would answer only to each other led by, perhaps, a global assembly of the sort that already basically exists in several guises, from the UN to the

Bilderberg Group. The superelite would continue to control the economy and function as overlords.

In the middle will be national political classes, continuing with elections of carefully vetted candidates serving as vassals—preserving the illusion of democracy, if possible—along with probably tens of thousands of less visible players to administer the directives of the superelite and the visible political class in one way or another. Thousands of bureaucrats will oversee states and cities. These enforcers, we might call them, will maintain vast databases of information on workaday transactions and those conducting them. They will be the remnant of the middle class, their loyalty bought by salaries enabling them to live in comfort, doubtless inside gated communities. In this scenario there will be many neighborhoods, especially in large cities, where those perceived as having money and privilege will not be safe! Many such areas have already been consigned to oblivion by the Great Recession and look like sets from the science-fiction film *Blade Runner*.

At the bottom will be the masses of commoners—the "global workforce" and others who never found steady work under the new order but perhaps will pick up whatever jobs they can. To the superelite and even the new protected middle class of politicos and enforcers, the masses will be little more than human cattle. The entertainment marketplace will doubtless continue via mass media, etc., as will the production of gadgets. Since the majority of jobs will pay poorly, even those with stable employment will be chronically cash-strapped and in debt. Some will be products of conditioning through the incentive systems built into public education as envisioned through later permutations of School-To-Work-styled policies. They will have been trained for specific tasks—to be reeducated if those tasks are replaced by new ones in new forms of creative destruction. Those with stable jobs will be tied to them: for all practical purposes, owned by those who employ them as were medieval serfs tied to the land owned by nobility—hence the *feudal* in techno-feudalism. If incentives are not enough, then poverty will be their fate.

Those who attempt to circumvent the rules will be imprisoned until the rest get the message. Building more prisons will create jobs! The United States already incarcerates a larger percentage of its population than any other advanced nation in the world; the majority of those imprisoned are in on petty drug-related offenses, but one can also be incarcerated for the "crime" of inability to pay child support due to job loss. Many sectors of a future world like this will be plagued with the hopelessness that gives rise to alcoholism and drug abuse (yes, there will continue to be plenty of drugs, both legal and illegal). There will be an abundance of both personal and property crime that will go unpunished, except in cases where the enforcers seek to make an example of someone or get even with someone, or in cases involving celebrities or someone with connections. Corruption will abound; selective prosecutions will encourage cynicism and fear.

V.

The point is to have society as controlled as possible. The blue-print known as Agenda 21—a UN "soft law" document consid-ered the bible of the Sustainable Development movement—is taking much of the world toward total control by stealth, in true Fabian fashion. Agenda 21 is a program for centralization and total control of the world's resources. It was issued via a 1992 UN confab known as the Rio Summit, the confab which also pro-duced the Kyoto Treaty. Some 178 nations signed onto Agenda 21, including the United States. President George H. W. Bush was our signatory; the following year, President Bill Clinton cre-ated the President's Council on Sustainable Development.

What, precisely, is "Sustainable Development"? According to the UN-affiliated Brundtland Commission in a 1987 state-ment, it is "development that meets the needs of the present without compromising the ability of future generations to meet their needs." This is the kind of statement that sounds good until you ask, what, precisely, does it mean? What are the "needs of the present," how are these to be determined, and by whom? How does one determine the "needs" of future generations, especially given likely technological change? How could someone living just fifty years ago have determined *our* needs with any preci-sion? They couldn't of course. This hasn't stopped anyone. An early supporter of Sustainable Development was Prince Charles, the obvious connecting link to the City of London. He assem-bled the Prince of Wales International Business Leaders Forum, which held its first meeting in Charleston, South Carolina, in 1990 (see Joan Veon, *Prince Charles: The Sustainable Prince*, 1997).

The World Business Council for Sustainable Development, also organized through the Rio Summit, drew on the resources of more than two hundred corporations and formed a vast international network.

Within just a few years, local activists began organizing "community visioning" sessions, often pursuing "local Agenda 21s." Programs with names like *Vision 2020* emerged all over the country; behind them, one often encountered an organization called the International Council for Local Environmental Initiatives (ICLEI), which, as the name suggestions, is devoted to bringing local governments on board. Chambers of Commerce became involved as well. Most at this level were innocent; they believed the goal was to protect the environment, not pursue a more centralized and controlled society. In 1996, the President's Council on Sustainable Development issued a 186-page report titled *Sustainable America: A New Consensus for Prosperity, Opportunity, and a Healthy Environment for the Future*. It, too, was a blueprint for control: various chapters addressed restructuring corporations, impacting education, developing "visioning councils"— and dealing with recalcitrant members of the public, often by employing techniques such as Delphi to marginalize, isolate, and ultimately demonize dissent. The Delphi technique can be used by a trained facilitator to create an illusion of involvement while in fact conformity to a predetermined conclusion or agenda is being pursued and potential dissent is being squeezed out.

A useful critical guide to Sustainable Development is the short tract *Understanding Sustainable Development* (Freedom Advocates, 2004). This tract isolates the "three Es" of Sustainable Development: *equity, economy, environment*—to which I would add a fourth: *education*. The basic criticism: far from innocently pursuing environmental initiatives, Sustainable Development is a top-down agenda that requires individual wants, needs, desires, and aspirations to be conformed to the views, values, and dictates of central planners. As Harvey Ruvin, one-time vice chair of ICLEI and clerk of the Circuit and County Court of Miami-Dade County, Florida, put it, "individual rights will have to take a back seat to the collective." This, of course, is hard evidence of top-down Sustainable Development's status as just one more form of collectivism.

This form of collectivism takes commitment to *equity* to the global level: as long as Americans are, on the average, better off economically and financially than much of the rest of the world, policies ought to be encouraged to diminish the standard of living here at home while attempting to raise it overseas. Suddenly we see the ongoing assault on the U.S. middle class and its financial independence in a new light! The *economy* of the West must be transformed—very much in the fashion we have been documenting, but with one added component. The institution most at home in Sustainable Development is the *public-private partnership*, yet another entity that began to develop during the Fabianized so-called Reagan Revolution of the 1980s. Public-private partnerships may be thought of as the fundamental economic entity of our present time and are central to the techno-feudalist vision. In public-private partnerships, the *political* power of big government (the power of the sword) essentially merges with the *economic* power of big business (the power of the purse), leading both local politics and economic development in the desired direction.

Globalist and superelitist Maurice Strong, secretary general of the Rio Summit, summed up the conception of economy under Sustainable Development: "current lifestyles and consumption patterns of the affluent middle class—involving high meat intake, use of fossil fuels, appliances, home and work air conditioning, and suburban housing, are not sustainable." This just expands on the basic idea. To repeat: *individual wants, needs, and desires are to be conformed to the views, values, and dictates of central planners.* The central planners answer, knowingly or not, to the superelite. The operant assumption: a few are fit to rule as oligarchs; the rest, to obey.

Finally, there is *environment*. The brand of environmentalism fostered within Sustainable Development is a radical stance known as *deep ecology*. What differentiates deep ecology from more modest concerns (for example, guarding reasonably against pollution and punishing offenders) is it's not just giving rights to animals, but seeing natural resources themselves (and Nature Herself) as agencies with moral properties human beings are obligated to respect. Deep ecology accords Nature a higher moral standing than human beings. Deep ecologists argue that natural resources have a "right" to remain in their pristine condition, untouched by human hands. The idea goes back to Aldo Leopold, a forester turned conservationist who penned a number of essays collected under the title *The Sand County Almanac* (1962). In the Leopoldian view, human beings are just one biological life form among many in a very diverse ecosystem, with no inherent claim to moral privilege.

Consider the following, from the beginning of the 1997 Benchmark Draft of the *Earth Charter* (cowritten by Maurice Strong and former Soviet leader Mikhail Gorbachev): "Earth is our home and home to all living beings. *Earth itself is alive.* We are part of an evolving universe" (emphasis mine). This incorporates the pagan theology of Gaia, created in the 1970s by James Lovelock, author of *Gaia: A New Look at Life on Earth* (1982). Lovelock told a UN conference in Oxford, England,

"On Earth, she is the source of life everlasting and is alive now; she gave birth to humankind and we are a part of her." Principle 9 of the *Earth Charter* accordingly refers to Mother Earth. This pagan theology of nature-as-sentient infuses Sustainable Development's conception of our relationship to other forms of life: human beings are not inherently superior to other animals and have no right to interfere with their free movement. Thus not only must Sustainable Development call for massive controls over Western culture, in the name of "protecting the environment," it must call for restrictions on where human beings are allowed to live and roam. Human beings are the enemy!

Agenda 21 has components devoted to the further hijacking of education: the "fourth E." Its chapter 25 calls for "enlist[ing] and empower[ing] children and youth in reaching for sustainability." In accordance with the idea of education as social engineering, its chapter 36 states: "Both formal and non-formal education are indispensable to *changing people's attitudes* so that they have the capacity to assess and address their sustainable development needs" (*emphasis theirs*). Aspects of Sustainable Development have thus made their way into every classroom of every government school, with federal backing. They have made it into textbooks; even arithmetic texts came to incorporate more about the environment than they do about basic arithmetic. Much of this material is designed to employ powerful techniques of thought control, while thwarting parental oversight (even though parents foot the bill via their tax dollars). It dovetails with the ratcheting down of academics we have seen in government schools generally. Consider just one example, the *Education For Sustainable Development Toolkit*, issued in 2002 by the Energy, Environment, and Resources Center at the University of Tennessee. This book-length manuscript offers a very interesting observation early on, in a section titled "Education: Promise and Paradox":

> Generally, more highly educated people, who have higher incomes, consume more resources than poorly educated people, who tend to have lower incomes. In this case, more education increases the threat to sustainability. Unfortunately, the most educated nations leave the deepest ecological footprints, meaning they have the highest per-capita rates of consumption....Statistics... show that per-capita energy use and waste generation in the United States are nearly the highest in the world. In the case of the United States, more education has not led to sustainability. *Clearly, simply educating citizenry to higher levels is not sufficient for creating sustainable societies....It is also evident that simply increasing basic literacy...will not support a sustainable society.* (pp. 10–11; emphasis mine)

What ensues is a call for "reorienting" existing education that favors softer "values," to "address sustainability" (Values Clarification is explicitly mentioned as "useful to the values component of ESD"—*Education for Sustainable Development*, p. 22). The kinds of "values" that emerge include literacy—defined not in the conventional way, but as "questioning, investigating, critical thinking, problem-solving, and decision-making"—questioning, that is, "traditional" values and arrangements inherited from parents and from society as it has been. It also includes "aesthetic appreciation and creativity" ("students will be sensitive to the aesthetic dimension of the natural and human world"), "communication and collaboration" ("they will work cooperatively with others to achieve mutual understanding of common goals"), "information management" ("they will identify needs, conduct research, and seek solutions using a variety of sources, strategies, and technologies"), "responsible citizenship" ("our students will value the diversity of the world's people, cultures, and ecosystems. They will understand and actively promote equity, justice, peace, the democratic process, and the protection of the environment in their own community"), and finally "personal life skills, values, and actions" ("they will possess basic skills and good work habits, deal effectively with stress and change, and make wise choices for a sustainable future both personal and global") (p. 40). This is the description of the kind of population sought for the kind of economy to be furthered and managed under Sustainable Development: docile, cooperative collectivists, relatively uneducated (about history, etc.), their minds controlled, but with job skills necessary to participate in the global workforce envisioned.

How will the overall agenda of Sustainable Development be furthered? In their "visioning sessions," trained facilitators present glowing descriptions of communities consisting of multiuse facilities whose inhabitants can walk or bicycle everywhere—to work, to school, to shop for groceries, to the movies, and so on. These presentations play on many people's sincere weariness with long commutes to work, traffic congestion, and inflated gas prices, and portray as idyllic an existence where automobiles can be dispensed with. They sometimes present pictures of physically attractive, happy-appearing twentysomethings, prospective dwellers in Sustainable urban high rises atop businesses or government offices. What they will not tell you is that the dwellers in these new urban high rises will not have the options traditional homeowners enjoyed. For one thing, Agenda 21 does not speak of *property*, much less of property *rights*. It speaks of *human settlements*. For example, from Agenda 21's Chapter 7:

> The objective is to provide for the land requirements of human settlement development through environmentally sound physical planning and land use so as to ensure access to land to all households and, where appropriate, *the encouragement of communally and collectively owned and managed land.* (emphasis mine)

Thus the facilitators will not tell the "human settlers" in their mixed-use facilities that their domiciles will not be "theirs" (even if they paid for them!) but belong to a local collective for which they will be required to pay a membership fee (which may be automatically deducted from their bank accounts). This collective will be empowered to micromanage activities ranging from how much water and energy they may use, how they are to dispose of waste, whether they will be allowed to hang plants or otherwise decorate front balconies, if and under what circumstances they will be allowed to own firearms, and so on. Their lives and health decisions such as whether to take dietary supplements may not be theirs. One of the chief manifestations of Sustainable Development in large- and medium-sized cities is Smart Growth. The purpose of Smart Growth as a form of urban planning is to concentrate human populations into small urban areas, where people—especially their mode of transportation, as well as their commercial activities—will be under various degrees of control by the public-private partnerships that many of them will work for. In the "sustainable communities" of the techno-feudalist future envisioned by the superelite and those working on their behalf, public-private partnerships will provide the lion's share of workaday jobs. "Business owners" will be partners, carefully licensed and managed (and taxed). Bona fide entrepreneurship, based on private property rights and a quest for financial independence, will be a thing of the past.

How realistic is this? The idea that *all* people can be controlled is, of course, absurd and would probably not be attempted beyond a certain point. Were government or private activists to seriously pursue criminalizing private gun ownership for personal protection, for example, such attempts would merely empower gangs to thwart law enforcement with superior firepower that would be increasingly difficult to deal with. Even if efforts were made to force commoners to have RFID chips embedded in their arms as a condition of buying groceries, some would find ways to circumvent the system (both sellers and buyers!). But again, chronic lawlessness makes people afraid, and fear will further social control. Those commoners whose incomes enable them to afford it would probably live in mixed-use habitations, currently in various stages of planning. Those out of work and in some cases forced to survive by illegal means may well inhabit a very dangerous and sometimes violent world. One thinks of British philosopher Thomas Hobbes's description of lives in the state of nature: "solitary, poor, brutish, nasty, and short." This may well be an accurate description of many people's lives in a techno-feudalist economy. Hobbes was wrong to think of *state of nature* and *civil society* as a sharp dichotomy, with the latter firmly established by a social contract, and not as a continuum involving various states of order versus dysfunction. We are already probably closer to the state of nature than we think!

Now in closing: there is nothing wrong with rational, intelligent concern about the environment. There are elements of Sustainable Development that make sense. Industrial pollution indeed created problems that needed to be addressed. We do not want to foul our own nests: poison our water and food, or render our air unsafe to breathe. The most responsible means of addressing these problems was through new technology that eliminated harmful pollutants. When presented with the evidence and given the opportunity, technologists usually solve problems. As policy analysts Joseph L. Bast, Peter J. Hill, and Richard C. Rue concluded in their landmark study *Eco-Sanity: A Common-Sense Guide to Environmentalism* (1996), addressing legitimate concerns by legitimate means has actually meant that our land, water, and air are all getting *cleaner*. *Good stewardship* of our natural surroundings both is, and always has been, a sound idea that we should require of ourselves, and in large measure, our civilization has risen to the occasion.

But what of the reasonably well-documented global warming—or climate change? It is certainly likely that climate change is occurring, but there remain more than a few legitimate doubts about the cause. Some climate scientists are skeptical of the claim that human activity can cause the kinds of changes being attributed to it. The climate has changed many times throughout geological, and even within human, history. Moreover, melting ice caps have been observed on Mars, suggesting that increased activity on the sun, not human industrial activity, is the primary cause of global warming (see Kate Ravilious, "Mars Melt Hints at Solar, Not Human, Cause for Warming, Scientist Says," *National Geographic News*, February 28, 2007).

Thus the answer to Sustainable Development is that *no such broad-based, top-down agenda is needed or is capable of helping*. Good stewardship can be practiced, and is practiced best, in the context of private property rights protected by Constitutionally limited government within the worldview supplied by Christianity—with a legal apparatus involving strict liability (if you pollute my property, I can sue you for damages). The biblical perspective avers that man has "dominion" over the Earth and all living things on it (Gen. 1:26). In this sense, we *are* the supreme species. Sustainable Development turns this on its head. It makes Mother Earth the supreme entity, morally speaking: the deep ecologist's surrogate for God. Thus it provides the kind of surrogate for Christianity capable, for some, of inspiring allegiance to a kind of warm and fuzzy New Age "global consciousness" that plays directly into the hands of the superelite, who, of course, want nothing to do with Christianity but are comfortable with a hijacked globalist "interfaith" message that is, on the surface at least, religious in nature and quite compatible with the goal of social control

VI.

Of course, there may be too many commoners for the global central planners and Sustainable Developers! The ongoing economic crisis, after all, has thrown millions of people out of work. As of this writing, some 48 million people are dependent directly on the federal government for basic necessities, whether through unemployment benefits or food stamps. There are no guarantees that these payments either will or can be continued indefinitely. This is bad news, especially because some economists claim that some who have been out of work for as long as two years will never find reliable employment again. Moreover, many people in this population are over fifty and already experiencing significant health problems likely to worsen with time. This will add to the growing population of elderly nursing-home residents in need of round-the-clock care. The sixth chapter of *Sustainable America: A New Consensus for Prosperity, Opportunity, and a Healthy Environment for the Future* openly advocates population control, both in the United States and across the world. Others have written ominously not just of population control, but of actual population reduction, up to and including *eliminating* "useless eaters" through malnutrition, disease, war, and other life-shortening measures, possibly including violent death at the hands of street-level criminals.

Is it possible that official policy might enable population-reduction measures? Those who believe the idea impossibly paranoid have probably never heard of, or seen, the peculiar monument near Elberton, Georgia, called the Georgia

Guidestones. This monument's origins are shrouded in mystery. In 1979, a man known only as "R. C. Christian" appeared one day at the Elberton Granite Finishing Company and announced that he wanted them to build a monument to transmit a message to mankind. He had money from ten anonymous donors. The monument was constructed to his specifications and was engraved with ten new commandments written in eight languages—including this one: "Maintain humanity under 500,000,000 in perpetual balance with nature." How might one do that? There is only one answer, and it has been echoed by reputable scientists: *reduce the present population*. How might someone with the means reduce the present population? The answer should give every reader of this book any number of sleepless nights: *exterminate slightly over ninety percent of all human beings now living.*

The idea is not as crazy as it looks. It need not be conducted as a new Holocaust. The superelite need do nothing specific. All they need do is maintain what has become the standard American diet while moving society into techno-feudalism. Despite a strong interest in healthy eating among some of those involved in the sustainability movement, much of the standard American diet remains unhealthy. Much of our food marketplace encourages poor eating habits that have already given us the sickest population in human history, with epidemic levels of obesity and high rates of cancers, diabetes, heart disease, Alzheimer's disease and other dementias, breathing disorders, sleep disorders, bone problems, chronic fatigue, and so on. Common processed foods on every grocery-store shelf or in freezers contain preservatives; flavor enhancers (e.g., monosodium glutamate, or MSG); bovine growth hormone, which is blamed for girls beginning to develop breasts as young as age eleven; high-fructose corn syrup, which is known to cause obesity; aspartame, a known carcinogen, in diet drinks—and so on. Studies—ignored by mainstream science and media—have linked childhood vaccines to autism. Add to all this the lives permeated by varying degrees of stress experienced by most Americans today. The negative health effects of chronic stress are well-known. The "cures" for all these may be worse than the diseases. The many drugs marketed by the multibillion-dollar pharmaceutical industry ("Big Pharma") for a wide variety of ailments may have long-term effects that cannot be known—although some are discovered relatively quickly (think of Vioxx!).

In the end, however great our technological successes, it seems likely that the human body is just not suited to sitting behind a desk hunched over a computer terminal all day, five days of every week, and then reclining watching television the rest of the time—in Sustainable communities or otherwise. We are not even close to being as physically fit as our ancestors who settled this country and worked its land, or even those who built the first industries. Finally, much of our cubicle work damages our mental fitness as badly as it does our physical fitness. Taken cumulatively, we have a recipe for a growing population of chronically sick people—with both physical and mental illnesses!

Consider now that the excess population of human beings on this planet is hardly limited to the United States. Poverty is worsening all over the globe, especially as the cost of basic foodstuffs is driven up by the devaluation of fiat currencies, the destruction of local agricultural lands by forced industrialization, and new practices such as diverting corn harvests into producing biofuels. The idea of abortion as a means of population control has been floated for several decades now—doubtless one of the reasons that opposition to the practice by Christian conservatives has been rendered toothless. Consider these words of John P. Holdren on the possibilities of coerced abortion, from a text coauthored with alarmist biologist Paul Ehrlich as far back as 1977:

> Indeed, it has been concluded that compulsory popula-
> tion-control laws, even including laws requiring com-
> pulsory abortion, could be sustained under the existing
> Constitution if the population crisis became sufficiently
> severe to endanger the society. (*Ecoscience*, 1977, p. 837)

The fact that Holdren is now President Barack Obama's top science advisor ought to give us sleepless nights! Holdren's and Ehrlich's commitment to globalism is seen in the following:

> Perhaps those agencies, combined with UNEP and the
> United Nations population agencies, might eventu-
> ally be developed into a Planetary Regime—sort of an
> international superagency for population, resources,
> and environment. Such a comprehensive Planetary
> Regime could control the development, administration,
> conservation, and distribution of all natural resources,
> renewable or nonrenewable, at least insofar as interna-
> tional implications exist. Thus the Regime could have
> the power to control pollution not only in the atmos-
> phere and oceans, but also in such freshwater bodies as
> rivers and lakes that cross international boundaries or
> that discharge into the oceans. The Regime might also
> be a logical central agency for regulating all interna-
> tional trade, perhaps including assistance from DCs to
> LDCs, and including all food on the international mar-
> ket. The Planetary Regime might be given responsibility
> for determining the optimum population for the world
> and for each region and for arbitrating various coun-
> tries' shares within their regional limits. Control of

> population size might remain the responsibility of each
> government, but the Regime would have some power to
> enforce the agreed limits. (*Ecoscience*, p. 942–43).

The authors advocate eliminating national sovereignty under a globalist-created international police force:

> If this could be accomplished, security might be pro-
> vided by an armed international organization, a global
> analogue of a police force. Many people have recognized
> this as a goal, but the way to reach it remains obscure
> in a world where factionalism seems, if anything, to be
> increasing. The first step necessarily involves partial sur-
> render of sovereignty to an international organization.
> (p. 917)

Abortion might not be enough. There is every reason for a certain amount of paranoia about what the supcrelite plan to do with an excess population through the corporations its members own and the political classes it controls. The United Nations has published documents by well-known scientists supporting such figures. In the *UNESCO Courier* of November 1991, celebrated oceanographer Jacques Cousteau wrote:

> The damage people cause to the planet is a function of
> demographics—it is equal to the degree of develop-
> ment. One American burdens the earth much more than
> twenty Bangladeshes....This is a terrible thing to say. In
> order to stabilize world population, we must eliminate
> 350,000 people per day. It is a horrible thing to say, but
> it's just as bad not to say it.

Biologist Eric Pianka of the University of Texas at Austin was quoted as having said (in a March 3, 2006, speech before the Texas Academy of Science), "I actually think the world will be much better when there's only 10 or 20 percent of us left." The Texas Academy of Science later issued a statement that Pianka's words had been taken out of context and that he was actually warning us that our highly mobile society was placing us at risk to newly emerged diseases such as the Ebola virus; but a much-discussed online essay of Pianka's does contain the following: "I do not bear any ill will toward people. However, I am convinced that the world, including *all humanity*, WOULD clearly be much better off without so many of us" (emphases his). Again: the context is his belief that if *we* do not initiate population control, nature will "do it for us in ways not of our choosing" and "these ways...will not be much fun" ("What nobody wants to hear but everybody needs to know," at http://uts.cc.utexas. edu/~varanus/Everybody.html).

Other far wealthier and more influential people, including media mogul Ted Turner and Bill Gates of Microsoft, have endorsed the idea that the world would be better off with fewer people. Turner was quoted in the *McAlveny Intelligence Advisor* as saying: "A total population of 250–300 million people, a 95 percent decline from present levels, would be ideal" (June, 1996). Gates told a TED (Technology, Entertainment, Design) conference in February 2010: "The world today has 6.8 billion people. That's heading up to about 9 billion. Now if we do a really great job on new vaccines, health care, reproductive health services [i.e., abortion], we could lower that by perhaps 10 or 15 percent." Careful readers should note the working assumption here about vaccines and wonder what Gates knows about them that parents do not know, especially given the above-mentioned allegation of a connection between vaccines and autism; other studies link vaccines to infertility. If such allegations are true, we would expect their use as a means of population reduction.

The Gates Foundation—now ranking with the Rockefeller Foundation in terms of having very deep pockets—has joined with Rockefeller and the United Nations to form the Global Alliance for Vaccination and Immunization (GAVI) to promote vaccination on a global scale. Gates has praised the Rockefellers. "It seems like every new corner we turn," he said back in 2000, "the Rockefellers are already there. And in some cases, they have been there for a long, long time." Can there be any doubt that the financial empire begun by the founder of Microsoft has followed that of the Rockefellers into globalism—and into a commitment to control populations from the very top, including culling the herds if possible? If this seems unbelievable, go back and read David Rockefeller Sr.'s remark about the "successful" Chinese revolution under Mao, especially that "*whatever the price.*" One you become a superelitist (or are born to that station, as was Rockefeller), you stop valuing the lives of common people and can advocate culling the herds!

The UN may again have the key. Consider now Codex Alimentarius (Latin for "Food Code"), originally created back in the early 1960s by the Codex Alimentarius Commission. It is a program to globalize control over food in as much of the world as possible, including the United States, in the name of "food safety" by "harmonizing" all food-safety standards at the global level. What Codex Alimentarius "standards" would do is *rob* food of its nutritional content, resulting in populations that are even weaker, sicker, and more disease-prone than they are at present; it would also eliminate vitamins, natural herbs, and other dietary supplements that had not been strictly tested by Big Pharma's bought-and-paid-for "scientists," and by forcing would-be buyers to obtain doctors' prescriptions to purchase them. This would be accomplished by the expedient of reclassifying them as narcotics, which would severely limit their availability and provide Big Pharma an absolute monopoly over whatever was left of the dietary-supplement industry. Genetically modified foods, moreover, would be sold without any legal requirement that they be labeled as such. Again, the long-term health risks of such foods are unknown.

In placing "food safety" under federal control (with "federal control" subject to global standards), Codex Alimentarius would eliminate private "backyard" agriculture of the sort that has been practiced throughout this country's history, which enabled many families to survive the Great Depression, and remains a very good source of healthy food. If Codex Alimentarius is fully embraced here, many people, especially the elderly which will soon include a lot of aging baby boomers, will begin to die of preventable diseases traceable to inadequate nutrition and from a multitude of mysterious ailments that will doubtless defy specific medical determination. (See Scott Tips, ed., *Codex Alimentarius: Global Food Imperialism*, 2007; cf. also F. William Engdahl, *Seeds of Destruction: The Hidden Agenda of Genetic Manipulation*, 2007.)

The problem in a nutshell: in a techno-feudalist world, *there just plain will not be enough work for 6 billion to 7 billion people!* Worse, many will be directly dependent on the state for their basic needs as *their capacity for independence will have been destroyed, and there will be insufficient resources to sustain them!* This includes those whose health will have been compromised by poor nutrition or from ingesting preservatives and artificial sweeteners their entire lives—not to mention what genetically modified foods might have done to them!

These multiple agendas, converging on concentrating wealth and power at the center while rendering common people dependent and possibly chronically ill or disabled, possibly as expendable "useless eaters," perhaps explain even further why relevant academic subjects have been neutered or skillfully turned down paths of "academic radicalism" that may turn groups against one another (women against men, for example, by radical feminism), leaving them impotent from the standpoint of producing critiques of real power. This matters, because it should be clear that the ethical implications of what we have been considering are horrifying! They make the infamous Tuskegee syphilis experiment (in which approximately six hundred poor black sharecroppers with syphilis were left untreated from 1932 to 1972 so that the medical community could study the natural progress of the disease) look like a schoolyard prank by comparison! Where, moreover, were the "tenured radicals" when the superelite-led banking cartel and those on Wall Street most responsible for the Meltdown of 2008 were the first to receive massive bailouts at taxpayer expense? The superelite, of course, have no interest in becoming wise Platonist philosopher-kings who seek to benefit those in their charge based on an abstract *eidos* of perfect justice. It will be sufficient for them to be overlords of controlled populations in which commoners are conditioned to stay in their work cubicles, where university professors stay in their classrooms and library cubicles and remain irrelevant, and where *refuseniks* are either imprisoned or compelled to live at a subsistence level in dangerous urban jungles. Under ideal techno-feudalism, *no one* has the resources to mount an effective challenge to power.

Techno-feudalism is just a scenario, of course. It may look like standard dystopian science fiction. It is not intended as prophesy, just as possibility. As I stated in the introduction, I do not have a crystal ball. I am not an insider. But one can argue plausibly that this is either the kind of world the superelite want or what will emerge regardless of their intentions, as the global system they are building evolves according to its own dynamic. In the final chapter, we will consider some possible avenues *we the people* might pursue, in the hope of ensuring that this scenario *remains* in the realm of dystopian science fiction. In so doing, we might encounter reasons for believing *it* unsustainable—because for all their power, it is likely that in one very specific respect, to be encountered in our final chapter, the superelite *literally do not know what they are doing.* Their "new world order," as I already observed above, is doomed. Not that this will help commoners once the dynamic we just spoke of is in full play!

6

What now? The superelite have done their work well. A large body of evidence shows a United States in decline and a world on its way to global techno-feudalism. In nations such as China, the long-term decline of the United States is now a given. Because of incorrect premises about economic law, the entire Western world might be about to enter a Greater Depression. So where do we go from here?

• • •

I believe it will soon be clear, if it is not already, that the former republic called the United States is in decline: economic, political, educational, and cultural. We have raised the pressing question of our present moment: was the Meltdown of 2008 a mere misadventure, or was it planned? There were plenty of warning signs that trouble was coming. Political mavericks like Ron Paul saw them. Gerald Celente, a longstanding authority on long-term trends, has been pontificating on them for years. Other authors, many of them professional investors and financial advisers, such as Peter Schiff and William Bonner, foresaw the trouble. All spent years warning that printing-press money is not the key to sustainable prosperity, that growing indebtedness (personal, corporate, governmental) is trouble, and that the piper would one day come demanding payment. That day has arrived. The conclusion is irresistible: either key decision-makers in the upper-echelons of the superelite are utter fools completely out of touch with reality, or they were responsible for the Meltdown of 2008 and the Great Recession—or (what amounts to the same thing) they allowed it to happen by allowing average Americans' poor education, preference for short-term quick fixes over long-term solutions, and sometimes plain old-fashioned greed and lust to own *things*, to automatically work against them: as, for example, when many were cajoled into buying houses they couldn't afford.

So what now?

I.

Before answering, I believe it necessary to be as clear as possible about where we stand—particularly in the present environment, in which mainstream economists and media are urging enthusiasm about an "economic recovery" that has so far benefitted only the political class and that of corporate elites. The main sources for what follows are *TheEconomicCollapseBlog. com* and *EndoftheAmericanDream.com* blogs created by Michael T. Snyder, a one-time Washington lawyer and respected independent researcher on the economy. Each of his claims is referenced on one or the other website, and sometimes on both; each claim there contains a hyperlink to the supporting documentation. Keep in mind that this is only a small fraction of a much larger body of information.

Healthy economies make what they need or develop trade relationships based on mutual advantage. They don't export a significant portion of their manufacturing base to potentially hostile nations, and they don't become dependent on others or on illusions about the possibilities of fiat-money creation to sustain their standard of living! Consider, in this light, the relative disappearance of our manufacturing base:

- The major U.S. "export" over the past forty years has been jobs. In 1970, 25 percent of all jobs in the United States were in manufacturing. Today, just 9 percent of U.S. jobs are in manufacturing.
- The United States has lost a staggering 32 percent of its manufacturing jobs since 2000.

- Since 2001, more than 42,000 factories have closed down for good. The United States is being deindustrialized. Our standard of living would already have dropped precipitously were it not for credit cards. Hundreds of new factories are appearing in China. The standard of living there is rising.
- At the end of 2009, fewer than 12 million Americans worked in manufacturing. The last time that was true was in 1940. Keep in mind that in 1940, the U.S. population was 132 million and that we now have more than 300 million people living in the United States.
- Every year since 2000 we have lost 10 percent of our middle-class jobs. In the year 2000, there were around 72 million middle-class jobs in the United States. By 2010, there were just 65 million middle-class jobs.
- For those who insist that the disappearance of manufacturing is due to changing technology and is actually evidence of advance: per-capita employment in the computer industry in the United States was lower in 2010 than it was in 1975.
- Back in 1998, the United States had 25 percent of the world's high-tech export market and China had just 10 percent. By 2008, the United States had less than 15 percent and China's share had risen to 20 percent.
- Back in 1985, the U.S. trade deficit with China was a mere $6 million for the entire year. In 2010, for the month of August alone, the trade deficit with China was over $28 *billion!* That is to say, the U.S. trade deficit with China in August 2010 was *56,000 times larger* than it was for the entire year of 1985.

- In 2008, 1.2 billion cell phones were sold around the world. How many were manufactured in the United States? None. Zero. Zilch.
- What is the major U.S. export to China? "Scrap and trash."
- The United States continues to ship jobs overseas. Nobel Prize-winning economist Robert W. Fogel projects that if present trends continue, by 2040, the Chinese economy will be almost three times the size of the U.S. economy: China will account for 40 percent of total gross domestic product, while the United States will account for just 14 percent. While several specifics of Fogel's projections are challenged by other economists, the bottom line is: *the United States is losing economic ground to China—rapidly*.

Unemployment has become epidemic in the United States where, as noted in chapter 1, we long ago shifted from an economy of independent entrepreneurs, craftsmen, and the like, to an economy of employees. Employees are more easily controlled and tend to develop work philosophies of dependence on an employer. They do not think entrepreneurially. Unemployment therefore disrupts and sometimes devastates their lives; becoming an entrepreneur only occurs to a few, and many of those become discouraged in the face of the hurdles one must clear to start a legal business of any size in the United States. There is a myth, though, prevalent among Republicans, that the unemployed would rather receive unemployment benefits than work. All one need do is consider the erosion of the availability of jobs in America that match the needs and skills of the common people or that pay wages one can live on, and the willingness of many to apply anyway:

- The *official* U.S. unemployment rate was over 9 percent from April 2009 until March 2011. The *actual* rate, which counts those "discouraged workers" who have not applied for work within the previous four weeks because they have given up, has not been under 17 percent since April 2009. The number of "persons not in the labor force" in the United States has reached an all-time high.

- In 2000, 7.2 percent of blue-collar workers were either unemployed or underemployed. As of this writing, that figure is 19.5 percent. (*Underemployed* means having taken a job because the job is available but does not utilize the person's actual education, abilities, or skills.)

- At the start of 2007, there were just slightly more than a million Americans who had been unemployed for half a year or longer. Today there are more than 6 million Americans who have been unemployed for half a year or longer.

- The United States has lost more than 7.5 million jobs since the start of the Great Recession.

- At present there are roughly five applicants for every job opening, as one would expect with a real unemployment rate hovering above 17 percent.

- According to one survey, 28 percent of all households have at least one member who is seeking full-time work.

- An announcement by Delta Air Lines that they had a thousand job openings garnered more than one hundred thousand applicants! These positions paid "in the upper $20,000s," which is barely enough to live on.

- Thousands of people lined up to apply for one of four hundred announced job openings at a Ford plant in Chicago's Hegewisch neighborhood—jobs that paid $15 an hour plus benefits. Eventually the company ran out of applications and had to turn people away. Some

of those turned away had been waiting in line for hours in frigid weather.
- Far more than a thousand people applied for a handful of temporary positions picking up, packing, and shipping orders for Zappos.com. These jobs paid between $8.25 and $9.75 per hour.
- A newly opened IHOP restaurant in the D.C. area advertised 120 job openings and received more than 500 applications—for jobs paying just $3.32 an hour plus tips.

This is only a handful of examples. A more complete list would run to several pages. The economy would have to create an average of 235,120 jobs per month to restore the *official* unemployment rate to its pre-recession level by 2016. At the time of this writing, the "recovery" hasn't even begun to approach this; in fact, Paul Craig Roberts has written numerous columns criticizing BLS jobs numbers as employing a methodology that vastly overstates the number of jobs actually being created, while underreporting those lost to outsourcing.

As much of the above testifies, the job market in America is *terrible*—especially for the college-educated, despite all the promotion of higher education as necessary for the "jobs of the future." This includes those with scientific and technical degrees, not merely the intellectual class, which admittedly gravitates to the humanities and the social sciences. Consider these facts:
- More than 2 million recent college graduates are currently unemployed.
- In 1992, there were 5.1 million underemployed college graduates in the United States. In 2008, according to the Center for College Affordability and Productivity, there were 17 million underemployed college graduates

in the United States. Jobs for educated people have disappeared.

- Some 317,000 waiters and waitresses in the United States today have four-year college degrees.
- Some 24.5 percent of all retail salespersons in the United States today have four-year college degrees.
- There are 365,000 cashiers in the United States today with four-year college degrees.
- More than 18,000 parking lot attendants in the United States today have four-year college degrees.
- According to a recent survey by *Twentysomething Inc.*, an unbelievable 85 percent of college seniors planned to move back in with Mom and Dad after graduation in May 2010!

Some of the unemployed and underemployed doubtless have advanced degrees, including doctorates in their fields. As an academic myself, I can testify from personal experience that knowing the right people and graduating from the right university is a *necessary condition* for obtaining decent academic employment—prior to the added constraints created by political correctness in the context of an overcrowded job market that ensures hiring conformists and weeding out dissidents.

These kinds of figures ensure rising poverty in the United States:

- According to a 2009 poll, 61 percent of Americans "always or usually" live paycheck to paycheck—up from 49 percent in 2008 and 43 percent in 2007. (The author did not supply the 2010 figure, but it is anticipated to be higher still.)

- As of this writing, the number of Americans on food stamps is 42.9 million. One out of every six Americans is enrolled in at least one federal antipoverty program. Many of the hardest hit by the Great Recession are children. Approximately 21 percent of all children in the United States now live below the poverty line. This is the highest rate in twenty years.

- More than 1.4 million Americans filed for personal bankruptcy in 2009, a 32 percent increase over 2008. Again we do not yet have the final number for 2010, but it is clearly going to be higher than the 2009 number.

- In 2009, approximately 4 million Americans joined the ranks of the poor.

- More than a thousand homeless people, doubtless including families, now live in the two hundred miles of flood tunnels under Las Vegas.

- Tent cities—makeshift communities created spontaneously by the homeless—have sprung up outside major metropolitan areas all around the country.

- Large areas in once-thriving cities in Michigan, California, and elsewhere stand abandoned, many of the houses in them having been foreclosed on. Many others have been abandoned by people who found themselves "underwater": due to falling housing prices they owe more than their house is worth on the market. There is serious discussion of bulldozing entire neighborhoods.

Or consider the projected erosion of the possibility of retirement in America. Social Security has been a politically untouchable mainstay since the 1930s and has adequately supported the World War II generation. The generations that came later, including the post-war generation and the baby boomers, have all willingly paid into it. Many are counting on its being in place when their turn to retire comes. If you ask ten "experts" about the future of Social Security, whether it will remain solvent well into the future and for how long, you will get ten different opinions: a strong suggestion that the "experts" are clueless. But consider:

- Beginning in 2011, every day at least ten thousand baby boomers will reach the age of sixty-five. That will continue every day for the next nineteen years.

- Some 35 percent already older than sixty-five rely almost entirely on Social Security; roughly half of Americans have less than $2,000 set aside for their retirement years! This is because with the relative disappearance of good-paying jobs, they are living from check to check.

- Approximately three out of four Americans have to start claiming Social Security benefits the day they reach eligibility (age sixty-two). They have no other choice. However, by claiming Social Security benefits this early, they are locked into a lower rate than if they had been able to wait. Many will die in poverty or from treatable illnesses.

- In 2010, 55 percent of Americans between sixty and sixty-four were in the labor market, up from 47 percent ten years ago. The number of older Americans who find they can't retire is rising rapidly.

- As the population ages, there will be too many retirees and not enough people working. In 1950, each retiree's Social Security benefits were paid for by 16 workers. This past year, each retiree's benefits were paid for by approximately 3.3 workers. By 2025—other things being equal—that number will have fallen to around

2 workers for every retiree. Obviously, if the U.S. economy tanks again, that year will move closer to the present.

- We are not assuming here that "Obamacare" is going to prove workable or that it will save the common people money. Its demand that people purchase private health insurance against their will has already prompted rebellion against it. If anything, the added bureaucracy will cost us all more, while driving a lot of doctors and medical professionals out of the field. In the final analysis, even if implemented as stated, it will do nothing to improve public health—which is probably not "Obamacare's" aim.

A major problem is that no one's money goes very far any longer. Our dollars have been devalued, as noted in several places above. Consider the following:

- The Federal Reserve has been debauching our currency for decades, and when Nixon closed the gold window, money printing grew a little at a time. Since the Meltdown of 2008, the money-printing spigot has been going full blast. This means every dollar in our pockets buys less.

- The devaluing of the dollar has wiped out middle-class savings. Recent rounds of money printing created the conditions for the spending spree, and the mentality that tries to live beyond its means. The party began in the mid-1980s. It accelerated during the late 1990s, the era of "irrational exuberance." It ended in 2008.

- Elderly readers will remember when a gallon of gasoline cost between $0.20 and $0.30; today the price of a gallon of gasoline is averaging over $3.50 per gallon in the United States. To some extent, it is true that increased demand for crude oil coming from the growing economies in China and India has resulted in higher prices; but our dollar's declining purchasing power is also a major factor.

- An item that cost $20 in 1913, other things being equal, would cost $440.33 today.
- Over the past several decades, China has accumulated around $2.5 trillion in foreign currency reserves. The U.S. government now owes China almost $900 billion.
- Ben Bernanke recently denied (during a widely publicized *60 Minutes* interview) that Quantitative Easing 2, inaugurated on November 3, 2010, amounted to money printing: "One myth that's out there is that what we're doing is printing money. We're not printing money." Yet back on November 21, 2002, prior to his becoming Fed chair, Bernanke said: "The U.S. government has a technology, called a printing press (or today, its electronic equivalent), that allows it to produce as many U.S. dollars as it wishes at no cost." Will the real Ben Bernanke please stand up?
- In point of fact, on that date—November 3, 2010—the Federal Reserve pledged to create $600 billion out of thin air and pump it into the U.S. economy—"buying $600 billion in U.S. Treasury securities by the middle of 2011"—in a desperate effort to get the U.S. economy off life support. (If the economy was really recovering, why would he pursue so radical a move?) Bernanke has not ruled out a QE3 or a QE4 to continue the effort to resuscitate the economy.

- Other nations have grown nervous. We have seen moves, including at a secret meeting in April 2010 that included Russia, China, France, and several other nations, to end the dollar's status as the world's reserve currency. We noted that Russia and China have resolved to cease using dollars when doing business with one another and instead use their own currencies.

- The end of the dollar's status as the world's reserve currency is manifestly on the table, despite Treasury Secretary Timothy Geithner's denials, with all that would follow and set the stage for the techno-feudalist scenario sketched above.

Could things get that bad? Things are bad *now*. Consider the infrastructural falling out, especially from the malinvestments in housing during that bubble, but also due to the fact that state, city, and local governments are flat broke:

- Above we mentioned entire neighborhoods of abandoned houses. According to the U.S. Census Bureau, there are currently 6.3 million houses in the United States standing vacant—a few for sale and a few for rent, but many simply abandoned.

- During the third quarter of 2010, 67 percent of mortgages in Nevada were "underwater," 49 percent of mortgages in Arizona were "underwater," and 46 percent of mortgages in Florida were "underwater." What happens if housing prices drop even further in 2011?

- All over the United States, asphalt roads are being ground up and replaced with gravel because gravel roads are cheaper to maintain. South Dakota has transformed over one hundred miles of asphalt road into gravel; thirty-eight of eighty-three counties in Michigan are doing the same thing.

- Dave Bing, mayor of Detroit, wants to save that city money by cutting 20 percent of Detroit off from services such as road repairs, police patrols, functioning street lights, and garbage collection.

- Camden, New Jersey, called the "second most dangerous city in the United States," is about to lay off half its police in a desperate attempt to save money.

- At the end of November 2010, Newark, New Jersey, laid off 13 percent of its police force.

- Other local governments have begun instituting "police response fees." New York Mayor Michael Bloomberg has come up with a plan whereby a fee of $365 would be assessed whenever police respond to an automobile accident where no injuries are involved; if injuries are involved, the fee would go up!

- In Oakland, California, the chief of police recently announced that due to budget cuts, there are circumstances, including crimes, that his units will simply not be able to respond to any longer. These include grand theft, burglary, vandalism, identity theft, and car wrecks.

- Police responsible for patrolling communities in Arizona along our open border with Mexico increasingly say they are outmanned, outgunned, and in fear of being taken out by Mexican drug cartels or their hired assassins. In Mexico, once-peaceful cities like Ciudad Juarez, across the border from El Paso, Texas, have become war zones.

- As this book goes to press, unionized public workers in Madison, Wisconsin, have taken to the streets in response to Wisconsin's state government pushing through a bill that would end most of their collective-bargaining rights and compel them to pay some of the cost of their pensions. All one needs do to see the entitlement mentality in action is observe how these public unions operate.

The federal government is technically broke! Consider the escalating federal expenditures and national debt:

- According to a U.S. Treasury Department report issued in 2009, soaring interest costs on the national debt, plus the escalating cost of Social Security and Medicare, will absorb approximately 92 cents out of every dollar of federal revenue by 2019. This is before a single dollar is spent on anything else!
- The U.S. national debt will have surpassed $14 trillion by the time this book reaches print. According to one U.S. Treasury Department report to Congress, other things being equal, the debt will reach $15 trillion before the end of 2011 and soar to an estimated $19.6 trillion by 2015!
- The U.S. government budget deficit rose to $150.4 billion in November 2010 alone—the hugest November deficit in history!
- According to economist John Williams of *Shadow Government Statistics* (http://www.shadowstats.com), federal debt has reached the point of no return. It is now mathematically impossible for us to "grow" our way out of it:

The government's finances are not only out of control, but the actual deficit is not containable. Put into perspective, if the government were to raise taxes so as to seize 100 percent of all wages, salaries and corporate profits, it still would be showing an annual deficit using GAAP accounting on a consistent basis. In like manner, given current revenues, if it stopped spending every penny (including defense and homeland security) other than for Social Security and Medicare obligations, the government still would be showing an annual deficit. Further, the U.S. has no potential way to grow out of this shortfall. (*www.shadowstats.com*, December 2010)

The U.S. federal government has no trouble with spending on the military-security complex, however, as these facts demonstrate:

- The U.S. military has more than 700 military bases in 130 countries around the world. It is costing us around $100 billion per year to maintain these bases. Total military spending by the U.S. government is nearly equal to the military spending of the rest of the world, including China, Russia, Japan, India, and all of NATO, combined.
- The U.S. government has spent over $373 billion on the war in Afghanistan and over $745 billion on the war in Iraq, totaling over $1.118 trillion in combined expenditures for two unnecessary wars. No special efforts were made to cover the costs of these wars.
- When you add in all the "off-budget" items and other categories of "defense" spending, you get a total of additional spending on national "defense" in 2010 of somewhere between $1.01 trillion and $1.35 trillion.
- The Pentagon absorbs upward of 56 percent of all discretionary spending by the federal government.

- Hundreds of millions have been sunk into highly invasive full-body scanners still being installed in airports around the country—purportedly to protect Americans from terrorism.
- We have no means of estimating the total amount of taxpayer dollars sunk into projects like HAARP, the top-secret installation in Alaska allegedly able to control weather patterns and cause violent storms—nor is there transparency in accounting for many other federal "black ops" projects—because the information is classified.

But the federal government has no trouble taking care of its own, as these facts show:

- In 2005, 7,420 federal workers were making $150,000 or more per year. In 2010, 82,034 federal workers were making $150,000 or more per year. All members of Congress are paid at least $175,000 per year.
- The total compensation the U.S. government workforce received in 2010 was approximately $447 billion!
- According to a recent Heritage Foundation study, federal workers earn 30 percent to 40 percent *more* on average than do their counterparts in the private sector.
- Also according to the Heritage Foundation, private-sector employers pay out an average of $9,882 per employee in annual benefits. The federal government pays out an average of $32,115 per employee in annual benefits.
- According to *The Hill*, which publishes daily when Congress is in session, House Speaker Nancy Pelosi's net worth went from $13.7 million in 2008 to $21.7

million in 2009. The median wealth of a U.S. senator in 2009 was $2.38 million.

- With the country outside the Beltway mired in the Great Recession, the personal wealth of members of Congress increased by an average of more than 16 percent from 2008 to 2009.
- Insider trading—a practice that would land any commoner caught doing it in prison—is legal for members of Congress. No one should take bets on Congress passing a law that will end this blatant double standard.

Consider, finally, the likelihood that higher education in the United States—now absurdly overrated, both due to the prevalence of political correctness and pseudosubjects like "gender studies" and "queer theory," and because of the fact that the majority of jobs currently being created in the United States do not require a four-year college degree—has also become a bubble that will burst in the near future, possibly leaving still more members of the intellectual class unemployed (and unemployable). Focusing on the student-loan debacle:

- Since 1982, while the cost of medical care in the United States has gone up by over 200 percent, the cost of a four-year university degree has gone up by more than 400 percent!
- The ready availability of student loans is the key to explaining the rise in the cost of education. Students are not thinking about the long-term effects of borrowing huge sums of money to obtain a degree.
- Approximately two-thirds of all college students graduate with student-loan debt.
- Total student-loan debt in the United States is increasing at a rate of approximately $90 billion per year!

- Americans now owe more than $900 billion on student loans, which is more than is owed on credit cards!
- Only about 36 percent of students graduate in four years. Taking additional years to finish only drives up their level of debt.
- The Project on Student Debt estimated that 206,000 Americans graduated from college with more than $40,000 in student-loan debt during 2008 alone. Student-loan balances have been known to soar to over $100,000 for those pursuing advanced degrees.
- Federal bankruptcy laws make discharging student-loan debt almost impossible. Thus many new college graduates are saddled with devastating levels of debt at a time when they are simultaneously looking for some means of supporting themselves.
- Defaults on student loans are at an all-time high.
- Many graduates report a sense that actually having a degree is counting against them in their job searches; some lie on job applications by not reporting all their degrees or credentials in order to move from unemployment to underemployment.

We are becoming a nation with a controlled population. Most people are unaware of the controls. Some are in denial. Some actually support them! Some of the controls are over business; some are over food and health; others are over our own bodies. Consider the following:

- At one time, starting one's own business was the way to live the American Dream. Today, however, small businesses are being regulated out of existence. Starting a business of any size that involves the purchase of facilities and equipment and the hiring of employees has become a legal and bureaucratic minefield. A person starting a business in today's environment needs a team of lawyers who can interpret the federal, state, and local regulations that apply to one's business and one's *kind* of business. No entrepreneur can possibly learn them all. Lawyers do not know them all, as they change from year to year.

- The United States now has one of the most (possibly *the* most) repressive business tax schemes in the world. A new entrepreneur needs a tax lawyer to work out his total tax liability. This creates jobs for lawyers; and the money spent to pay lawyer fees cannot be used to create jobs for workers.

- "Obamacare" (somewhere in the 2,409 pages that Congress had to pass to find out what was in it) may require new entrepreneurs to provide health insurance for their employees. This, of course, will again kill any incentive to create jobs—a new entrepreneur will simply not hire new employees. If he or she needs the employees, his inability to hire them may cause his business to fail.

- Can entrepreneurs handle all this and simultaneously compete with similar businesses based overseas—especially if they are attempting to manufacture something? One of the reasons businesses have moved operations overseas is to avoid having to deal with health-insurance benefits for employees, retirement benefits, unions, worker's comp, environmental regulations, payroll deductions, and crushing taxes. Each of these has its own paperwork, which often requires an extra layer of employees to sort out. Big businesses have an advantage because they can afford the extra employees whose only purpose is to deal with the government.

- Is any entrepreneur going to be motivated to operate in a country whose government can change the relevant laws, arbitrarily, at any time?

- (Are these facts not going to encourage the formation of an "underground economy" of people who go around the laws in order to survive? This is what happened in the Soviet Union. Ridiculous laws and overbearing regulations just encourage disrespect for the rule of law.)

- As of this writing, the Senate is on the verge of passing S.510, the so-called "Food Safety Modernization Act," a power grab by the FDA over food production and corporate concerns that control the FDA. The corporations approve of this legislation because again, the expense of compliance will drive small, local growers out of business (another illustration of how large corporations do not really believe in free markets). This is unfortunate because it is the small, local growers who tend to produce the healthiest food, free from preservatives, flavor enhancers, and other additives. The product of the large firms will ensure that the standard American diet remains in place. People who suffer from chronic fatigue or frequent illnesses, are on medication for diabetes or other health conditions, or have physical problems brought on by inadequate nutrition are easier to control. Hence it is arguable that we do not really have a "health care" system in the United States, but a "sick care" system. Sick people spend money on drugs, doctors, hospitals, and so on.

Healthy people are healthy because they have spent their money on healthy food and health-promoting activities.

- The issues and abuses surrounding the adoption of the above-mentioned full-body scanners and "enhanced pat-downs" by the Transportation Security Administration have been sufficiently well publicized that I probably do not need to explain or elaborate on them here. What is astounding is the poll conducted in late November 2010 indicating that four out of five Americans believe these procedures are keeping Americans safer. Public schools have done their job all too well! Meanwhile, our borders remain as open to potential terrorists from hostile nations who might do Americans harm as they are to illegal immigrants. This leads us to ask:

- *How, precisely, does a nation fight a "war on terror" with its southern border wide open, with millions of people having entered that nation illegally since the worst terrorist attack in its history?* I've raised this question in a variety of forums and have yet to receive an intelligent response. Is it reasonable to wonder if the "war on terror" is really a war on Americans' civil liberties, or if the government's account of that terrorist attack includes more than a few fabrications? These appear to be questions we commoners are not supposed to ask!

The superelite are, of course, increasing their wealth and thereby their capacity for control over the global economy—and hence over the various political machines of nations:

- Financial and other corporate assets are concentrating in fewer and fewer hands. The "big four" (superelite-owned)

U.S. financial institutions (Citigroup, JP Morgan Chase, Bank of America, and Wells Fargo) had approximately 22 percent of all deposits in FDIC-insured institutions back in 2000. As of mid-2009, that figure had risen to 39 percent.

- CEO salaries in global corporations have skyrocketed, while the commoners of the world have seen their incomes stagnate.

- As of the end of 2009, if you totaled all debt in the United States—federal government, state governments, local governments, corporations, and individual consumers—the figure comes to $50.7 trillion. At this writing we are in the second quarter of 2011, and that figure is undoubtedly much higher. We are living in the biggest debt bubble in human history! Who is benefiting from this ocean of debt? The superelite, of course! They own the banks that do the lending! They are becoming fabulously wealthy while the common peoples, not just in the United States but everywhere in the world, are becoming poorer.

- European Union nations, too, are on the brink of bankruptcy; several nations (Greece, Portugal, Spain, Italy, France, Belgium, Ireland, etc.) are also swimming in oceans of red ink; some—Greece, for example—have seen riots when cuts in government spending necessary for bailouts led to the adoption of austerity measures.

- The wealthiest 2 percent of the world's population owns more than half of the world's assets. Within this 2 percent you will find the superelite.

- Over 80 percent of the world's population lives in countries where the gap between rich and poor is widening.

- An average of one person starves to death every 3.6 seconds. Three-quarters are children under the age of five. In 2008 alone, 9 million children died of starvation.
- Approximately one billion people throughout the world go to bed hungry each night, despite all our advanced communications and transportation technology. Many live in countries whose economies have been wrecked by superelite interference and whose political systems are controlled by superelite-controlled puppet regimes. Unrest in the Middle East may be bringing down some of these regimes one at a time, although the jury is out whether what will replace them is better or worse.
- The United States' own political class is reaping its share of windfalls. Recently, President Obama spent an average of $181,757 per hour flying on Air Force One.

II.

The above *tour de force* of data depicts *part* of the predicament we face. The question is still staring at us: *what now?* What, if anything, can we do about it? Where do we go from here?

One way of responding is just to say: *we the people take back this country from the superelite, or the United States will not survive as a major power*. If we do not take our country back, present trends will continue unabated, their consequences will gradually worsen, and our standard of living will drop precipitously over the next decade or so as our society becomes techno-feudalist. It may do so anyway, because the time has come to pay the piper for over four decades of mounting false prosperity. Matters are as stark as that. And time is rapidly running out. What are the odds of this happening, though? I would place them at less than 50-50. This is the main reason I gave this book the subtitle *Reasons for the Decline of the American Republic*. Republics have risen before, usually turning into empires and then collapsing to become mere shadows of their former selves on the world stage. Rome is the most obvious example: it rose, became decadent, materialistic, and overextended—then went into long-term decline, resulting eventually in its people fleeing across the borders to live amid the "barbarians" who finally "sacked" Rome on multiple occasions, the first of which was in 387 A.D. (by the Gauls; the Visigoths attacked in 410 A.D. and the Vandals in 455 A.D.). We have also experienced turning points with our defeat in what was South Vietnam and its fall to Hanoi in 1975, the 9/11 attacks, and finally the Meltdown of 2008. Arguably, despite setbacks the United States has become an empire—one intent on spreading "democracy" across the world especially after the fall of the Soviet Union. The effort is clearly tottering.

There are no cases—none—*zero*—of an empire being turned back into a republic.

The Tea Parties are attempting to turn the country around. The Tea Party movement considered as a whole, however, is hardly unified. While specific groups like the Tea Party Express have formed around politicians like Michele Bachmann or Sarah Palin, not everyone who considers him- or herself a Tea Party supporter accepts the leadership of one of these two. By and large, the Tea Parties as a whole remain decentralized at the grass-roots level. This is a drawback. The rest of the movement is in danger of being co-opted by the Republican Party and by moneyed interests (the Koch brothers, who have bankrolled the Tea Party Express, come to mind). Thus it is questionable that the Tea Party movement can get the job done. I do not think we can count on more mainstream Republicans to turn us around, anymore than we can the Democrats. Anyone who believes me wrong about this should flip back to this book's introduction and read Carroll Quigley again. The upper echelons of both major parties are Fabian permeated and superelite controlled. For all practical purposes, we have been under one-party rule for at least thirty years and possibly longer. I am therefore simply assuming for our purposes here that working within the machinery supplied by one of the major parties is no longer viable.

Many libertarians and libertarian-leaning Republicans have flocked to Dr. Ron Paul as the sole hope for Republicans. He refuses to support any legislation he believes violates the Constitution—often making him the sole vote against much Congressional legislation today and winning him the nickname "Dr. No." The Ron Paul movement was shut down cold in 2008, however, despite record-setting "money bomb" fundraising events that spanned the country. Efforts were made to exclude Dr. Paul from the Republican debates in 2008. His supporters have been physically ejected from GOP events, including the Republican National Convention itself that summer. A popular Paul-led effort to subject the Federal Reserve to a comprehensive audit in 2009 (H.R. 1207) was blocked, despite 320 cosponsors of the House bill alone. Dr. Paul has positioned himself to run again in 2012, but he will turn seventy-seven next year. As this book goes to press, he has announced his plans to retire from Congress. There is no replacement for him on the horizon. His son Rand, recently elected to the Senate, has a similar philosophy but is too inexperienced so far to fill his father's shoes. There are a few mavericks in the Democratic Party (Dennis Kucinich comes to mind), but no Ron Pauls. This is all the more reason not to see any hope in the two-party system.

This leaves us with the following options. Some are options that states (or alliances of states) can pursue; some can be pursued by private groups; a few are recommended for individuals in the event the others are impractical. All are already being pursued to some degree without much unity or coordination. (1) Start a new national political party whose primary purpose is to expose the Fabians and the superelite. (2) Work at the level of the states to nullify federal laws judged to violate the U.S. Constitution, possibly even working toward secession; alternatively, work to form "Continental Congress"-styled groups prepared to pick up the pieces if the dollar collapses or loses its status as the world's reserve currency, along with whatever destabilizing effects or loss of legitimacy of the U.S. government results. (3) As individuals or small groups, retreat from the political process altogether and "hunker down," expecting and preparing for the worst—economic destabilization and likely political upheaval in the United States if hyperinflation hits or if the dollar's status as the world's reserve currency is ended, with whatever chaos ensues. We may well see clashes between "left" (e.g., public unions and their supporters) and "right" (e.g., the Tea Parties) as things deteriorate—or other violence by those attempting to obtain food at any cost. (4) Expatriation: relocate to one of many nations outside the United States and eventually give up one's U.S. citizenship, preferably before currency controls are put in place or other restrictions make it impossible for U.S. citizens to take their assets with them. Let us consider each of these.

(1) Starting a new political party has been tried multiple times. If one works under the assumption that their purpose is to win elections, one must concede: third-party efforts have usually proven futile, and when they have had influence, they have backfired. Usually they garner no attention outside immediate supporters. If they do begin to gain mass support, they serve as spoilers. Confining ourselves to the last hundred years, the first prominent third-party effort was Theodore Roosevelt's Bull Moose Party. Ironically, it was this effort, exploited by the superelite of the time, that placed Woodrow Wilson in the White House. Roosevelt's well-intentioned effort was used. Arguably, Ross Perot's Reform Party effort in 1992 backfired by drawing enough votes away from the first George Bush to elect Bill Clinton, clearly that year's superelite favorite (CFR member, Rhodes Scholar, Carroll Quigley protégé).

The Libertarian Party is the best example of a third party with a definite philosophy that has run candidates for high office in every election since 1972. They have never received an electoral vote and rarely received more than a million votes nationwide.

In recent elections, their numbers have actually been dropping. The reasons are many. On the one hand, of course, third parties that are not capable of being used by the superelite have ballot-access laws to overcome; these laws vary from state to state, but usually require a specific number of signatures to have their candidates placed on the ballot in those cases when, in the previous election, their candidate received less than 5 percent of the popular vote. The Electoral College is the problem. It is simply not designed to accommodate more than two major parties. The only means by which a third party could pose a significant challenge to the status quo is if either the Democratic or the Republican Party were to disintegrate from within. While this is possible, it is not likely. The superelite have too much invested in both of them to allow either one to collapse without a very good reason. Be this as it may, Libertarians have never taken into consideration the lack of both education and interest in their message on the part of the general public. As suggested earlier, I have reached the judgment that libertarian political philosophy vastly overestimates the rationality of the masses, made worse through dumbing down in government schools.

This man-the-rational-animal idea behind most libertarianism is worth examining, even though a thorough examination would require a separate book! We ought to note that Bernays-style strategies were successful well before dumbing down through Progressive Education set in. Hume had argued against the idea long before Freud and Bernays came along. Sooner or later, we have to confront the reasons why such strategies have proven so successful. The Aristotelian man-the-rational-animal view of human nature imported into the political arena from the Enlightenment and from there into the Jeffersonian wing of our own founding, in its modern guise easily coupled with materialism, is vastly overrated. Hume was right: most men and women are not moved to action by appeals to abstract rationality; most are creatures of habit; most look at what those around them are doing and follow the crowd instead of thinking independently. They are moved by what affects them directly and immediately, usually on an emotional level. The fact that people tend to buy on emotion has been known to good salesmen for decades.

Moreover, the vision of *laissez-faire* capitalism seen amongst most Libertarians leaves the role of one's social conscience too ambiguous for most common people. The latter might reasonably join Libertarians in objecting to specific legislation—draconian marijuana laws, for instance, which have jailed hundreds of thousands of people unnecessarily. They might want to promote smaller government in a general sense, but few Americans want to live in a society where, for example, those made poor due to severe chronic illness or some other circumstance beyond their control are left to starve. It is unclear that private charities would prevent such starvation because unless the person had some means of reaching them, they would not know about it. Most people would permit some coercion in such circumstances to prevent the helpless from starving if they saw no alternative. Moreover, recent history has shown that while the idea of cutting federal spending has wide general appeal, when specific cuts are proposed for specific programs that begin to affect one's own, most Americans quickly turn against them. Newt Gingrich, who as Speaker of the House proposed sweeping changes when the Republicans took over Congress during the Clinton years, learned this the hard way. Or consider today's reactions of older Americans to the mere suggestion of cuts to Social Security or Medicare. For this reason, whether for better or for worse, Libertarianism as a political philosophy has so far proven to be a nonstarter in the United States as it is presently constituted—however sound much of the economic reasoning behind it.

Perhaps we should not count Libertarianism out completely, however. In 2003, a number of pro-liberty activists, as they described themselves, conceived of what they called the Free State Project. Their plan: select a state for liberty-minded people to move to in sufficient numbers—20,000 is the number they have in mind—to make a difference there, eventually securing political representation and bringing about change back toward liberty: government limited to protecting life, liberty, and property. The state they selected was New Hampshire. It is a small state with a population of hardy, hard-working people ("live free or die" being the state's well-known motto). The idea was endorsed by a number of authors and others who have been fairly visible in the Libertarian movement more broadly, ranging from past presidential candidates such as Bob Barr and Michael Badnarak to writers such as Claire Wolfe and Mary Ruwart. The Free State Project, whatever its potential, has not affiliated itself with the Libertarian Party, however; and while more than 10,000 people have joined, according to its website, only around 900 have actually moved there. Whether the Free State Project will show promise as a hotbed of pro-liberty activity or be just one more quixotic effort going up against some very large hurdles remains to be seen. Much the same can be said for the movement begun by Rev. Chuck Baldwin, who moved with his group from Florida (where he pastored a large Baptist church) to Kalispell, Montana. Rev. Baldwin sees in that area and its people a potential for independence and therefore liberty not seen elsewhere.

There are other third parties besides the Libertarian Party. The Constitution Party (of which Baldwin was the 2008 presidential candidate) is today the largest alternative to the Libertarians, but to my mind suffers from many of the same drawbacks, with one additional matter to consider. The Constitution Party's strong Christian bent would be used to bash any candidate who actually rose to visibility and began to generate a following among the masses. The usual arguments, however spurious, about "separation between church and state" would be raised. The candidate would be accused by mainstream media of being a closet theocrat. These charges would be believed; money would be spent to ensure that. Other third parties are not facing this problem. The problem, in just about all these other cases, is lack of visibility. Unless you are in the party founder's (or founders') immediate network, you won't even hear of it. This is sad, because I have no doubt there are some good ideas out there, especially on the Internet, which has become a huge repository of information. One must have produced something *very* new and *very* dramatic in the arena of "alternative" political parties to be noticed these days—and this has dangers all its own. We would be remiss, after all, not to note that there are also some *evil* third parties out there—genuinely racist and neo-Nazi groups that, if they could somehow stage a revolt against the superelite, would only replace it with collectivist tyrannies of their own—tyrannies with the potential to be more sadistic and brutal than anything we would face under the superelite's techno-feudalism!

Now some might respond further that we do have a counterexample to the idea that third-party candidates can at best be spoilers: the election of Jesse Ventura to the governorship of Minnesota in 1998. He ran on the Reform Party ticket—the one candidate from that party to win an election—though it is telling that he left that party before the end of his one term when the Buchananites took it over in 2000. Ventura never had the mainstream media on his side, though, and was often lampooned, including by Garrison Keillor, who called him Jimmy "Big Boy" Valente, a former Navy WALRUS. (water, air, land, rising up suddenly). Ventura was able to push through some initiatives of his own, but by and large he was seen as an outsider—which he was—and this limited his effectiveness. Doubtless his past career as a professional wrestler and his demeanor in office contributed to this. Many people likely voted for him not because of any ideas he might have had, but because he was a celebrity— the same thing that would help Arnold Schwarzenegger become governor of California a few years later. The Reform Party, we should note in closing, was dysfunctional by the time Ventura left office. Infighting, including a likely sabotage of Buchanan's 2000 candidacy by a splinter group within the party, effectively ruined it.

One might argue that *all* these efforts made a major strategic blunder: they failed to name the enemy. For the most part— though as always we can find exceptions—neither Libertarians, members of the Reform Party, nor those of the Constitution Party talk openly about the superelite: the globalist banking cartel and the Fabians. Again, many react mechanically to such exposés as "conspiracy theory."

I know one person who is undertaking the herculean task of organizing a movement around the idea of exposing the Fabians, drawing on Schumpeter's thinking to expose their building up the kind of British-American capitalism that will transform into socialism. His name is Terry Hayfield, and he operates out of Fostoria, Ohio. He has the experience of a former union leader and organizer. He is very well read (a trained speed reader, in fact), can spot Fabian permeation a half-mile away, and would be very persistent—a formidable enemy of the superelite if he created a movement that caught on. I am doubtful about the potential of any such movement, however. For starters, Hayfield explicitly names the enemy of this republic as *British-American capitalism*—not communism or socialism. He uses a phrase more associated with a Marxian approach to society than that of our founding fathers: the *Permanent Revolution* (of Schumpeterian creative destruction serving the interests of the Crown). He believes capitalism was never a sustainable system in *any* form. Many will see this and dismiss him as a closet Marxist without hearing him out: what he believes is that *capitalism, socialism, and communism are parts of a single process, both guiding and guided by superelite activities in a kind of symbiosis.* The superelite, Hayfield argues, do what they do not because they want to, but because they *have* to. The flaw of capitalism—his phrase—is that it tends to overproduce, while consumers tend to underconsume. Means must be found of getting money into consumers' pockets, or the system falls into crisis and must resort to some form of fascism. Means must be had to get money into the hands of entrepreneurs so they can produce, or the system stagnates. Only central banks and fractional-reserve lending can do this. In so doing, they empower and further the Permanent Revolution of creative destruction (capitalism revolutionizing itself from within, as Schumpeter says). And they must do so globally: a specific global capitalism will evolve into global socialism, which in turn will evolve into communism. Communism is not dead because it hasn't happened yet! In other words, the enemy is *capitalism itself*, not just the superelite. The *process* must be targeted. As Hayfield explained the matter to me, "conspiracy theories" fail because they do not recognize the reality of the Permanent Revolution.

Hayfield has begun the task of presenting this to audiences he can find (and he has found some). I wish him well, but I am not especially hopeful that his conclusions can catch on in a population that cannot define *capitalism* (but associates criticisms of it with *communism*), and has not heard of Schumpeter or the Fabians. Those who support the idea of "conspiracies" in modern history, moreover, often do see the Council on Foreign Relations or the Trilateral Commission (or is it the Bilderberg Group?) at its center. Will they be prepared to accept a considerably more complex and difficult body of ideas and recommended strategies?

(2) Thomas E. Woods Jr., a very prolific historian and economist associated with the Austrian school, recently published a bold book titled *Nullification: How to Resist Federal Tyranny in the 21st Century* (2010). Unlike Hayfield, he is a proponent of free-market capitalism who insists that we haven't had true capitalism in the United States for many years. An earlier work, *Meltdown: A Free-Market Look at Why the Stock Market Collapsed, the Economy Tanked, and Government Bailouts Will Make Things Worse* (2009), analyzed the Meltdown of 2008 from that perspective. Woods correctly points the finger at the Federal Reserve System, and therefore at the superelite (not employing that term, of course). He correctly observes that the bailouts that occurred that year and continue to occur will not work over the long run, although they enriched a very few and, alongside the American Recovery and Reinvestment Act that President Obama signed the following year, created an appearance in elite circles of recovery. Indeed, at our most optimistic, extensive efforts, including more fiat-money creation, may conceivably set in motion one more

frenetic boom-bust cycle, especially if accompanied by a steady supply of popular new gadgets before the system disintegrates.

In his more recent work, Woods argues that the legal process of nullification will thwart the imposition on states of federal laws deemed unconstitutional—many of them unfunded mandates. The states, he argues, were originally conceived as bulwarks against uncontrolled federal expansion. The locus of nullification in the Constitution is the Tenth Amendment. Woods documents his claims with extensive use of primary source material from the time of the American republic's founding. Unlike Hayfield, Woods has a large readership—primarily, of course, though the Austrian economics network centered at the Ludwig von Mises Institute in Auburn, Alabama. Through their sponsorship of Mises Circle events, he makes appearances all across the country. His ideas are catching on with at least some decision makers, having dovetailed with other recent efforts such as those refusing to implement the REAL ID Act of 2005. The latter include my own state of South Carolina, whose General Assembly passed a law signed by then Governor Mark Sanford in 2007 making it illegal to implement REAL ID in the state. At present, a number of states are considering legislation to nullify "Obamacare." The legislation would declare it unconstitutional and therefore null and void in that state. They would refuse to appropriate the money necessary for its provisions to be implemented. These battles are making their way through the courts. Efforts also exist in some states (South Carolina again, Utah) to create conditions for restoring the legal-tender status of gold and silver coins as a safeguard against dollar decline—effectively nullifying federal laws that assign a monopoly to the dollar and prohibit competing currencies.

My fear is that these strategies, too, will fail in the long run, despite the advantage of forward momentum lacked by option (1). They will lack staying power in the face of the likely federal response. States that opposed the REAL ID Act have been worn down over time; new problems have overwhelmed the old—especially given their budgetary crises—and many of those who opposed REAL ID from inside state governments have simply lost interest. REAL ID has not gone away, however. The Department of Homeland Security *has* had staying power, and we have reached the point where, if the agency wanted to play hardball with recalcitrant states, it could do so. In principle, it could turn entire states into no-fly zones (the DHS actually threatened to do this to Texas, using as justification an inability to ensure the safety of air travelers, when the Texas state legislature was considering a bill that would criminalize at the state level the use of "enhanced" pat-downs by Transportation Security Administration personnel in Texas airports without probable cause). Ordinary citizens would suffer more than those in government would when they could not board planes or enter federal buildings or otherwise do business with the federal government. They would turn their wrath on their own state leaders, not on the feds. Mainstream media would demonize opponents of what those in power wanted, of course. The same kinds of things will happen if states attempt to nullify Obama/Pelosi "Obama-care." For starters, states long ago allowed themselves to grow dependent on federal largesse. If that largesse were to disappear, their citizens, again, would be the ones to suffer when long-standing services cease. Thus all the federal government need do to compel compliance with its mandates is threaten to withhold federal money and then follow through on the threat if need be. The sad fact is that, other things being equal, many states—especially in the South and in the Midwest—would descend almost immediately into third-world conditions without federal dollars. The best means to avoid that would be to begin using alternative currencies (especially gold and silver, as mentioned above), and work out systems of entrepreneurship employing those currencies. Again, however, such activities would fall outside the law; those employing them would place themselves at risk of having their operations forcibly closed down and being prosecuted and made into political prisoners.

Much the same can be said for movements such as neosecessionism, as we might call it. Neosecessionism takes its cue from the idea that "the South was right" back in 1860–61, or that if our own war of independence from Great Britain was legitimate, then the secession and formation of the Confederacy was legitimate (see Walter Kennedy and James Kennedy, *The South Was Right!*, 1984). I will not get into these issues here, or whether the Constitution somehow leaves the door open for states to secede. I will note that neosecessionist movements of various stripes exist in a number of states or groups of states around the country: the Southeast, Vermont, Texas, Arizona, Montana, Alaska, Hawaii, and elsewhere. They differ from one another. None, thus far, have developed an adequate power base or support network. Some, moreover (especially those based in the Southeast), are easily stigmatized as racist themselves or sympathetic to racist groups. Such are the arguments that portray the Confederate battle flag as a racist symbol, an argument accepted by a substantial percentage of the public. The entire movement has a formidable enemy in the powerful Southern Poverty Law Center, the radical leftist organization based in Montgomery, Alabama, that has the ear of (and funding from) upper echelons of law enforcement.

From a standpoint of what is practicable, neosecessionism could succeed only if (a) the secessionists could get their members elected to office in that state or states, (b) the seceding state or group of states has a self-sustaining economy, or could establish stable trade relations to obtain what they need, and (c) the federal government has grown sufficiently dysfunctional that it cannot use force to prevent seceding states or groups of states from establishing independence. For (a) to happen would require more votes than for mainstream candidates. The situation in the United States would have to get much, *much* worse for that to happen. A sizeable fraction of the population would have to be really, *really* mad at the federal government. A candidate for governor would have to appear who could mobilize this anger and remain free of stigma despite, again, not having mainstream media on his/her side. An alternative possibility is that an existing governor would have to mobilize public anger in response to some presumably reprehensible action taken by the federal government, and call for the state general assembly to introduce secession legislation. Were all this to transpire, it is conceivable that the federal government would mobilize troops to occupy the capitol or capitols, arrest and imprison the governor, his/her aides and legislative supporters, and place the entire state government in a kind of receivership. Posse Comitatus would no longer apply. Those involved would doubtless respond, *does this make secession wrong?* No, but that isn't my subject, which is whether or not secession is *practicable*. Under present conditions, it is not. The U.S. federal government would have to decline into such dysfunction that it loses control of its own military apparatus for the secession of any state or group of states to be possible—and this assumes that the military apparatus hasn't staged a coup to continue national government that would make separation even less practicable.

Perhaps more productive are the activities of groups such as the Southern National Congress, which is not a neosecessionist group as such, just a committee that has organized to articulate a set of principles and build a network, including scholars, in the event of situation (c): if the U.S. system were to break down and become dysfunctional for whatever reason—a dollar collapse/hyperinflationary spiral being the most commonly discussed—structures of order must be recovered quickly, a semblance of authority maintained, and economic stability based on sound money restored now. Also among the goals of such groups is to study the mistakes of the present order, learn from them, and make preparations for offering an eventual alternative to it in the event federal authority simply disintegrates.

We have been emphasizing recent groups and efforts, but would be remiss not to mention one of the oldest—the John Birch Society (JBS). Dating back to the 1950s, the JBS worked tirelessly to expose what they saw as Communist infiltration into American institutions, especially governmental ones. They published monthly periodicals *American Opinion* and *Review of the News*; later, their flagship publication became the biweekly *The New American*. Following the fall of the Soviet Union, they turned their attention to organizations such as the Council on Foreign Relations. As we would expect—the mass media dismissed the JBS out of hand. They continued researching and publishing anyway. Their information always checked out. Sadly, in their case the label *conspiracy nut* became impossible to live down. They had a substantial audience which opened the door to new organizations and kept it open for discussions such as this one, but they themselves remained without significant influence.

Yet as we survey the number of groups, a certain discomfort ought to emerge. There are just too many. There is little coordination among them; their members often bicker over minor points of doctrine. Some groups refuse to work with others or even talk to them. Libertarians are especially bad about this last; followers of Ayn Rand are the absolute worst! Organizing the various liberty movements has been compared to attempts to herd cats. In going up against a centralized, more or less monolithic system such as the U.S. federal government, the Federal Reserve, and the corporations that have grown up all around them, our very independence and tendencies toward individualism are working against us, as these leave us unwilling or unable to support one another and pool our often very limited resources against the much greater and consolidated resources of those who do the bidding of the superelite. Some, of course, have grown frustrated and simply stopped participating in (1) and (2). That brings us to (3).

(3) One will find individuals who not only advocate becoming "survivalists," but are actually practicing it: withdrawing to the greatest extent possible, growing and/or storing their own food, using their own generators for electricity, and in general, turning their homes into private, self-sufficient enclaves around which they have erected walls to separate themselves from the outside world. There are entire websites devoted to the topic, such as *RogueTurtle.com*. There are businesses, mostly online, that supply buyers with dried food packaged to last months, if not years. It goes without saying that the political establishment in this country looks askance at such activities, describing such people with one of their favorite words—*extremist* (or *right-wing extremist*)—and their homes as *compounds*. The fact that such individuals frequently do have supplies of firearms and a knowledge of how to use them for protection often works against them in the mainstream media, even if they are not violating any laws.

The survivalist assumption is that the U.S. economy and infrastructure will experience a cataclysmic breakdown—possibly through a cascade effect—leaving millions of people stranded and ultimately unable to obtain food. Numerous scenarios are possible. I will leave aside those that would be so devastating if they occurred that little would remain of the country, including survivalists, such as all-out nuclear war or an EMP (electromagnetic pulse) attack. More modest scenarios picture the U.S. government having started yet another war of aggression in the Middle East. Example: the United States, alone or in a joint operation with Israel, begins air strikes on Iranian targets. This backfires terribly. Iran retaliates by mining the Strait of Hormuz, blocking the exit of fresh crude oil to the West. Perhaps Venezuela, another major oil supplier to Western powers with no love for the U.S. government (or Western-based global corporations), cooperates with Iran. Gas prices immediately skyrocket not to $4 per gallon but to $8, then $10, then $12 per gallon, perhaps even higher. If gasoline got that expensive, the U.S. economy would shut down. Truckers would walk away from their rigs; food would not be delivered, leaving grocery shelves empty; millions of people would be stranded, unable to afford the commute to work. Food riots would quickly break out; martial law would be declared to contain them, although in many parts of the country, martial law would be unenforceable; police, who also need to eat and feed their families, would demand higher pay and walk away from their jobs when the government couldn't provide it. The United States would go down in flames in a matter of weeks, if not days.

This scenario is not impossible, but I do not think it especially plausible. The fact that the federal government has rattled sabers for years against Iran without doing anything is telling.

Federal officials doubtless realize that an unprovoked attack on Iran would precipitate disaster for the West. I think we can be reasonably sure the superelite do not want the chaos that would ensue, or the responsibility for cleaning up the mess necessary for their continued control. We can be reasonably sure that the superelite want global domination—that is, economic control over as many of the world's political systems as possible. Part of achieving this will be the eventual institution of a global currency. This we know: superelitist George Soros recently *told* an interviewer, in another of those open statements confuting those who dismiss such things as "conspiracy theory," that the United States should prepare itself for a managed collapse of the dollar. The emphasis here should be on the word *managed*. He believes that the process can be carried out in such a way that those with economic power do not lose control. Time will tell whether he is right. If he is right, the United States loses its status as a world power without a shot being fired and without the sort of chaos that the above scenarios predict. If he is wrong, then of course all bets are off and those who have prepared will be glad they did; those who haven't will wish they had.

Other things again being equal, survivalism does have drawbacks of its own. We should ask the survivalist: does he have the means of warding off the government should it, again, criminalize his activity or some part of it, such as growing and storing his own food? Does he have the firepower and the manpower (consisting, perhaps, of his own extended family or perhaps others who have come inside his walls for protection and food in exchange for work) to repel an army of police and possibly federal troops who have him surrounded? More people will be affected by the mainstream media's descriptions of him as an extremist than by anything on his website, if he has one. He can count on some support, but not on the bulk of popular support, which—again, given the job done by government schools—will invariably be on the side of the government, which will have the larger number of guns (also tear gas and other means of driving someone out from behind closed-in walls).

(4) This leaves emigration and expatriation, the final strategy we will discuss here. Emigration, of course, involves persons or families simply packing up and leaving this country, hopefully for locations more favorable to personal freedom and economic liberty. Expatriation involves the further step of formally renouncing one's U.S. citizenship. Communities of expatriated former Americans have formed in many countries around the world; some of these communities number in the thousands. The idea, which makes some patriots see red, first came to my attention via a Web article "Why Americans Should Be Packing Their Bags Now" (http://www.whatreallyhappened.com/emigration.php, 2005), authored by someone calling himself Ezekiel. (Such authors use pseudonyms for obvious reasons.) The author paints a very grim picture of a United States turning into a police state, a process he deems irreversible. This is certainly compatible with our observation that republics tend to turn into empires and then fall from within; empires do not tend to turn back into republics. Ezekiel notes the unlikelihood that either Democrats or Republicans will be effective at turning back the slide toward more and more repression in the United States.

For most Americans, emigration is probably not a live option. Many have family members who refuse to leave or—perhaps for health reasons—cannot leave. For those who can, there are specific procedures one must follow, and the process involves money. Obviously, a passport is a must; but one must also obtain a legal residency status in the prospective country, and this will usually require demonstrating that one has the means to support oneself either with a job or business in the new country or assets in hand, or that one has retired with sufficient assets. For most people, the lion's share of their personal assets is tied up in their home—and as everyone reading this doubtless knows, the American housing market is in the toilet, meaning that the prospect of selling one's home to obtain the assets might not be realistic. Finally, there are hurdles to clear in getting established in one's new home, such as setting up an account in a foreign bank. Many foreign banks have grown increasingly reluctant to do business with Americans because of past experiences being bullied by the IRS, which is even now in the process of hiring more agents, some of whom will no doubt investigate the movement of assets offshore for whatever evidence of impropriety they can find. You will be assumed guilty until you can prove yourself innocent!

For those able to emigrate but with specific hurdles to clear (e.g., obtaining a U.S. passport under new and far stricter rules, establishing contacts in their target country, caring for aging relatives who do not want to leave), time is against them. Events are happening apace. The longer one waits, the less one's dollar-based assets are worth as the dollar loses its value, and the more difficult it may become to get assets out of the United States, especially if currency controls are put in place. Emigration does not free a U.S. citizen from the clutches of U.S. power. The United States is one of the few nations that continues taxing its citizens even while they are living and working abroad and also paying taxes to the other nation's government, meaning that a U.S. citizen living abroad has to contend with not one but two tax schemes. Moreover, during the 2000s decade, more and more Americans living abroad had to contend with banking problems stemming from unintended consequences of the USA Patriot Act. The only means of freeing oneself from these problems is to renounce one's U.S. citizenship altogether—and this will not absolve a person of taxes the IRS claims are owed. Renunciation must be done at a U.S. embassy or consulate in the foreign country. One's name is recorded in the Federal Register (although there is reason to believe this does not always happen, so that the actual number of renunciations is underreported). The federal government has seen to it that there are numerous hoops to jump through, some of them costly. The process is getting more complex and difficult as the years pass. Whether it is worth it, each person must consider for himself. Many patriots thus choose to remain in the United States and ride out whatever occurs. But if the economic and political situation in the United States continues to deteriorate, or if an organized resistance emerges, you may wish to be on the far side of the nearest border when those in power in the United States decide they've had enough and crack down.

III.

Expatriation and renunciation of one's U.S. citizenship is a bold step, and will not be for everyone who is capable of it. It has the obvious benefit for individual expats and their families that they are free of the U.S. federal leviathan once and for all. There is a larger picture, however: *expatriation will not stop the spread of the forces that have almost ended the American republic*. In response is the contention that the United States is the last bastion of liberty in the world; if it falls, then none of the countries to which one might expatriate will remain free in the long run, even if they have more freedom now. Critics of the expat movement argue that it concedes personal defeat—perhaps even cowardice. This is what bothers many patriots who choose to "stay and fight." The fundamental problem is the encircling of the world's economies by the superelite, who are engaged in dragging ever more economies into their orbit—utilizing (usually the United States') military force where necessary. Nearly every nation in the world to which one might expatriate still has a central bank wired into the Rothschild-Rockefeller behemoth. Those that do not are isolated and impoverished by tyrannies of their own, and hardly desirable places to live. North Korea and Cuba come to mind.

But is there really anything to be gained by "staying and fighting"? How is it working out, anyway? Not very well, it seems! As we've seen, the various strategies for opposing the superelite here all have serious and debilitating drawbacks, including refusal to name the enemy. Is there anything capable of stopping the forces of globalism, the superelite's rising to world domination, and its establishing some variation on the kind of techno-feudalism sketched above? Should we expect an act of God? Asking the question this way probably sounds sarcastic. It need not be. According to Christians, after all, our fundamental problem is sin, and only God can fix our failure to organize socially and economically. It is very possible, however, that even if no human force can stop the superelite, something nonhuman other than God will: *reality* (which Christians believe was created by God, of course).

Recall the observation we made during our discussion of capitalism on the difference of perspective between those who contributed to building it up and those who did not but inherited the fruits of their parents' labors. The latter developed a sense of entitlement that began to work against them, because it is out of touch with the way the world really works. Let us extract the core insight here. It goes like this: *the superelite, being multigenerational, now comprise mostly people who inherited everything but have produced nothing. Their skills are limited to moving money around and using their control of nations' finances to bully them. For all their power, they are sufficiently out of touch with the realities of economic production that they no longer understand how it works.* Clearly, only someone completely out of touch with reality can believe that creating printing-press money and pumping it into circulation can generate real wealth indefinitely. *Those who have had to work—to produce—instinctively understand real wealth creation better than those who have inherited their wealth or done nothing other than move money around—even if they have studied at the prestigious LSE!*

Most readers will probably agree if they think about it. But what explains this insight?

The most important working premise of our entire discussion here, from start to finish, is that the physical universe has determinate properties that render it "indifferent" to human life. The second is that the world around us is intelligible to the human mind. Were it not, it is dubious that beings such as ourselves could survive at all. This is not to deny Providence. What we are saying is that the physical universe, as it is manifested in human experience anyway (at the quantum level, matters might be different), is governed by specific versions of cause and effect. We laid out the basic idea in chapter 3. It is useful to reiterate it here, that one of the most important realizations, which occurred over and over again as human beings conquered one problem situation after another, was that from causality, they could infer that if they undertook specific actions, they could obtain specific results—and by avoiding other actions, they could avoid bad consequences. The process of production begins with realizing that specific, intelligence-directed, and coordinated actions taken on raw materials found in nature could transform them into something useful and therefore sellable—satisfying needs for food, shelter, and so on, eventually including energy to enhance the process. This is the logic and physics of civilization!

Physics tells us, moreover, of a law of conservation of matter and energy. This law ranges across the hard sciences, where it is probably the best-confirmed principle of all time. Matter and energy might be interchangeable, but in physical reality, neither can be created nor destroyed. *This principle is not domain-specific; it is a general law of reality.* Other sciences typically don't make use of the principle because it is not immediately pertinent to the problems in their domains. But they presuppose it. If applied to economics, the idea that neither matter nor energy can be created or destroyed comes out as follows: *nothing* can be created by human hands out of *nothing.* This includes wealth, which must be produced. Why fractional-reserve banking should be seen as the sole exception to one of the most important laws of reality is a mystery; but economists who believe that any human agency—be it a government or a private central bank—really can create wealth out of thin air without *someone* having labored to produce something of value are in fact saying, no doubt unintentionally, that fractional-reserve banking repeals the law of conservation of matter and energy.

Economists sold on the benevolence of the practice would not put it this way, of course. They would shake their heads with confusion, tell us we are mixing up disciplines, misapplying concepts, and as evidence, they would point to the successes of fractional lending in building up large enterprises. These successes are local and are achieved at a price: the slow but inevitable devaluation of our currency, which is inherent in the process. The more units in existence, the less a particular unit buys and the more individual goods cost. It's called inflation. What is being inflated is the money supply. What is unfortunate, perhaps, is that the consequences of long-term inflation of the money supply by their very nature do not appear for a long time. Please allow me to explain further.

Physical systems may be complex. But the consequences of ignoring laws governing them are immediate. Ignore gravity by stepping out your third-floor window, and you'll appreciate this fact—for a few seconds. Physical systems involve components that unthinkingly obey laws of cause and effect specific to them. There is no mentality or action present to influence outcomes. *Economic systems* differ because they involve human actions, not mere causality. Human beings are not machines. While all have many of the same needs (for water, food, etc.), the specifics differ widely, and so there is a huge variety of ways needs can be satisfied. Thus civilization has a magnitude of complexity much greater than any mere physical system. The actors in economic systems are persons, all of whom have goals of their own; organizations take on the goals of their dominant members, along with their interactions and the interactions with other such systems, serving to increase the complexity geometrically. The most important point here is that the consequences of violating the manifestation of the laws of nature in economics may not manifest themselves for decades—or even generations. Humans have proven very clever at quick-fixing the problems created by money creation, which in any event were comparatively small in the Federal Reserve's early years.

The Fed has been around since 1913. We nevertheless built up a solid civilization. Common people were prosperous in any reasonable sense of this term. They were able to accumulate savings. Historically this had not happened before. There seemed every reason to believe this civilization would go on expanding indefinitely; it would be onward and upward forever! There were storm clouds on the horizon, but they were very distant and one had to know exactly where to look in order to see them. But government was expanding to offer safety nets and correct perceived inequities, and this had financial consequences. Government needed money, and people tended to chafe at higher taxes when they were instituted. In 1971, with Nixon, our currency became fiat currency exclusively. Consequences manifested themselves again relatively slowly, as, for example, wages failing to keep up with inflation. A "cooked" inflation statistic hid the inflation. Eventually the middle class began to struggle, despite the sense of its being "morning in America" when Ronald Reagan assumed the presidency after the disastrous Carter years. Middle-class struggle deepened with the passage of NAFTA thirteen years later, the outworking, as we saw, of an agenda that was in motion before Reagan even set foot in the White House. Globalism was moving into high gear. In 1999, Glass-Steagall was repealed; but the worst of the consequences of an unsound money system were not felt until unbridled greed reached a crescendo pitch shortly after the middle of the 2000s decade. In truth, several decades of mistakes on top of one another combined their effects. The system nearly collapsed because its key processes—money creation and spending money one does not have—are unsustainable over the long run. Hundreds of billions in pseudoprosperity disappeared in a matter of months, taking millions of jobs with it.

Do the Anglo-European superelite not understand this? Greed and the hunger for power, one might say, conquers all! One might argue that the superelite had embarked on a course intended to destroy this country. That is probably true, though likely with the intention of preserving the U.S. military-security might, which would remain able to pull additional nations (e.g., those of the Middle East) under superelite dominance. But the use of fiat currency and the avalanche of debt are hardly limited to the United States. It is a worldwide phenomenon. Indebtedness has almost become an economic universal. If the dollar ceases to be the world's reserve currency, the effects on the U.S. economy will be immediate and severe. The adoption of SDRs (if that is what takes the dollar's place) will postpone, rather than solve, the problem. SDRs as reserve currency will replace one fiat currency with another form of fiat money. Perhaps the techno-feudalist elite will restore gold backing—once the price of gold has risen sufficiently, relative to the world's fiat currencies (perhaps to between $4,000 and $5,000 per ounce). This may buy time. It may allow the institution of world government at last. There might even be a period of relative stability and calm. But within a decade or so, the same problems will reemerge. And there will be no "higher order" financial system to bail out a global fiat-money system should the children of today's superelite who would be running it continue on the same path.

As long as the belief persists that wealth can be created out of thin air, adoption of a new global currency will only postpone the worst economic collapse ever—when the pseudoprosperity made possible by the money-creation spigot disappears all at once. Such a collapse might have occurred in 2008; the spigot bought the superelite some time. But money creation to stave off economic collapse is a quick fix, not a long-term solution. The absolute bottom line here: *an economic system based on fiat-money creation and on the accumulation of debt is unsustainable!* Hence even if they instituted the techno-feudalist order we sketched above, it would eventually destabilize amid a new round of financial crises and finally collapse.

IV.

Much of this will doubtless strike many readers as extremely pessimistic: and it is, if you are in the business of laying up treasures exclusively on Earth. Theological implications of the preceding remark aside for now, isn't it possible that we have missed something? Just recently, Warren Buffett—one of the wealthiest men alive—made the following statement to shareholders of Berkshire Hathaway:

> Throughout my lifetime, politicians and pundits have constantly moaned about terrifying problems facing America. Yet our citizens now live an astonishing six times better than when I was born. The prophets of doom have overlooked the all-important factor that is certain: Human potential is far from exhausted, and the American system for unleashing that potential—a system that has worked wonders for over two centuries despite frequent interruptions for recessions and even a Civil War—remains alive and effective. We are not natively smarter than we were when our country was founded nor do we work harder. But look around you and see a world beyond the dreams of any colonial citizen. Now, as in 1776, 1861, 1932, and 1941, America's best days lie ahead. (quoted in *Stanberry's Investment Advisory*, March 2011, p. 1)

Buffett, no less than others we have been quoting, is doubtless "in the know" about what is really going on. Do his words— this is just one statement of many he has made over recent years—make him a kind of contemporary Edward Louis Bernays marketing propaganda to shareholders? It is easy to impugn his motivates. Others, though, representing various disciplines and perspectives, have also managed to be optimistic about our prospects as a civilization, despite the massive problems we face in the present: Stewart Brand (of *Whole Earth Catalog* fame), Matt Ridley, Kevin Kelly, others associated with organizations such as the forward-looking, West Coast-based Long Now Foundation or with impressive culture-of-technology publications such as *Wired* magazine.

My answer to the above question, in light of Buffett's remarks and the thoughtful works of these latter authors, may be surprising: *yes*, it *is* possible that we have missed something, and that the main line of analysis here underestimates human ingenuity, the ingenuity that built this country—indeed, that built Western civilization as a whole and has been spread elsewhere by globalization. We have created massive problems for ourselves, many due to inattention toward things we should have been paying attention to, such as the lust for power on the part of a few; but human beings are problem solvers by nature. We often solve problems in surprising and inherently unpredictable ways. Some of us, moreover, are far better at it than others! Many human inventions were barely imagined before the circumstances that gave rise to them. Consider George Orwell's *1984*, which portrays its frightening future in the grip of totalitarian thought control without foreseeing the personal computer or the Internet. "Prophets of doom" often find their predictions repeatedly postponed. Could such developments in the future prove our pronouncements of the decline of the United States as a world power premature? Yes, I concede that it is possible—if only because the future is always changing and surprising us.

Be this as it may, one thing is for sure: no form of human ingenuity or inventiveness can violate physical, natural, or economic law indefinitely without consequences. Unrestrained greed, moreover, is clearly just as dangerous as unrestrained government. The Meltdown of 2008 should have taught us these things. That means that if, perhaps through some combination of the above strategies or through some means yet unseen, we somehow recover this country's founding principles and can place ourselves on a road to real prosperity, perhaps a prosperity derived from the good things that can go on between *people* in a community instead of from the untrammeled desire to accumulate and consume *things*, it will have been done *without* fractional-reserve banking, *without* centralization in education or in economy, *within* a philosophical aegis that rejects materialism and recovers what was best in Christendom, and which *insists* on a sound money system and transparency in leadership.

Such a foundation could provide a new beginning, but *it does not purport to be utopian*. We will not eliminate the tendency of human beings to group themselves into elites and masses—because some people are born to be leaders and most are not. The need to contain greed and the lust for power will continue to be a problem for as long as fallen man remains the dominant species in this world. But by promoting sounder worldviews and philosophies of civil society, we can hope for elites that comprise a benign *aristocracy* of excellence and not an *oligarchy* driven by greed and the lust for power: elites who will control themselves through a transcendent morality embraced by all. Nor will we ever eliminate factions as long as different groups have different interests and different priorities. Allowing factions the freedom to flourish, but allowing no one faction, including a political class, to dominate can provide a potentially useful check on the lust for power of all. Whether any of these hopes is realistic, only time will tell. From a Christian perspective, of course, only when Jesus Christ really does establish His Kingdom here will these problems cease. Until then, as the saying goes, there will be no permanent happy endings, just new battles to fight.

The discussion here has gone as far as it can. At this point, readers should go back and dig out some classics on how the world works: classics that integrate economics, history, philosophy, and fallen human nature. I would begin with Frederic Bastiat's slim volume, *The Law*—arguably the best short treatise on the subject ever produced—an amazing piece of work that situates a sound economic philosophy within a larger Christian perspective that is sensible about the limitations of human nature. For its combination of brevity and stunning acuity, I would follow up with the much-lesser-known allegory, "The Earth Plus 5% " (1971, available at many places online, although the original is at http://www.larryhannigan.com/EarthPlus.htm). This allegory is the best short presentation of how the belief that one can create money out of nothing might seem a stroke of genius at first, but eventually dislocates economies, sidetracks political systems, and ultimately destroys cultures. It is doubtless significant that the author named his central character Fabian. Then I would turn to another short allegory: Leonard Reed's "I, Pencil" (http://www.fee.org/library/books/i-pencil-2/, 1958). The reader will find a clever and colorful account of what is wrong with the idea of centralization/central planning in economics. The more advanced or braver reader might then turn to a work like Carl Menger's *Principles of Economics* (1871) or some of Ludwig von Mises's or F. A. Hayek's works, though I would not neglect more personal works such as George S. Clason's *The Richest Man in Babylon* (1926), from which I obtained numerous useful ideas and habits for saving instead of spending—for example, *ten percent of everything you earn is yours to keep*. Since in the future many people might find themselves having to live closer to nature, it will be helpful if they can begin by appreciating the wonders of nature. If one needs a book capable of doing this, I know of no better one than biologist Loren Eiseley's meditative *The Immense Journey* (1946), although no amount of reading can communicate the wonders of nature as well as a long walk, hike, or occasional bicycle ride away from buildings and super-highways and machines. To be sure, nature (we have returned, obviously, to the lower-case *n*) remains as indifferent to civilizations as it is to persons. Its systems operate according to the laws governing them, and no others. Should superelite activities bring about global economic collapse in the future—or even a slow downward slide, perhaps punctuated by a series of worsening economic shocks—people would be wisest to follow survivalist preparations. The best book-length guide I have found to all aspects of preparedness, from financial to ensuring that one can obtain food for oneself and one's family, is Sean Brodrick's *The Ultimate Suburban Survivalist Guide: The Smartest Money Moves to Prepare for Any Crisis* (2010).

It is clear that civilization, no more than a person, can live beyond its means on borrowed money indefinitely, conducting quick fixes and considering only short-term consequences. The person who lives this way will end up broke, in debt, and bankrupt—and so will the civilization. Nor should we ever lose sight of the fact—for fact it is—that we all will answer to a Higher Power for our deeds in this mortal life. Losing sight of this fact was perhaps the most tragic of the Four Cardinal Errors. What has become clear to many common people appears completely opaque to those who would be overlords over all of civilization. This is the most important message that can be communicated right now—because the combination of the superelite being so terribly wrong in their basic view of how the world really works, along with their immense power, does not bode well for the world, however creative we are. It suggests that were the right catalyst to strike—it could be a war gone terribly wrong or a natural disaster or a combination of such—their policies will be the root cause of the worst calamity the world has ever seen. Survivors will literally have to build civil society over again—if they can. We can only hope and pray that there is still time to avoid so catastrophic an end to a civilization that was once so promising.

CONCLUSION

In this short treatise, we have spelled out Four Cardinal Errors that have brought our republic into a state of decline. Again: (1) We failed to secure full economic independence from British bankers. Eventually these bankers set up the Federal Reserve system, hijacked the U.S. economy, and set us on a course for economic self-destruction. (2) We embraced an educational system set up on principles alien to those of our Founding Fathers, putting us on a path toward educational self-destruction. (3) We rejected Christianity and embraced materialism; left ethically and philosophically adrift, we were vulnerable to the multiple avenues available for moral self-destruction. (4) We failed to recognize Fabian penetration and permeation, leading first to the embrace of entitlements and then to political self-destruction amid spiraling, out-of-control indebtedness, given a sense that banks can create real wealth out of thin air.

The pivotal moments or events should be clear: (1) 1790s: Alexander Hamilton was allowed, over Thomas Jefferson's explicit objections, to create the first Bank of the United States, allowing the bankster class of the day to establish a presence here—which never left—and the Jay Treaty ensured the capacity of the Crown/banker axis to continue meddling in our affairs, once the banking leviathans were established. (2) 1840s: the creation of government schools based on an ideology hostile to individuality and freedom; naturally they slowly ceased to produce citizens educated for a free and sovereign republic. (3) 1865: President Abraham Lincoln saved the Union but in so doing established the political supremacy of the federal government over state and local governments, thus paving the way for further economic as well as political centralization. (4) Early 1900s: Americans did not recognize the arrival of Fabian socialist thought when it came to our shores under the assumed names of *progressivism* and *liberalism*. (5) 1913: President Woodrow Wilson signed the Federal Reserve Act, in effect granting superelite control over the U.S. economy through control over its monetary system; that same year saw the creation of the IRS and of the Anti-Defamation League, which made it possible to smear critics of the Federal Reserve with bogus charges of anti-Semitism. (6) 1930s: with the country in the grip of the Great Depression, the economics intelligentsia embraced the *General Theory* of Fabian socialist John Maynard Keynes. (7) 1940s: under the guidance of Keynes and his cohorts, several institutions were established to permit the migration of financial power to the global level (the UN, the International Monetary Fund, the World Bank); GATT set the precedent as the first globalist trade agreement. (8) 1971: burdened with the Johnson era's expansions of federal power, President Richard Nixon severed the dollar's ties to gold, allowing free reign to the Federal Reserve/U.S. Treasury Department money-creation machine, which created the contemporary frantic boom-bust cycle, encouraged the largest spending spree in history, and allowed the build-up of our present edifice of debt. (9) 1993: NAFTA was passed and went into effect on January 1, 1994. Since that day, America has lost millions of middle-class jobs that will probably never return; an equivalent destruction of Mexico's economy, meanwhile, sent those workers here. The long-term effect may be the dissolving of our southern border.

(10) 2008: the financial system nearly collapsed. Americans have since struggled with an economy that remains stubbornly on life support as of this writing, the many pundits who see "recovery" in government numbers notwithstanding. What our Establishment is doing to spur recovery, however, will just inflate the bubbles of recent years and increase the size of the edifice of debt to the point of uncontrollable collapse at a global level.

The implication of all this is that for America—possibly for much of civilization itself—time is growing short! Indeed, the likelihood of success in saving the U.S. *qua republic*—a system founded on transcendently grounded morality, Constitutionally limited government, and sound money—is unlikely, even if it remains possible. I am writing under the assumption that future historians, if there be such, will want to know why the greatest civilization in human history lost its sense of direction and self-destructed.

In the final chapter, I suggested some strategies, the last of which was an exit strategy out of our former republic. The beginnings of *de facto* colonies of American ex-pats already exist in many Central and South American countries, and also elsewhere around the world. Of course, without guiding principles, efforts by expatriated Americans to form colonies elsewhere will only delay the inevitable arrival of world government and the "scientific" totalitarianism of techno-feudalism to their new doorsteps. Based as it is on unsound economics, techno-feudalism will eventually collapse. It might take a number of years before the right catalyst hits, but hit it will. Can we do anything to prevent it? We discussed the options. We end with: read, study, learn. Turn off your television and close your mainstream newspaper. Work on maintaining sound nutritional habits. Spend time with your family. Establish networks of friends and associates within your community. Learn new skills. Develop the habit of always taking the long term into consideration, as well as willingness to answer to the Higher Power that ultimately governs this world. Allow these values to direct your economic life and the condition of your spirit. Do not succumb to the illusion that you can change the world by yourself; but do be conscious of the fact that you are an example to others. If enough of us build from the bottom up, perhaps we can work toward a civilization that avoids the Four Cardinal Errors. That, of course, is another long story.

WORKS CITED

Author's note: this works-cited list omits classic historical works of philosophy, as well as works of fiction.

Alinsky, Saul. *Rules for Radicals*. Vintage Books, 1989 [orig. 1971].

Bast, J., P. Hill., and R. Rue. *Eco-Sanity: A Common-Sense Guide to Environmentalism*. Madison Books, 1996.

Bastiat, Frederic. *The Law*. Foundation for Economic Education, 1987 [orig. 1850].

Beard, Charles A. *An Economic Interpretation of the Constitution*. Free Press, 1965 [orig. 1913].

Benson, William J. *The Law That Never Was*. Constitutional Research Association, 1985.

Bernays, Edward Louis. *Propaganda*. Ig Publishing, 2004 [orig. 1928].

Bessinger, Maurice. *Defending My Heritage*. Lmbone-Lehone, 2001.

Brodrick, Sean. *The Ultimate Suburban Survivalist Guide: The Smartest Money Moves to Prepare for Any Crisis*. Wiley & Sons, 2010.

Brzezinski, Zbigniew. *Between Two Ages: America's Role in the Technetronic Era*. Viking Press, 1970.

Canfield, Joseph A. *The Incredible Scofield and His Book*. Ross House Books, 1988.

Capaldi, Nicholas. *Out of Order: Affirmative Action and the Crisis of Doctrinaire Liberalism*. Prometheus Books, 1985.

Clasen, George S. *The Richest Man in Babylon*. Signet Books, 1988 [orig. 1955].

Codevilla, Angelo. *The Ruling Class*. Beaufort Books, 2010.

Cole, Margaret. *The Story of Fabian Socialism*. Wiley & Sons, 1964.

Cox, Harvey. *The Secular City*. McMillan, 1965.

Crane, Philip. *The Democrats' Dilemma: How the Liberal Left Captured the Democratic Party*. Henry Regnery Co., 1964.

Cuddy, Dennis. *New World Order: The Rise of Techno-Feudalism*. Bible Belt Publishing, 2010.

Dewey, John. *Democracy and Education*. The Free Press, 1968 [orig. 1916].

DiLorenzo, Thomas J. *The Real Lincoln: A New Look at Abraham Lincoln, His Agenda, and an Unnecessary War*. Three Rivers Press, 2003.

Eakman, Beverly. *Education for the New World Order*. Halcyon House, 1991.

Eakman, Beverly. *The Cloning of the American Mind*. Huntington House, 1998.

Ehrenreich, Barbara. *Nickled and Dimed: On (Not) Getting By in America*. Henry Holt, 2001.

Eiseley, Loren. *The Immense Journey*. Random House, 1957 [orig. 1946].

The Energy, Environment and Resources Center at the University of Tennessee. *Education for Sustainable Development Toolkit*. 2002.

Engdahl, F. William. *Seeds of Destruction: The Hidden Agenda of Genetic Manipulation*. Global Research, 2007.

Epperson, A. Ralph. *The Unseen Hand*. Publius Press, 1985.

Estulin, Daniel. *The True Story of the Bilderberg Group.* TrineDay, 2007.

Ezekiel. "Why Americans Should Be Packing Their Bags Now." http://www.whatreallyhappened.com/emigration.php. 2005.

Ferguson, Niall. *The House of Rothschild: Money's Prophets.* Viking Books, 1998.

Frankl, Victor. *Man's Search for Meaning.* Simon & Schuster, 1984 [orig. 1946].

Freedom Advocates. *Understanding Sustainable Development.* Freedom Advocates, 2004.

Flesch, Rudolf. *Why Johnny Can't Read.* Harper & Bros., 1955.

Fremantle, Anne. *This Little Band of Prophets: The British Fabians.* New American Library, 1959.

Gardner, Richard N. "The Hard Road to World Order." *Foreign Affairs*, April 1974.

Gatto, John Taylor. *The Underground History of American Education.* Oxford Village Press, 2000.

Greenspan, Alan. *The Age of Turbulence.* Penguin Press, 2007.

Griffin, Des. *Descent into Slavery.* Emissary Publications, 1980.

Griffin, G. Edward. *The Creature from Jekyll Island: A New Look at the Federal Reserve.* American Media, 1994.

Griffin, G. Edward. *The Future Is Calling: Part One, The Chasm.* Freedom Force International, 2004 version.

Hannigan, Larry. "The Earth Plus 5 %." http://www.larryhannigan.com/EarthPlus.htm, 1971.

Hapgood, Charles. *Maps of the Ancient Sea Kings.* Adventures Unlimited Press, 1997 [orig. 1966].

Harrington, Alan. *Life in the Crystal Palace*. Jonathan Cape, 1960.

Hayfield, Terry. "The Permanent Revolution." *Idaho Observer.* http://proliberty.com/observer/20030115.htm, 2003.

Henkels, Stan V. *Andrew Jackson and the Bank of the United States*. Privately Printed, 1928.

Herman, Edward S., and Noam Chomsky. *Manufacturing Consent: The Political Economy of the Mass Media*. Pantheon Books, 1988, 2002.

Hertz, Emanuel, ed. *The Hidden Lincoln; from the Letters and Papers of William H. Herndon*. Viking Press, 1938.

Holdren, John P., and Paul Ehrlich. *Ecoscience, 2nd Ed.* Freeman & Co., 1977.

Holgate, Karen. "School-To-Work: A Formula for Failure." *Radio Liberty.* http://www.radioliberty.com/school.htm, 1997.

Hornbeck, David W., and Lester M. Salamon, eds. *Human Capital and America's Future: An Economic Strategy for the '90s*. The Johns Hopkins University Press, 1991.

Hospers, John. *Libertarianism*. Liberty Press, 1973.

House, Edward Mandell. *Philip Dru: Administrator*. RWU Press, 1998 [orig. 1910].

Iserbyt, Charlotte Thomson. *the deliberate dumbing down of america*. Conscience Press, 2000.

Iserbyt, Charlotte Thomson. "United States—Russian Merger: A Done Deal?" *NewsWithViews.com*, http://www.news-withviews.com/iserbyt/iserbyt9.htm, 2003.

Jefferson, Thomas. *The Writings of Thomas Jefferson*. ed. Albert Ellery Bergh. http://www.constitution.org/tj/jeff.htm [orig. 1905].

Kennedy, Marilyn Moats. *Office Politics: Seizing Power, Wielding Clout*. Warner Books, 1980.

Kennedy, Walter and James Kennedy, *The South Was Right!* Pelican Publishing, 1994.

Keynes, John Maynard. *The Economic Consequences of the Peace.* Macmillan & Co., 1920.

Keynes, John Maynard. *The General Theory of Employment, Interest and Money.* Macmillan Books, 1964 [orig. 1936].

Kinzer, Stephen. *All the Shah's Men: An American Coup and the Roots of Middle Eastern Terror.* John Wiley Sons, 2003.

Kissinger, Henry. "With NAFTA, U.S. Finally Creates a New World Order," *Los Angeles Times*, July 18, 1993.

Knuth, E. C. *The Empire of the City.* The Book Tree, 2006 [orig. 1944].

Korten, David C. *When Corporations Rule the World.* Berrett-Koehler Publishers, 1995.

Kristol, Irving. *Two Cheers for Capitalism.* Mentor Books, 1978.

Kupelian, David. *The Marketing of Evil.* WND Books, 2005.

Leopold, Aldo. *The Sand County Almanac.* Oxford University Press, 1962; enlarged ed., 1969.

Levine, Michael. *The Big White Lie.* Thunder's Mouth Press, 1994.

Lionni, Paolo. *The Leipzig Connection.* Delphian Press, 1988.

Love, Susan et al., *The Incredible Bread Machine.* World Research, 1974.

Lovelock, James. *Gaia: A New Look at Life on Earth.* Oxford University Press, 1982.

Lynch, Frederick R. *Invisible Victims: White Males and the Crisis of Affirmative Action.* Greenwood Press, 1989.

Machan, Tibor R., ed. *The Libertarian Alternative.* Nelson-Hall, 1974.

Marcuse, Herbert. *Eros and Civilization*. Vintage Books, 1955.

Marcuse, Herbert. *One-Dimensional Man*. Routledge & Kegan Paul, 1964.

Marcuse, Herbert. "Repressive Tolerance." *A Critique of Pure Tolerance*, eds. R. P. Wolff, B. Moore and H. Marcuse. Beacon Press, 1965.

Martin, Rose L. *Fabian Freeway: The High Road to Socialism in the U.S.A.* Fidelis Publishers, 1968.

McDonald, Forrest. *Novus Ordo Seclorum: The Intellectual Origins of the Constitution*. University of Kansas Press, 1986.

McIlhany, William H. *The Tax-Exempt Foundations*. Arlington House, 1980.

Menger, Carl. *Principles of Economics*. Institute for Humane Studies, 1976 [orig. 1871].

Mills, C. Wright. *The Power Elite*. Oxford University Press, 1956.

Mises, Ludwig von. *Human Action: A Treatise on Economics*. Yale University Press, 1949.

Mises, Ludwig von. *The Anti-Capitalistic Mentality*. D. Van Nostrand Co., 1956.

Moore, E. Ray. *Let My Children Go!* Gilead Media, 2002.

Morton, Frederic. *The Rothschilds*. Curtis Publishing, 1961.

Mullins, Eustace. *Secrets of the Federal Reserve*. Kasper & Horton, 1952.

Nicolay, John. "A Popocratic Forgery." *New York Times*, Oct. 3, 1898.

Packard, Vance. *The Hidden Persuaders*. David McKay, 1957.

Packard, Vance. *The Status Seekers*. David McKay, 1960.

Palast, Greg. *Armed Madhouse*. Dutton, 2006.

Paul, Ron. *End the Fed*. Grand Central Publishing, 2009.

Pease, Edward R. *The History of the Fabian Society.* Echo Library, 2006 [orig. 1916].

Pianka, Eric. "What Everybody Needs To Know but Nobody Wants To Hear." University of Texas, http://uts.cc.utexas.edu/~varanus/Everybody.html, 2008; most recently accessed June 28, 2011.

Podhoretz, Norman. *Breaking Ranks.* HarperCollins, 1980.

President's Council on Sustainable Development. *Sustainable America: A New Consensus for Prosperity, Opportunity, and a Healthy Environment for the Future.* President's Council on Sustainable Development, 1996.

Putney, Snell & Gail. *The Adjusted American.* Harper & Row, 1964, 1972.

Quigley, Carroll. *Tragedy and Hope: A History of the World in Our Time.* CSG & Associates [orig. 1966].

Quigley, Carroll. *The Anglo-American Establishment.* CSG & Associates, 1981.

Quist, Allen. *FedEd: The New Federal Curriculum and How It's Enforced.* Maple River Education Coalition, 2002.

Quist, Allen. *America's Schools: The Battleground for Freedom.* EdWatch, 2006.

Ravilious, Kate. "Mars Melt Hints at Solar, Not Human, Cause for Warming, Scientist Says." *National Geographic News*, February 28, 2007.

Read, Leonard. "I, Pencil." http://www.fee.org/library/books/i-pencil-2/. 1958.

Rees, John Rawling. "Strategic Planning for Mental Health." *Mental Health*, 1940.

Reisman, Judith. *Kinsey: Crimes and Consequences: The Red Queen and the Grand Scheme.* Institute for Media Education, 1998.

Rhodes, Cecil. "Confession of Faith." *The Last Will and Testament of Cecil John Rhodes,* ed. W.T. Stead. Review of Reviews Office (London), 1902.

Richman, Sheldon. *Separating School and State*. Future of Freedom Foundation, 1994.

Rockefeller, David. "From a China Traveler." *New York Times,* August 10, 1973.

Rockefeller, David. *Memoirs.* Alfred A. Knopf, 2002.

Rothbard, Murray N. *America's Great Depression.* Richardson & Snyder, 1963.

Russell, Bertrand. *The Scientific Outlook.* W.W. Norton, 1962 [orig. 1931].

Russell, Bertrand. *The Impact of Science on Society.* Simon & Schuster, 1953.

Schiff, Irwin A. *The Biggest Con: How the Government Is Fleecing You.* Freedom Books, 1977.

Schiff, Irwin A. *The Federal Mafia: How the Government Illegally Imposes and Unlawfully Collects Income Taxes.* Freedom Books, 1990.

Schumpeter, Joseph M. *The Theory of Economic Development.* Transaction Publishers, 1982 [orig. 1911].

Schumpeter, Joseph M. *Capitalism, Socialism and Democracy.* Harper & Row, 1942, 1947.

Shaw. A. H., ed. *The Lincoln Encyclopedia.* Macmillan, 1950.

Shortt, Bruce. *The Harsh Truth about Public Schools.* Chalcedon Foundation, 2004.

Snyder, Michael T. *TheEconomicCollapseBlog.com* (website). http://theeconomiccollapseblog.com, 2010–11.

Snyder, Michael T. *EndoftheAmericanDream.com* (website). http://endoftheamericandream.com, 2010–11.

Sommers, Christina Hoff. *Who Stole Feminism? How Women Have Betrayed Women.* Simon & Schuster, 1994.

Sowell, Thomas. *Preferential Policies: An International Perspective.* William Morrow, 1990.

Spengler, Oswald. *The Decline of the West, rev. ed.* Alfred A. Knopf, 1929 [orig. 1918].

Sunstein, Cass, and Adrian Vermeule. "Conspiracy Theories: Causes and Cures." *Journal of Political Science*, 2008.

Swanson, Mary Elaine. *The Education of James Madison.* Hoffman Education Center for the Family, 1992.

Tips, Scott. *Codex Alimentarius: Global Food Imperialism.* Foundation for Health Research, 2007.

Tonelson, Alan. *The Race to the Bottom.* Basic Books, 2002.

Toynbee, Arnold J. "The Trend of International Affairs Since the War." *International Affairs*, 1931.

Tucker, Marc. *Tough Choices or Tough Times.* National Center on Education and the Economy, 2004.

Unknown. "The Rothschilds' International Plot to Kill Lincoln." *New Solidarity*, 1976.

Veon, Joan. *Prince Charles: The Sustainable Prince.* Huntington House, 1997.

Veon, Joan. "Who Runs the World and Controls the Value of Assets." *Rense.com* http://www.rense.com/general75/wrus.htm, 2007.

Walbert, M. W. *The Coming Battle.* Walter Publishing & Research, 1997 [orig. 1899].

Weller, Marvin. *The Course of Evolution.* McGraw-Hill, 1969.

Wells, H. G. *The Shape of Things to Come.* Penguin Classics, 2005 [orig. 1938].

Wells, H. G. *The New World Order, 3rd ed.* Secker & Warburg, 1940.

Whyte, William H. *The Organization Man.* Doubleday Anchor Books, 1957.

Williams, John. *Shadow Government Statistics* (website). http://www.shadowstats.com. 2006–11.

Willis, Henry Parker. *Banking and Business (rev. ed.)*. Harper, 1925.

Wilson, Robert McNair. *Monarchy or Money Power*. Eyre & Spottiswoode, 1933.

Wilson, Woodrow. *The New Freedom*. Prentice-Hall, 1961 [orig. 1913].

Woods, Thomas. *Meltdown: A Free-Market Look at Why the Stock Market Collapsed, the Economy Tanked, and Government Bailouts Will Make Things Worse*. Regnery Publishing, 2009.

Woods, Thomas. *Nullification: How To Resist Federal Tyranny in the 21st Century*. Regnery Publishing, 2010.

Yates, Steven. *Civil Wrongs: What Went Wrong With Affirmative Action*. ICS Press, 1994.

Yates, Steven. "The Dangers of Growing Up Comfortable." *The Freeman* (Foundation for Economic Education), 2000.

Yates, Steven. *Worldviews: Christian Theism versus Modern Materialism*. The Worldviews Project, 2005.

ABOUT THE AUTHOR

Steven Yates *earned his doctorate in philosophy at the University of Georgia in 1987 and has taught the subject at a number of Southeastern colleges and universities. He is the author of two previous books:* Civil Wrongs: What Went Wrong With Affirmative Action *(ICS Press, 1994) and* Worldviews: Christian Theism versus Modern Materialism *(The Worldviews Project, 2005). His articles and reviews have appeared in refereed philosophy journals such as* Inquiry, Metaphilosophy, Reason Papers, *and* Public Affairs Quarterly, *as well as on websites such as* LewRockwell.com, NewsWithViews. com, FreedomAdvocates.org, TheNewAmerican.com, AmericanDailyHerald.com, *and elsewhere. He also writes semiregular columns for a conservative weekly based in Greenville, South Carolina,* The Times Examiner. *He lives in a rural area of Greenville County, South Carolina, with two extremely spoiled cats named Bo and Misty.*

www.ingramcontent.com/pod-product-compliance
Lightning Source LLC
Chambersburg PA
CBHW071221290326
41931CB00037B/1506

* 9 7 8 0 6 1 5 5 1 6 4 1 7 *